JANET BALASKAS

with Cathy Meeus

the

WATER

BIRTH

BOOK

 thorsons

Also by Janet Balaskas

Easy Exercises for Pregnancy
The Encyclopedia of Pregnancy and Birth (with Yehudi Gordon)
Natural Baby
New Active Birth
New Natural Pregnancy
Preparing for Birth with Yoga

The publishers wish to thank the following for the use of the photographs:
© Saskia van Rees: pages xii, 24, 34, 270
© Genna Naccache: pages x*, 74, 102*, 132*, 158, 200, 232
* Special thanks also to Yehudi Gordon who kindly allowed the publisher to reuse this photograph from his book, *Birth and Beyond.*

Thorsons
An Imprint of HarperCollins*Publishers*
77–85 Fulham Palace Road,
Hammersmith, London W6 8JB

The website address is: www.thorsonselement.com

thorsons™

and *Thorsons* are trademarks of
HarperCollins*Publishers* Ltd

First published by Thorsons 2004

10 9 8 7 6 5 4 3 2 1

© 2004 Janet Balaskas and Cathy Meeus

Janet Balaskas and Cathy Meeus assert the moral right to be
identified as the authors of this work

A catalogue record of this book is
available from the British Library

ISBN 0 00 710817 6

Printed and bound in Great Britain by
Martins The Printers Ltd, Berwick upon Tweed

Contents

Foreword by Yehudi Gordon, MD   v

Preface   vii

Acknowledgements   ix

Chapter 1: The history of birthing in water   1

Chapter 2: The power of water   24

Chapter 3: How water can benefit you during labour and birth   34

Chapter 4: Choosing a waterbirth   74

Chapter 5: Preparing for birth and motherhood   102

Chapter 6: Starting labour   132

Chapter 7: Labour and birth   158

Chapter 8: Midwives and waterbirths   200

Chapter 9: Medical backup for waterbirths   232

Chapter 10: What women say   270

Resources   295

Index   301

This book is for my children,
for their loved ones and friends,
and for pregnant women everywhere

Foreword

I am very pleased to write the foreword to *The Waterbirth Book*. Janet Balaskas and I have worked together for many years and I know that she has had a seminal role in changing birth practice, initially in the UK and subsequently throughout the world. Janet is a visionary and is the founder of the Active Birth Movement. She has inspired many people: some joined her as colleagues in the Active Birth Movement and others became converts and firm admirers of the concept of 'active birth'. Active birth arose as a counterbalance to the obstetric medicalization of birth, with its active management of labour. Water was initially introduced into the birth room decades ago by Michel Odent in Pithiviers in France as a pain relief for labour and to help a woman give birth actively. Waterbirth evolved from that.

In 1990 Janet and I wrote a book called *Waterbirth*, but this new book is more comprehensive and provides a detailed overview of the information that is now available. *The Waterbirth Book* contains sage advice from Janet, who has had 25 years of experience with active and waterbirth. This book looks at all aspects of water for labour and birth, beginning with the history of waterbirth and including details of the physiological benefits and potential risks of using water. Janet gives useful guidance for prenatal preparation and details on the practicalities of using the pool for mothers and midwives. This book is primarily addressed to mothers and it contains many quotations and practical case studies to help the reader get a 'real life feel' of what the experience could be like. Compared to women who have given birth out of water, waterbirth mothers have a higher level of satisfaction.

The Waterbirth Book also addresses potential complications of labour and birth and using water, and emphasizes the value of good midwifery care in all labours and births. The vast majority of babies who are born in water do very well and many people would say that they are particularly calm. Babies have a protective dive reflex, which ensures that water is not inhaled after the head is born – a baby will not begin to inhale and breathe until he or she reaches the surface of the water. Fortunately, complications related to birth in water are extremely rare and the skill of experienced midwives allows close monitoring of mother and baby. This book guides women to be aware that while the pool may have been useful in labour, it may be safer to give birth out of the water. The emphasis is that if there are concerns for the baby's safety or the labour is prolonged it is important to leave the water.

The accent is on safety and giving birth actively and this is portrayed in the book with a rhythm reminiscent of the rhythm of labour. The book is comprehensive and balanced – Janet reminds us that birth does not always go to plan, and that each labour has its own unique rhythm. Waterbirth is not a panacea or the holy grail, and labour and birth are influenced by many factors. This book encourages women to prepare and yet remain open to the possibility that birth is unpredictable. It is a valuable tool, empowering women to make choices, be active in the birth of their children and approach labour and birth with an open mind and an open heart.

Yehudi Gordon, MD

Preface

An extraordinary revolution in childbirth has been happening since the 1960s, when the first waterbirths took place in Moscow. For it was there that the simple idea of a labouring woman finding comfort and relief in a deep pool of warm water led to the births of the first water babies. Today in the UK waterbirth is becoming an increasingly accepted alternative to the medical model, with more than half of our hospitals now having installed birth pools, and more midwives learning how to include the use of water in their practice. As you will discover when you read the chapters that follow, the benefits of water in labour are numerous and research findings are encouraging and impressive. This has been achieved at a time of change, when both women and midwives, drawn to the idea of using a birth pool, may naturally be a bit hesitant and cautious. However, in places where confidence has grown, we are beginning to see exciting new models of how birth can be, with many more spontaneous natural births, fewer complications and less need for intervention, thanks to the simple expedient of a birthing pool and the philosophy that goes with it.

Women who give birth in water are often ecstatic and sometimes even evangelical about the experience. Through their enthusiasm a wave of inspiration flows out to other women. This also happens to the midwives who attend them. It is an unstoppable tide that has the power to transform birthing practices in our culture and beyond that, and may even change the culture itself. Time and again, mothers who have given birth in water tell me that their baby smiles a lot and seems unusually relaxed and calm. The sight of an older sibling first meeting their new baby sister or brother as they peer over the rim of a birth pool is incredibly moving to observe. This new generation will remember the birth of a baby as a time of joy, love and celebration – a far cry from the trauma that can result from the inappropriate use of medical technology.

Of course, the use of a birth pool is not always an option and is relevant only to the majority of women who have a healthy pregnancy followed by an uncomplicated birth. And it is precisely for these women that the use of a birth pool has the potential to prevent the cascade of unnecessary interventions that so often robs women of the possibility of an empowering birth experience and can also compromise the baby. I feel pleased and privileged to have had the opportunity to write this book. It is born out of my excitement about the great changes that have occurred in the span of my career, which began in the 1970s when most women gave birth on their backs in hospital labour rooms that resembled operating theatres. A pool room is a radically different concept that invites a very different outcome. Anyone who has witnessed the scenes of love and ecstasy that are common after a waterbirth will agree that this is a major innovation which deserves to become part of normal midwifery practice and to be widely available to women wherever they choose to give birth.

Janet Balaskas
London
May 2004

Acknowledgements

Thanks go firstly to the mothers and their families who have generously contributed their stories and photographs to this book. My sources of inspiration come from the home births which have taken place throughout the UK in birth pools hired from the Active Birth Centre and from the birth centres and hospitals that have installed birth pools and created a welcoming and conducive environment for birth. I would like to thank the pioneering midwives who attended these births and contributed to this book, in particular Pat Scott and Anita O'Neill, and also the obstetricians and waterbirth pioneers Michel Odent and Yehudi Gordon. Sheila Kitzinger and Beverley Lawrence have been staunch supporters of the waterbirth movement.

Many other colleagues, too numerous to mention by name, have also worked tirelessly to campaign for women's choices to include the option of a waterbirth. I appreciate them all for their efforts, commitment and contributions. I would also like to thank Keith Brainin who was my partner for 20 years and who designs and produces the birth pools that make it possible for so many women to benefit from the use of water. Using one of them during the birth of our son Theo is a memory that I treasure. It has been a pleasure working on this book with Cathy Meeus, and with Wanda Whiteley and Susanna Abbott from Thorsons.

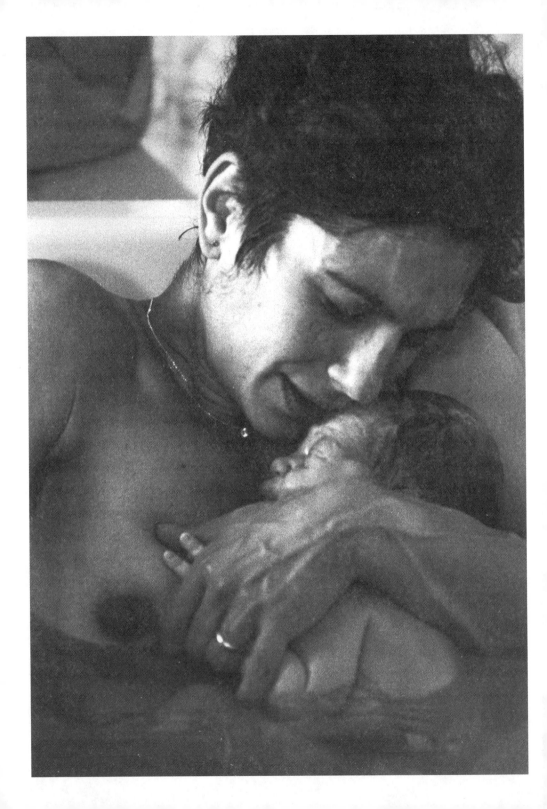

Before you were conceived
I wanted you
Before you were born
I loved you
Before you were here an hour
I would die for you
This is the miracle of life

Maureen Hawkins, 'The Baby Blessing'

chapter one

The history of birthing in water

'The pool was wonderfully relaxing and calming for me. Within half an hour of entering, my waters broke and my daughter's head was born, the next contraction delivered the shoulders. As she emerged I reached down and brought her to the surface. She blinked and quietly looked around. We cut the cord. The birth was quiet, tranquil and wonderful, and we the parents did it!'

Birth is a primal event. As we are propelled from the shelter of the womb into this world we make the hugest transition of our lives. Such elemental experiences of early life shape our future. Yet until recently, the 'primal period' from conception through infancy received very little attention. The emotional and physical sensitivity of newborn babies was not generally recognized – nor was it understood that what happens to us from conception onwards may establish the response patterns of a lifetime.

The 1960s heralded a turning point. The dawning of a new awareness that babies are born with already highly developed senses began in the field of psychology – following upon what philosophers and poets had been telling us for a long time. There was an explosion of different kinds of therapeutic work with adults, surrounding the events that happened in their early lives during pregnancy, birth and early infancy.

In the 1970s the psychiatrist R.D. Laing wrote:

> 'To be born is a momentous event in our life cycle. In recent years hundreds of thousands of people have been going through experiences as adults which they themselves feel to be related to their actual birth experience. Traces of the experience of being born seem to occur in dreams, myths, fantasies, physical events or to be acted out in different ways.' [1]

Laing was a radical psychiatrist and one of a few thinkers in the world who observed that patterns of behaviour may have their origins in earliest life – as early as conception or inter-uterine life. He believed that these primitive experiences, including what occurs during birth, make a profound impression on the psyche and resonate within us for a lifetime. At the time, this way of thinking was revolutionary.

In 1974 the French obstetrician Frederick Leboyer published a book called *Birth Without Violence* that shocked readers all over the world into recognizing that the high-tech birth practices prevalent at the time were often highly insensitive to babies. It became a bestseller and influenced a revolution in birthing culture. [2]

---

1 R.D. Laing, *The Facts of Life*, Penguin Books, 1977
2 Frederick Leboyer, *Birth Without Violence*, Knopf, 1975

His film with the same title was compulsory viewing for anyone interested in childbirth. The stark contrast of this film to the harsh reality of what was going on in hospitals at the time was a wakeup call.

While Leboyer did not propose that labour or birth might take place in water, he introduced the practice of immersing the newborn baby in a warm bath immediately after the birth. His concern was to relax the baby and make the transition from the womb to the world as gentle and easy as possible. Immediately after a natural birth, the film focuses on the newborn baby being sensitively and slowly bathed by Leboyer's hands in a bath of warm water. It ends with the baby smiling serenely less than one hour later as the dawn breaks on a new day.

The impact of Leboyer's work was astounding and began a welcome trend towards more gentle births all over the world. This involved creating a more sympathetic environment in the birthing room, including silence and a peaceful atmosphere with low lighting.

In a later film, *The Art of Breathing*, Leboyer used sounds and powerful images of water as a poetic metaphor for the 'tides' of labour, starting with a trickling stream and ending with strong river currents and huge ocean waves preceding the baby's first cries – which, in retrospect, seems to anticipate what was to come.

Within this context, women searching for alternatives to an obstetrically managed birth began to hear news of the extraordinary work of the Russian researcher Igor Tjarkovsky with the pioneering women in Moscow who were labouring and giving birth in warm water.

The reclaiming of birth

The obstetric model of birth which was widely prevalent in the 1970s originated just three centuries ago. It started in Europe with the invention of obstetric forceps in 1588 by the English surgeon Peter Chamberlen, who attended the labours of the queens of James I and Charles I. This heralded the appropriation of childbirth by male surgeons. By the late 18th century, the takeover of birth by physicians had begun to lead to the loss or denigration of much of the wisdom of traditional midwifery. With the development of modern obstetrics, generations of women were encouraged to believe that instinct and intuition about their own bodily processes had no role in childbirth and that the only safe labour and birth was a technologically managed one. While the benefits of obstetric intervention in the event of a complication or difficulty are clear to any sensible woman, it became increasingly difficult for healthy women to give birth normally without professional intervention in the clinical atmosphere of the hospital birth room. Understanding of birth physiology and the birth environment that supports it were lost. Against the traditions of every culture on Earth, women began to lie on their backs for birth – a posture that is more practical and convenient for the birth attendant than the woman or the baby. The trend to medicalize and control birth in hospitals was dramatically reflected in the statistics for home births in the 20th century. Barbara Harper cites the American experience in which 95 per cent of births took place at home in 1900, compared with 50 per cent in 1939, and 5 per cent in the 1990s.[3]

Yet just at the dawn of the era of technological birth, in 1805 there was the first documented account of a birth in water. A French woman had laboured for two days before being encouraged to get into a warm bath by her enlightened doctor.[4] She gave birth to a healthy baby within an hour. Sadly for millions of women, at the time there was no recognition of the importance of this event.

3　Barbara Harper, *Gentle Birth Choices*, Healing Arts Press, 1994
4　M. Embry, *Observation sur un accouchement terminé dans le bain*, AnnSoc Méd Prat Montpellier, 1805

Where did the idea of waterbirth originate?

Since the beginning of recorded history, humans have used water for the relief of pain and for relaxation. Women in particular have found respite from the pain of menstruation and labour through bathing in warm water. There are accounts of women of the South Pacific islands giving birth in shallow sea water, and oral traditions of similar practices among the Maori, the Indians of Central America, and the Ancient Greeks and Egyptians. The American childbirth educator Barbara Harper has written movingly about accounts told to her by a tribal elder of childbirth in water in Hawaii, where for generations this way of giving birth was common.[5]

'Grandfather [Semu] described...how as a young boy...he followed his mother and a group of women to the beach...On this day, the women began building a small lodge out of palm fronds. The structure quickly took shape and was entered by a few women, one of whom was very pregnant. Before long a group of men came onto the beach and began digging a pit in the sand not far from the lodge. After determining that the size was right, a large skin was rolled out over the pit and staked into the sand. Four men then stood on the taut skin and began to dance...The waves set the beat and the Chumash dancers followed along. They sang beautiful songs and they danced and some of the women joined in. There was a fire pit dug in front of the lodge and the children gathered dry wood and kindling. The woman who was pregnant emerged on hands and knees from the lodge, stood up and looked out across the waves...The woman walked into the ocean, accompanied by four other women. There she played, swam, laughed and labored. Just as the sky was deepening into scarlet and pink, the laboring woman appeared to be coming out of the water. Instead she squatted with the help of one of the women in the shallow water...There in what seemed a brief instant she

5   Barbara Harper, *Gentle Birth Choices*, Healing Arts Press, 1994

birthed her baby into the salty ocean. She picked the baby up out of the water and cradled it in her arms...She emerged from the sea and went into the lodge, warmed now by the roaring fire in front of it. There she rested, nursed and was cared for until it was time to walk back to the village.'

Barbara Harper, *Ojai Village Voice*, 1992

This story gives us a sense of how birth might have been celebrated among peoples where there is a natural source of shallow warm water. In such traditional societies, however, the rituals and practices of childbirth have usually been kept secret, and many cultures have a wide range of taboos surrounding childbirth. Knowledge has been passed down through generations of women without ever being recorded in the public history of a tribe or culture. And for this reason our knowledge of the history of this area of human experience is often sketchy.

What is true is that before the modern era there are no accounts of a tradition of childbirth in water in Europe or other northerly regions. The reason for this may be a simple matter of climate and plumbing. In places where there are shallow, warm seas, rivers and pools, the attraction of immersion in water during labour is easy to understand. In a climate where the oceans and inland waters are cold, to give birth in water would be uncomfortable and dangerous for mother and baby. Only with the widespread availability of artificially heated water and birthing pools in comparatively recent times has labouring or giving birth in water become a real option for women in colder parts of the world.

Pioneers of waterbirth

The inspiration to discover the power of water during birth came from the visionary work of the controversial Russian researcher Igor Tjarkovsky in the 1960s. A swimming instructor by profession, Tjarkovsky had studied the behaviour of animals in water and discovered that a variety of mammals could be trained to give birth and nurture their young underwater. The young raised in this way seemed to thrive.

When his daughter Veta was born 2 months prematurely, he created a warm water environment for her as a replacement for the womb. He cared for her much of the time in a tub filled with lukewarm water. He was convinced that her need for oxygen would be less and therefore the strain on her immature lungs would be reduced. Although the doctors had previously doubted that she would survive, she developed surprisingly rapidly and soon caught up with her peers. When Tjarkovsky observed her unusually fast development compared with her peers, he became convinced of the power of water to enhance human development. Tjarkovsky was inspired to continue his research into the beneficial effects of water in childbirth. He installed a glass tank in his own home in Moscow in which many mothers gave birth to healthy babies. Stunning photographs of these extraordinary births were published in the book *Water Babies*, written by the Swedish journalist Erik Sidenbladh on Tjarkovsky's work, and this book brought the first visions of waterbirth to the West.[6, 7]

For today's generation of mothers, the key figure in the use of water for labour and birth is the French obstetrician Michel Odent, who has done so much to increase our understanding of birth physiology in general and the key role of hormones in the birth process in particular. In the 1970s he created an ideal environment for birth which he called the 'primitive' birthing room at the

6　While this experiment demonstrates that treatment of premature babies in warm water could be beneficial, this has not been followed with further research as yet and is therefore not yet safe practice for parents.

7　Erik Sidenbladh, *Water Babies*, A & C Black, 1983

General Hospital in Pithiviers, northern France. The room bore no resemblance to the standard hospital delivery room of the time. It was designed to allow the woman in labour the freedom to follow her own instincts without being disturbed or distracted. Dark, earthy colours and heavy curtains encouraged a feeling of seclusion and intimacy. In this sympathetic environment, women were able to labour in whatever positions they found comfortable. Odent emphasized the need for privacy, to enable the mother to secrete her own natural hormones and thus ensure good progress of the labour and birth.

In 1977 Odent installed a pool in the room, not with the idea of promoting birth in water, but primarily as an additional option for pain relief and rest during long or difficult labours. He has said 'the reason for the birthing pool is not to have the baby born in water but to facilitate the birth process and to reduce the need for drugs and other interventions'.[8] However, births did sometimes inevitably occur in the water. Over the next few years many women laboured in the pool and by 1983 over a hundred births had taken place in water. Odent published his findings in *The Lancet*, and his recommendations in this article provided the basis for the first midwifery guidelines for waterbirths.[9]

Inspired by news of what was happening in Moscow and France, the earliest waterbirths in the West took place at home in pools that were often improvised by the couples themselves and attended by independent midwives. The parents created birthing pools using any large waterproof container they could find – including refuse skips, cattle troughs, inflatable paddling pools or garden ponds lined with a plastic sheet. This happened simultaneously in several parts of the world and began to cause ripples in the world of obstetrics.

8   M. Odent, *Abstract MIDIRS Midwifery Digest*, March 2000 10:1
9   M. Odent, 'Birth Under Water', *The Lancet*, December 24/31, 1983

The spread of waterbirth

A key element in the spread of the popularity of waterbirth has been the design of birthing pools, both installed and portable. Providing the right equipment in terms of size and depth, provision for temperature and infection control and, not least, convenience, has made waterbirth a practical option for most women anywhere in the world.

Waterbirths continued to happen during the 1980s and 1990s in Europe, America and Australasia. In the southern hemisphere, New Zealand waterbirth activist Estelle Myers organized two conferences, promoting ideas of human affinity with dolphins and the benefits of birth in water. A few Japanese midwives began to use portable birth pools in traditional Japanese birth houses where the woman gives birth in the midwife's home. Even close to the North Pole in northernmost Norway, a midwife attending rural home births began using one of our portable birth pools in the late 1980s.

In various parts of Europe knowledge of waterbirthing was promoted by several individuals, in addition to Michel Odent. Notable among these is Dr Herman Ponette, working at Ostend, Belgium, who had assisted at more than 1,000 waterbirths before 1995, and Josie Muscat, whose use of a birth pool in a hospital in Malta revealed a very high percentage of natural births.[10]

When reports and images of the first waterbirths were published, the world looked on in amazement. The women who chose this way of birthing and their attendants were variously regarded as crazy, deluded, foolhardy or inspired. The medical establishment rallied to call the practice into question, citing theoretical risks, concerns about infection and fears of the baby drowning (see pages 10–11). Nonetheless a steady stream of journalists, midwives and doctors visited

10 Beverley A. Lawrence Beech (ed.), *Water Birth Unplugged*, Books for Midwives Press, 1996

Odent's birth unit in Pithiviers, and information about waterbirths spread all over the world.

Interest in waterbirth continued to grow. Experiences were generally so good that mothers and midwives were enthusiastic and often even evangelical about them. The midwives who attended them were impressed by the apparent benefits. Many were keen to participate in further research as they observed that a significant number of these women had easier births, fewer needed medical interventions and that the babies often seemed calmer and more relaxed.

However, some problems are bound to occur with any method of birth. Over the years there were also reports of a small percentage of problems that occurred at waterbirths in different parts of the world. Consideration of these identified the areas for many of the research projects that followed. Midwifery guidelines evolved which were carefully designed to exclude mothers and babies who were vulnerable to risk and to avoid preventable problems. Some problems were easily resolved with clear recommendations regarding practical issues such as the temperature and depth of the water, infection control and timing. A significant percentage of the reported problems were later revealed to be unrelated to the use of water *per se*. In the UK the issues of safe practice were addressed by the Department of Health, Royal College of Midwives, midwifery managers and supervisors and obstetricians, as the demand for waterbirths continued to increase.

The most tragic problem that can occur at a birth is the death of a baby. A small number of deaths have been reported over the years at births that may or may not have been associated with the use of water. In 1993 the death of a baby born in water in Sweden led to a furore in the press that gave waterbirth a lot of negative publicity. The professional evidence as to the cause of death in this case was scanty and inconclusive, but nonetheless the surrounding sensationalism temporarily set back progress. However, it did serve to highlight the need for more scientific evaluation of the risk of a baby drowning at a waterbirth.

However the birth is conducted, on rare occasions a few babies do die or are damaged around the time of birth for a whole variety of reasons, and waterbirth is no exception. Quite rightly, it is the task of paediatricians to raise questions about the relative safety of any birth method, including waterbirths, from the baby's perspective. Ongoing assessment in this area is a vital aspect of evidence-based care.

A large British study of adverse outcomes (death or admission to special care) following labour or delivery in water was reported in the *BMJ* in August 1999 (see page 22). The authors concluded that:

> *'Perinatal mortality is not substantially higher among babies delivered in water than among those born to low risk women who deliver conventionally. The data are comparable with a small increase or decrease in perinatal mortality for babies delivered in water.'*

This important study has been reassuring enough for the continued practice of waterbirth generally. While there are now few who question the benefits of water in labour, there is still uncertainty among some paediatricians about the practice of birth in water and its value to babies.

Waterbirth in the UK

In Britain, mostly inspired by Michel Odent, the use of birth pools began in the mid-1980s. A small number of independent midwives became known as specialist practitioners of home waterbirths. Roger Lichy, an independent general practitioner who specializes in obstetric homeopathy, attended and facilitated waterbirths in the southwest corner of England, famously travelling to home births with a birthing pool strapped to the top of his car![11]

Within the mainstream of hospital-based obstetric practice, particularly in the UK, there emerged a few enthusiasts for the use of water in labour who were already proponents of active birth. Yehudi Gordon, consultant obstetrician at the Hospital of St John and St Elizabeth, London, has been an inspirational advocate of the practice. He introduced the use of water in the birth unit at the Garden Hospital in the 1980s, and later transferred the practice to the Hospital of St John and St Elizabeth. Along with the team of committed midwives, including Jennifer Staritsky, Patricia Scott and Anita O'Neill, he developed reliable guidelines for best practice during waterbirths.

Another important waterbirth pioneer in the UK is Dianne Garland, Senior Midwife at the Maidstone Hospital birth unit, one of the UK's National Health Service hospitals where the use of water in labour and birth has become an example for birth units around the country. The first waterbirth at Maidstone was in 1986 in a pool hand-built by the father of the baby. What was key to this event was the open-mindedness and willingness to learn on the part of the midwives and doctors, who thoroughly researched what was then known about waterbirth in order to give the mother the birth she wanted. From this tiny beginning the hospital has developed into a national centre of waterbirth expertise where midwives, obstetricians and paediatricians confidently offer this option to women for whom it is appropriate.

A national survey conducted by the National Perinatal Epidemiology Unit in Oxford explored the extent of the use of waterbirth pools in England and Wales during 1992–3.[12] During this two-year period it was estimated that

11 R. Lichy and E. Herzberg, *The Waterbirth Handbook*, Gateway Books, 1993
12 F. Alderdice, M. Renfrew, S. Marchant, et al, 'Labour and birth in water in England and Wales: survey report.' *British Journal of Midwifery*, vol 3, no 7, Jul 1995

4,834 women gave birth in water and approximately twice as many used a pool in labour only. It was concluded in this survey that there was no evidence of any significant risk to mother or baby. Following the publication of this survey in 1995 the Department of Health cautiously endorsed the ongoing use of birthing pools and highlighted the need for further research.

Since then a burgeoning of interest in the use of water in labour in the UK has led to the development of a unique concentration of knowledge and expertise within the mainstream maternity system. Positive encouragement towards the use of water in labour and childbirth has come from the Royal College of Midwives, which recommends that midwives should develop the knowledge and skills to assist women at a waterbirth.[13]

Against this backdrop, more of the managers of maternity services in the UK are being persuaded that the option of using water in labour and for birth should be available to women. The extent of the use of birth pools in the UK has not been formally assessed since 1995, but has certainly increased. Pools are now used in hospitals as well as independent birth centres, some of which specialize in waterbirths, and in the community at home births with both independent and NHS midwives. The Edgware Birth Centre in North London is an example of a new type of forward-thinking birth unit in the UK. Set up in 1997 as a two-year demonstration project with central government funds and continued thereafter on the basis of its success, it is managed by midwives with a family-centred ethos. Designed for low-risk births, the centre is enthusiastically supportive of those women who want to use water in labour. It has two pools and typically 75 per cent of women who give birth at the centre use water during labour and 56 per cent give birth in water. Its outcomes show fewer interventions than for low-risk births at a conventional hospital birth unit. For example, at Edgware episiotomies are performed in only 3.6 per cent of births,

13 *The Use of Water in Labour and Birth*, Position Paper No. 1a, Royal College of Midwives, October 2000

compared with 18.9 per cent at a nearby hospital; 6.4 per cent of births involve epidurals, compared with 30.7 per cent; and inductions are performed in 7.3 per cent of births compared with 16.8 per cent.

The Albany Midwifery Practice based in Peckham, South East London are a self-employed and self-managed group contracted into the NHS who practise individual caseload midwifery in a socially deprived inner-city area. Though their mothers are both high and low risk, 40–50 per cent of their births take place at home and the rest in hospital. Around 80 per cent are spontaneous vaginal births. Many of these births occur in water in the two portable pools owned by the practice. Their philosophy to provide 'choice, control and continuity' free of charge to all women is a model of midwifery care that has integrated waterbirth in an inspirational way.

In the UK birth pools are now becoming a standard fitting in labour suites – or at least a goal to which financially hard-pressed hospitals aspire. In October 2000 the UK's Royal College of Midwives estimated that 50 per cent of maternity units provided facilities for labour or birth in water.[14] The usage of these facilities at the time varied between 15 and 60 per cent, which may be an indicator of the significance of the role of the midwife in encouraging women to consider the use of water. Since then the number of UK hospitals and birth centres with installed pools has risen to closer to 60 per cent. However, that does not always mean that the pools are being fully or enthusiastically utilized. It's not uncommon for women to be discouraged from using them or told that trained midwives are not available.

'One midwifery manager simply tells women: "We do not allow water births. My midwives are not trained for it." She said the same thing last year. And the year before. Meanwhile no training has been arranged.'[15]

14 *The Use of Water in Labour and Birth*, Position Paper No. 1a, Royal College of Midwives, October 2000

15 J. Robinson, 'Demand and supply in maternity care', *British Journal of Midwifery*, 9(8), 510, 2001

When introducing a birth pool some hospitals agree to use it for labour only at first with the birth itself happening on land. Inevitably, sooner or later a baby is born accidentally in the pool and this can be inspirational for the midwives, who may then begin to feel more confident to deliver babies in water. Sometimes stringent protocols around the use of a pool can limit its usefulness and frustrate both mothers and midwives. There is great variation in different parts of the country regarding availability of waterbirths. However, there has been tremendous progress, especially where the midwives, or a particular midwife, are passionate about bringing this beneficial option to women.

> '*The midwives were brilliant although they hadn't been trained to deliver in water and said they'd prefer me to get out for the second stage. I wasn't sure how I felt about that, but when it came to it, I was quite happy to step out of the pool and have the help of gravity to deliver the baby. I delivered in a squatting position and then held the baby for a short while. He sucked the breast a little and the placenta was delivered after 10 minutes.*'

Waterbirth in the US

Some of the earliest home waterbirths occurred in the US. Waterbirth pioneers such as film-maker Karil Daniels began to popularize the idea of birthing in water from the early 1980s. Her documentary featuring the first waterbirths in the US surveyed all aspects of the experience and proved an inspiration to many to pursue the idea of birth in water.[16] Currently the key person in the American waterbirth movement is Barbara Harper. A practising midwife, she was inspired by the idea of waterbirth in 1978 after visiting Pithiviers and observing the work of Michel Odent. She founded the organization Waterbirth

16 Karil Daniels, *Water Baby: Experiences of Water Birth,*1986

International (now renamed Global Maternal/Childhealth Association) in 1988 to provide education and resources for those wanting to experience a waterbirth. Her book *Gentle Birth Choices*[17] has been widely influential. At the Family Birthing Centre in Upland, California, another waterbirth pioneer, Dr Michael Rosenthal, assisted at over 900 waterbirths between 1985 and 1993.

In the US the culture of birthing is more deeply entrenched in the medical model and less driven by consumer pressure than the UK. The primary birth attendants are generally doctors. Although some of the first inspirational waterbirths happened at home births in the US, the percentage of hospitals offering waterbirths there is much smaller than in the UK. However, thanks to the campaigning work of progressive childbirth activists, the number of waterbirths have increased from just three in 1991 to 280 in 2003 (less than 10 per cent of hospitals have waterbirthing facilities).[18]

Interest in waterbirth is currently growing in the US as it is in most other countries. Without a national health service such as we have in the UK, facilities for birth pools are not yet widely available in hospitals in the US, although they can be rented through pool hire companies. The increase in waterbirths in the US is going hand in hand with the renaissance of midwifery. The hospitals offering waterbirth are overwhelmingly those in which midwives are the primary caregivers. As more midwife-led care happens, the pressure on US hospitals to install birth pools is being spearheaded by midwives who are keen to transform the birthing environment to be more conducive to natural birth. There is a strong revolutionary alternative birth community across the US who have fought long and hard for these changes for many years. It is hoped that the increase in waterbirth in the UK and the rest of Europe along with the work of dedicated researchers, midwives, birth educators and doulas will make waterbirths more easily available to American women.

17 Barbara Harper, *Gentle Birth Choices*, Healing Arts Press, 1994
18 Estimates provided by Waterbirth International (see Resources)

A changing attitude to childbirth choices

The expansion of waterbirth needs to take place in an atmosphere of increasing emphasis on consumer choice in maternity care. The reclaiming of responsibility for normal birth from the medical profession by women and midwives creates the right climate for waterbirths – which are essentially for low-risk mothers and come under the domain of midwifery rather than obstetrics.

A milestone in this process in the UK was the publication in 1991 of the Winterton Report on maternity services by the Parliamentary Health Select Committee. This recommended that birth pools should be provided as an option for labouring women 'wherever this is practicable' and led to the installation of the first birth pools in NHS hospitals.

This was followed in 1993 by a review of maternity care commissioned by Baroness Cumberledge, entitled *Changing Childbirth*. This important document set out to change the emphasis and quality of maternity care in the UK by giving more choice to mothers, providing greater accessibility to the services women want and greater responsiveness to their preferences in terms of obstetric care and the individuals who deliver it. This has given a great impetus to community-based services, one-to-one midwifery schemes and home births. These initiatives also led to the commissioning of further research into the effectiveness and safety of a variety of childbirth options including waterbirth.

Recognizing the huge shift in attitudes that was taking place, Baroness Cumberledge said in her opening address to the first International Waterbirth Conference in London in 1995, 'This is a moment of huge opportunity, this is a moment of professional fulfilment for midwives and doctors, and a time of enormous fulfilment for the women in their care.'[19]

19 Beverley A. Lawrence Beech (ed.), *Water Birth Unplugged*, Books for Midwives Press, 1996

This change in attitude has by no means been fully realized to date, but important progress has been made to the degree that we can now be more confident that the use of water in labour and for birth is here to stay.

> 'The birthing pool finally enabled me to have the birth I wanted – after two previous long, difficult, highly interventionist hospital deliveries. In the pool I felt relaxed, secure and in control. I was able to move freely, retire into myself to focus my natural instincts on the birth as I had never been able to previously. The waterbirth experience was uplifting, deeply satisfying and a thoroughly natural and appropriate environment to deliver my new son – from water into water – happy and with no complications!'

The research

Although anecdotal evidence from many countries was reassuring about the benefits and safety of the use of water in labour and for childbirth, the increasing numbers of waterbirths in the early 1990s created a need for more formal assessment.

Human beings have been developing knowledge of how to maintain the body in health and how to treat it at times of illness since the earliest times. Many treatments still in use today, including the use of water, have ancient origins. However, the modern scientific community demands increasingly rigorous standards of validation for any innovative treatments. The reasons for this are easily understood – few of us would want to take a drug or undergo a procedure that had not been thoroughly tested for safety and effectiveness. There are a number of different types of study used for assessing medical interventions. In order to appreciate the credence given to various waterbirth studies, it may be helpful to explain the basis of each of these.

As far as the scientific community is concerned, the 'gold standard' type of study – that is, the type most respected as being free from bias of any kind – is the 'double-blind' randomized control trial (RCT). In such studies subjects are allocated on a random basis to one of two groups. One group receives the treatment (often a drug) and the other group is given a placebo, an inactive substance. None of the subjects knows which group they are in, and the professionals treating them are equally unaware of the composition of the groups. In this way the results of the intervention can be compared without the risk of their being skewed by the placebo effect or the expectations of the doctors administering the treatment.

However, a double-blind trial is clearly not suitable for a study in which the subjects cannot fail to be aware of which group they are in – that is, whether or not they are receiving treatment. You are bound to know whether or not you are having a waterbirth, for example. In addition, such trials are not considered an ethical method of assessing interventions for which there is already strong evidence that patients will benefit – for example, it would be unacceptable to withhold a potentially life-saving treatment from a group of patients for the sake of a study.

Because of these problems, other types of study have been used to assess the benefits and possible risks of waterbirth. These include observational studies in which groups of patients who have received a particular type of treatment or intervention are compared with others who have not. The study groups may be tailored to match as closely as possible for other variables such as age or socio-economic grouping, but they are essentially self-selecting in their choice as to whether they have the treatment being studied, and they are aware of receiving it.

The fact that the subjects choose to have the intervention is regarded as important for practices such as waterbirth, which has been said to appeal mainly to more educated women from wealthier backgrounds, who are at lower risk from health problems of all kinds. However, as waterbirth becomes more widely available, this bias will be less critical for future studies.

Other studies include reviews and audits. Reviews involve a search through all the published data on a subject, with a view to gaining an overview. Audits are an evaluation of the outcomes of a specific practice against predetermined criteria. This could mean a birth unit evaluating the number of perineal tears, for example, for births in and out of water.

Key studies

In 1995 I was involved in organizing a ground-breaking international conference on the current state of knowledge about waterbirth. We invited all the leading international waterbirth practitioners, some of whom had experience of more than a thousand waterbirths. The proceedings were published as *Water Birth Unplugged*.[20] Speakers from many related disciplines pooled their experiences and knowledge of 19,000 waterbirths around the world. The results were inspiring.

One of the important speakers was Dr Paul Johnson, neonatal physiologist at the John Radcliffe Hospital, Oxford. His research on the mechanisms that trigger breathing in the newborn (later published as 'Birth Under Water

---

20 Beverley A. Lawrence Beech (ed.), *Water Birth Unplugged*, Books for Midwives Press, 1996

– to breathe or not to breathe')[21] provided scientific confirmation of the viability of birth underwater for babies who are not at risk. He described how the baby is protected against the possibility of breathing while underwater in the few seconds between emerging from the birth canal and being lifted out of the water. (This response, known as the dive reflex, is explained in more detail in Chapter 3, page 66.) This confirmation provided a confidence boost to all concerned, adding weight to the research on the dive reflex at birth by the German researchers Gerd Eldering and Konrad Selke.[22] Paul Johnson's findings helped in the design of safety guidelines for birth in water and gave reassurance to midwives assisting at waterbirths (see Chapter 8, page 214).

Other important contributors included a number of midwives and doctors who shared their experiences in assisting mothers to labour and sometimes deliver in water. The consensus was clear: water can help to alleviate pain, reduce the severity of perineal tears, speed labour and contribute to a positive birth experience. Midwives who regularly attended waterbirths agreed that the babies born in this way are on the whole more settled, alert and unstressed than babies born on land. Moreover, the midwives who regularly attended such labours found that working with water enhanced their own skills and sensitivities. The conference also showed that interest in waterbirth was a worldwide phenomenon, including contributions from midwives and obstetricians from America, Japan, Austria, Australia, Malta, Russia, Italy, Sweden and Denmark, and the UK.

One of the most notable outcomes of the conference was the conviction among waterbirth practitioners of the need to reinforce the positive results of their experience with solid scientific backing for the safety of the practice. A number of research studies and surveys were consequently designed and

21 Paul Johnson, 'Birth Under Water – to breathe or not to breathe', *British Journal of Obstetrics,*1996
22 Eldering, G., Selke, K., 'Water Birth – a possible mode of delivery?' *Water Birth Unplugged,* Books for Midwives Press, 1996

carried out, mostly looking at the benefits of using water in labour. These are listed on page 73.

However, the comparative risks of birth in water to the baby were not known until 1999, when Ruth E. Gilbert and Pat A. Tookey of the Institute of Child Health, London, published an important study in the *BMJ*.[23] This study set out to estimate mortality and morbidity rates for babies delivered in water. These were compared with other sources of data providing similar estimates for babies delivered conventionally to low-risk women. Although just one piece in the emerging jigsaw of research, this study has provided significant reassurance about the safety of waterbirths. The study examined adverse outcomes which were reported over a two-year period between 1994 and 1996 from approximately 4,000 waterbirths. In the UK, 1,500 consultant paediatricians were asked if they knew of cases where a baby died or was admitted to special care following labour or delivery in water. The study revealed a similarity in rates of perinatal mortality and morbidity in babies born in water and babies born to low-risk women on land. This suggests that delivery in water does not substantially increase adverse perinatal outcomes. The data were compatible with a small increase or decrease in perinatal mortality.

None of the five perinatal deaths recorded among the waterbirths was attributable to the delivery in water, and the rate of 1.2 deaths per 1,000 was in keeping with the rate for low-risk deliveries on land. Although the rate of admission for special care of 8.4 per 1,000 (34 babies in the study) of the waterbirth babies was significantly lower than for low-risk land births, the authors do have some reservations that some admissions may not have been reported and still have concerns about water aspiration and cord snapping which are detailed in Chapter 8.

23 Ruth E. Gilbert and Pat A. Tookey, 'Perinatal mortality and morbidity among babies delivered in water', *British Medical Journal*, Vol 319, no 7208, 21 August 1999

Waterbirth is now entering its fourth decade. Evaluations, research and experience from many places in the world during this 'trial period' reveal similar findings. Among practitioners there is general accord that waterbirth has significant benefits and comparatively few risks. Waterbirth has stood up well to scrutiny so far and the picture is not yet complete.

What is best for your baby must always be the priority – over and above your dreams and visions for your personal experience of the birth. The safety of any birth method can never be guaranteed. Research and assessment of waterbirth is ongoing, as with other approaches and technologies that assist birth. The best way to prevent problems at your birth is to keep an open mind and to be well informed, making your choices at the time with the help of your birth attendants. This will depend on how your labour progresses, how you and your baby are at the time and, most importantly, your intuitive sense and inner guidance. While the benefits and joys of waterbirth are very persuasive and women generally rate the experience very highly, this book is written in the spirit of providing you with up-to-date information you will need when considering using water at your birth.

> *'It was a magical experience, feeling the warm, enveloping water*
> *helping my body relax in between contractions. When her head*
> *was born it bobbed about under the water and I reached down to*
> *feel her velvety hair. The rest of her appeared within minutes and*
> *she floated to the surface and suddenly there was this tiny bundle*
> *on my chest. The depth of emotion and amazement was profound*
> *and unforgettable.'*

chapter two

The power of water

Water is the element that sustains life. Seventy per cent of our planet is covered by water and it is a key component of all living things. As much as 75 per cent of our body mass is water, and for newborns this proportion is 97 per cent.

The profound connection of life with water was understood by numerous ancient cultures throughout human history. Many creation myths describe human origins arising from a primordial body of water. For example, in Ancient Egypt it was believed that life arose from the watery chaos known as Nu. Creation stories from the Mesopotamian civilizations describe how the Earth was 'born' from the union of Apsu (sweet water) and Tiamat (salt water). In this myth Tiamat represents the feminine element, giving birth to the world. In the creation story of the Judaeo-Christian tradition told in the Book of Genesis, water is portrayed as the primal element, its existence preceding even the creation of light. In fact, scientists who study the earliest rocks and life forms on Earth are agreed that the first primitive life forms arose in the warm oceans that formed as the Earth cooled.

On an individual level, too, we all originate in the watery environment of the fluid-filled amniotic sac within the womb. Water is the first element we experience. It stimulates our first embryonic sensations on the skin, and throughout life it remains a source of refreshment, restoration and renewal – quenching our thirst and gently enveloping and soothing our body when we bathe or swim.

> *'Life began in the ocean; in amniotic fluid we recapture the history of life.'*
>
> Michel Odent, *Water and Sexuality*

Cultural associations of water

For practical reasons, the earliest settlements were situated near to reliable sources of water. As the provider of drinking water, irrigation and fertile soil, those springs and rivers often acquired a mythic or sacred status. The Ganges in India, for example, is regarded by Hindus as the sacred mother, and to die beside her is to find union with God. Bathing in the waters of the Ganges cleanses sin. On completion of the cycle of life, devout Hindus ask that their ashes be scattered on the waters of the Ganges. In the Hindu Vedas, water is referred to as 'matritamah' (the most maternal). The Ancient Egyptians revered the Nile, whose silt-laden flood waters brought fertility to the land. Its waters were believed to flow from Nu – the source of life. Muslims revere the holy spring of Zamzam at Mecca, and there are numerous holy springs, notably at Lourdes, that are a focus for Christian pilgrimage, many of these dating back to ancient pagan times.

Perhaps because of water's softness and mutability, many cultures have viewed it as a 'feminine' element. The oceans respond to the cycles of the

Moon, just as the female body resonates to a monthly cycle. In traditional Chinese philosophy water is yin – the female aspect. It is the first of the five elements and represents the primal life force. Associated with a state of rest, it contains the potential for growth and regeneration. In the ancient Mesopotamian language Sumerian, the word for 'sea' also means 'womb'. Some Native American traditions express the idea of water being the 'blood' of the Earth.

> *'There was a wonderful sense of timelessness when I was in the water.'*

Water is often regarded as a medium for change. This transformational quality is reflected in religious rites, such as Christian baptism, in which anointing with water symbolizes a transition of the individual from one state or community to another. Muslims wash their feet before prayer, an act of spiritual cleansing as well as simple washing. In Hindu marriages washing forms an important part of the proceedings, representing the casting off of one life before embarking on the new one. In the Jewish tradition the bride-to-be undergoes a ritual of bathing called the Mikvah to purify herself before marriage. And in the mundane setting of everyday life, we often use bathing as a way of marking the transition, for example, from the working day to the evening at home. In this context, it is not so surprising that parents often comment on the joy of experiencing the transition of a new life emerging into this world through the medium of water.

> *'I feel that my baby had the calmest, most peaceful and natural birth possible, with the transition from water-in-utero to water-in-pool. I cannot imagine giving birth in any other way.'*

The physical qualities of water

Composed of a simple molecule consisting of one oxygen atom and two of hydrogen, this wonderfully mutable substance can manifest in a variety of guises, as transparent liquid, as a gas and as a semi-opaque solid – ice. In its liquid form, the bonds that join the molecules are constantly breaking and reforming in different ways, creating its fluidity, but also the flexible tension that is its strength. Humans, whose bodies contain both air and fat, naturally float when submerged in water. For us it is a naturally supportive element that allows us to experience a sense of weightlessness.

We all know the feeling of peace that is engendered by being close to water, in a garden with the soothing sound of a fountain or on the shore of a great ocean. Or even the great feeling of relaxing in a bath at the end of a stressful day. This may have something to do with the preponderance of healthy negative ions (negatively charged molecules) in an atmosphere close to running water, but we may also be responding to a deeper affinity with this element.

> 'I was in labour all day with slow but steady progress – I danced, walked on the beach and danced some more. Got into the pool around 5.30 and felt contained and soothed.'

> 'I loved the sound of the water: I could concentrate better in my own little private space.'

A further subtle quality of water, perhaps associated with its liquid nature – less permeable than air, less rigid than a solid – is the gently protective barrier it forms around you. Many women who labour in water describe the sense of being enclosed or embraced by the water. It is as if the water has a benign, protective property in this situation. The woman feels protected in her pool without being isolated, creating an ideal environment for a natural labour.

> '*Labouring and giving birth in water was truly an amazing experi-*
> *ence. The sense of being cocooned and held by the water gave me*
> *peace and relaxation in between contractions. My most vivid memory*
> *is of the baby coming out under the water. He slowly turned to look*
> *up and it was fantastic. A very peaceful contented baby.'*

The healing energy of water

Many approaches to health and the treatment of disease or injury include work with water. From the healing baths prescribed by Hippocrates, the Greek founder of modern medicine, to the widespread use of health spas in 18th-century Europe, water has long been used for its health-giving properties. The popularity of pools, spas and steam rooms in health clubs today is testimony to the value of water in a healthy lifestyle. In the early 19th century, the founder of modern hydrotherapy, Vincent Priessnitz, devised treatments involving the use of baths. Since that time, both hot and cold water baths have been used in the alleviation of symptoms of a variety of conditions from arthritis to headaches. Both traditional Chinese medicine and Indian Ayurvedic medicine view water as the transmitter of life energy and therefore integral to health.

Modern physiotherapists use pools to enable those with physical disabilities to exercise more easily. The supportive qualities of water and the circulation-boosting effects of warm water in particular have helped to provide pain relief for many sufferers of chronic conditions involving muscle spasm. It is therefore

not a revolutionary idea that warm water baths could be soothing and comforting to women in labour.

> *'The pain was acute but the warmth of the pool was a very*
> *effective relaxant and source of comfort.'*

The power of water to re-establish emotional equilibrium is utilized in therapies such as Watsu, a form of shiatsu massage and bodywork done in water, and underwater rebirthing. The use of floatation tanks, in which you float and relax in warm water in an enclosed darkened space, is another form of water therapy. The unmistakable sense of tranquillity and wholeness that many people experience when immersed in or simply near to water can be of inestimable value to a woman in labour.

> *'The water was more helpful than I could have imagined – it was bliss!'*

Human affinity with water

Anyone who has observed children playing at the seaside will have noticed the instinctive attraction that water holds for them. As they splash and swim they seem to have a natural affinity with this element.

In recent years a number of studies have postulated theories about the origins and evolution of humankind that may contribute to our understanding of the adaptation to birth in water for humans. The writer Elaine Morgan popularized a theory first proposed in the 1960s by Alister Hardy. This suggests that modern humans evolved from primates who were forced by climatic conditions to adapt to a semi-aquatic existence, and then moved back to a predominantly

land-based lifestyle after having developed an upright stance.[1] She draws attention to a wealth of physiological characteristics that are not present in other primates, but that we share with aquatic mammals such as whales and dolphins.
These include a high proportion of fat under the skin, loss of body hair, and the
ability to control our breathing and hold our breath. She also suggests that the
development of the large human brain may have been due to the large amounts
of omega-3 fatty acids in a diet rich in fish and seafood. In the aquatic theory of
evolution, our ancestors would have lived at the water's edge, spending time
both on land and in the sea. These 'aquatic apes' would have been excellent
swimmers and divers, and have felt as safe in water as on land. An interesting,
and in the context of this book, significant observation Morgan makes is that
human babies have a very high proportion of body fat compared with the young
of chimpanzees, our nearest primate relatives, who have virtually none. She
makes the point that lightness is an advantage for young who have to cling on
to their mother's fur for safety as soon as they are born, like land- and tree-
dwelling primates, whereas the buoyancy provided by body fat would be more
advantageous for young who were likely to be born in water.

The idea of our possible aquatic origins is one that Michel Odent takes up in
his book *Water and Sexuality*,[2] in which he presents a fascinating argument to
explain the power and great attraction of water to humans. Through being
more in touch with water, he believes we have the opportunity to be more
in touch with ourselves, our sexuality and our basic human nature, and to
reconcile the gap between instinct and reason.

Aquatic mammals

It may be of interest to reflect on the habits of aquatic mammals that

1 E. Morgan, *The Descent of Woman*, Souvenir Press, 1985 and *The Aquatic Ape Hypothesis*, Souvenir
   Press, 1997
2 Michel Odent, *Water and Sexuality*, Arkana, 1990

commonly give birth under water such as the cetaceans (whales and dolphins). The cetaceans evolved from a group of mammals that adopted an aquatic lifestyle many millions of years ago. Although their body shape has adapted to swimming, they retain significant mammalian features. Like all mammals, these creatures give birth to live young and suckle them during infancy. They breathe air, although they are capable of holding their breath for long periods. They are also warm-blooded, that is, they regulate their own temperature.

Cetaceans are supremely well adapted to their environment and are believed to be highly intelligent, although their intelligence is very different from that of humans. Their complex and subtle communication systems enable them to operate as a group underwater over huge distances. They seem to form strong bonds within the group and protect sick or injured individuals, and some species appear even to mourn their dead.

Groups of mothers and young are often found well protected at the centre of the school. Such protection of mothers and children also occurs in most human societies. Interestingly, groups of cetaceans often contain numbers of non-reproductive females who seem to 'assist' other females as they give birth and defend them against the unwanted attentions of males. The young are well developed when they are born. After the birth, the umbilical cord snaps spontaneously and the newborn is gently nudged to the surface for its first breath by its mother or an attendant 'midwife' female. The mechanisms that trigger breathing and prevent inhalation of water are thought to be similar to those that operate at the birth of a human baby in water (see Chapter 3, page 66). The young cetacean is immediately able to swim but stays close to its mother for many weeks, protected at her side, coming up to the surface for air and suckling from her mammary glands until ready to feed independently.

Water in our lives

All these fascinating theories suggest a closer affinity of humans with water than previously acknowledged by modern science. But you don't have to take on board all of these ideas to benefit from using water in labour. The value of water at this time is clearly demonstrated by the experience of thousands of women and the midwives who have attended their labours. The inescapable conclusion is that for most, though not all women, the use of water can contribute significantly to making the experience of giving birth among the highlights of their life.

'My son was born at 4.15am in the pool and I remember looking through the glass roof and seeing the stars as he was being born. I could not have wished for a better birth experience.'

'The water gave me the support, pain relief and privacy to get on with dealing with the pain and concentrating on the contractions. I can't imagine not using water now – it helped so much. I could really stretch out and move about, but be supported and not waste energy on holding myself. In between contractions, it was bliss to lie in the water and refocus. The relief when my daughter came out was incredible and it was wonderful for her to have such a gentle transition into the world.'

'After my daughter was born, I nursed her in the pool. This was a beautiful experience, very relaxing and healing for me...being supported by water felt great. My husband thought that seeing me and our baby in the pool was the most moving experience of his life.'

chapter three

How water can benefit you during labour and birth

From the moment your baby is conceived, a natural continuum of physiological events is set in motion that leads to the birth of your baby. As soon as the fertilized egg implants in the wall of the uterus, your body begins to adapt to sustain the pregnancy and support the needs of your growing baby. These changes continue throughout the nine months and then through the transition of labour and birth into breastfeeding and motherhood.

It's reassuring to know that your body is perfectly designed for carrying and giving birth to a baby. The shape and structure of your pelvic bones and muscles, your organs and circulatory systems all play their part in adapting to the magnificent capacity your body has to produce a new life.

Labour and birth are initiated and stimulated throughout by natural chemical messengers we call hormones. These play a key role in the changes and physiological events that take place, rather like the conductor of the orchestra.

Understanding how this works can be the key to choosing and creating an environment that will make it easier for you to give birth to your baby naturally. It will also reveal the best way to use the help of water both during your labour and perhaps for the birth of your baby.

The 'love hormones'

We can be grateful to Michel Odent for bringing to our attention the crucial role of the mother's own natural hormones in a physiological birth and for much of the information that follows. In many ways he has created a new language for us to understand the true nature of birth. He encourages us to leave behind our preconceptions and observe the processes that commonly take place in all natural labours that we, as humans, share with other mammals.

At a lecture I attended recently, Michel Odent said 'in order to have a baby, mammals are supposed to release a complex cocktail of "love" hormones. Without this, birth is not possible.' He calls them love hormones because they are identical to the hormones we release during lovemaking and in all phases of the reproductive cycle including menstruation, ovulation, orgasm, sperm ejaculation and breastmilk ejection. Included in this 'cocktail' of hormones are prolactin, the 'mothering hormone', and endorphins, natural morphine-like chemicals that bring pain relief in labour, as well as oxytocin, the main birth hormone.

The love hormones are produced by the deep, most primitive part of the mother's brain, which is known as the hypothalamus. This is situated at the base of the back of the skull, behind the front brain, or neo-cortex, and includes the pituitary gland. The hypothalamus becomes very active when a woman is in labour, working hard to secrete huge amounts of love hormones – while the thinking part of the brain and home of the intellect, the neo-cortex, takes a back seat for the time being. You may notice this tendency building up already towards the end of your pregnancy when you are less inclined to be intellectual and become more 'spaced out' and easily forgetful.

The key love hormone is oxytocin. This has a multiplicity of physiological effects throughout the birth process and afterwards. It is the hormone that causes the muscular contractions involved in all phases of the sexual/reproductive cycle including the uterine contractions that open the womb, eject the baby at birth and then expel the placenta. Up to now only these contractile or mechanical effects of oxytocin have been well known.

However, oxytocin also has an important behavioural effect. In addition to stimulating muscular contractions, it is the primary hormone that promotes feelings of attachment and love. For this reason, Michel Odent calls oxytocin 'a typically altruistic hormone – the main hormone of love'. He reminds us that whatever facet of love you consider – oxytocin is always involved. For example, you may be familiar with the warm affectionate feelings you have for your sexual partner soon after lovemaking. This is the result of the altruistic effect of oxytocin secreted during the sexual response cycle, particularly during orgasm.

Soon after the birth of a baby, a woman has the highest peak of oxytocin in her life. This is because nature intends mother and baby to fall deeply in love – a powerful, unrepeatable stimulus to the bond of love that ensures the safety, protection and survival of the baby. Michel Odent believes that this high level of oxytocin shared by mother and baby at the time of birth is crucial in forming the capacity to love.

Oxytocin is never secreted in isolation, but is part of the complex cocktail of other love hormones that also promote attachment. While synthetic drugs such as Syntocinon (Pitocin in the US) used to induce labour pharmacologically can imitate the mechanical effects of oxytocin, they block the release of these natural love hormones and do not appear to have the same beneficial behavioural effects.

Mothers who have an interventionist birth can, however, be reassured that the love hormones continue to be produced throughout the primal period, albeit not at the same high level as in the first hour after birth. These hormones are released every time you hold your baby and especially during breastfeeding. Therefore an approach to baby care, known as 'attachment parenting', that involves a lot of body contact with your baby (for example, by 'wearing' your baby in a baby carrier and sharing a bed with your baby) is a way to promote ongoing secretion of the love hormones. I have expanded on this theme in my book *Natural Baby*.[1]

A hormone-led labour

Taking a closer look at the work of hormones throughout the birth process will help us to understand the context in which using a birth pool can be most beneficial. At the end of pregnancy the higher levels of oxytocin start to prepare the uterus for contractions by triggering the release of the female sex hormone oestrogen, while prostaglandin – a hormone produced in the tissues of the lower segment of the uterus – softens and ripens the cervix. When the baby's lungs are fully mature and ready to breathe, they

1   Janet Balaskas, *Natural Baby*, Gaia Books, 2001

produce a hormone that reaches the mother's bloodstream and sends a message to her brain that it's time for labour to start. Levels of another important hormone, prostaglandin E2, also rise before labour. This has the effect of inhibiting the baby's breathing reflex before he or she comes into contact with the atmosphere, and is therefore especially relevant to water-births (see page 66).

In the early phases of labour more oxytocin, secreted by the primitive brain, is released in pulses into the mother's bloodstream – each pulse resulting in a contraction. As labour builds up and intensifies the pulses become more frequent and stronger, so that labour establishes a rhythm of regular contractions with resting phases in between. The pulsatile secretion of oxytocin continues throughout labour. The increasingly high levels flowing through the mother's bloodstream gradually intensify the contractions and also cross the placenta into the baby' bloodstream.

'Being in the pool gave me the sense of being focused – meditative – at one with myself.'

Emotionally, the effect of the high level of love hormones during labour is to make the woman draw deeply into herself, as she concentrates her energies on the overwhelming sensations she is experiencing. Her behaviour becomes unthinking and instinctual. As Michel Odent observes, she dares to do what she would not do normally – to move and use unusual positions, to make a noise, shout or swear. As the time of birth draws near, she is likely to become more passive, perhaps resting and labouring in one position such as kneeling, lying on her side or floating in a birth pool.

> *'There was a wonderful sense of timelessness when I was in the water. I closed my eyes and the world outside the rim of the pool disappeared. I can't remember what happened until I began to feel the urge to push.'*

Michel Odent describes this as 'being on another planet' – when the mother instinctively wants to reduce stimulation of the neo-cortex. He points out that 'the hormones released during labour originate from the primitive part of the brain...When there are inhibitions during the birth process...such inhibitions originate in the new brain, or neo-cortex – that part of the brain so highly developed in humans.'[2]

He stresses the importance of protecting the labouring woman from disturbances such as bright lights, talking and asking questions or giving her a feeling of being observed with cameras or continuous electronic foetal monitoring devices. Hormone secretion is very sensitive to intrusive environmental factors and can easily be inhibited.

When the mother is disturbed, feels anxious or is afraid, her body is likely to produce adrenaline, the 'fight or flight hormone' from the family of hormones known as catecholamines. This is a kind of emergency hormone we release when there is a possible danger or in response to stimulation, fear and excitement. During labour adrenaline counteracts the release of oxytocin and can therefore slow or even inhibit the labour. We can understand this physiological response when we think of a mammal labouring in the wild who is suddenly threatened by a predator. In this case, stopping or inhibiting the labour could perhaps be life-saving, enabling her to escape and find a safer place to give birth. Our goal, however, should be to keep the level of adrenaline as low as possible during labour.

2 'Why Labouring Women Don't Need Support', *Mothering*, Fall 1996

'It was extremely comforting and relaxing to be in the pool. Also great for privacy. When I really wanted to get away from everything I ducked under the water. It was bliss.'

In a modern hospital setting and sometimes even at a home birth adrenaline is likely to be released in response to too much noise and activity, emotional stress, unsympathetic surroundings and in more extreme cases fear and distress. In this situation, the halting or slowing of contractions may lead to the need for a cascade of medical interventions to deliver the baby. In such a context the provision of a birth pool is likely to have little benefit, unless the woman finds the pool to be a private space where she can retreat and be protected from what is going on around her. Women in labour have a need to withdraw and cut themselves off from the world of ordinary events, and we can tell that a labour is going well when we observe this happening.

The transition to birth

'In labour I got into a kind of trance, sleeping between contractions and lifting my pelvis and legs to float and rock during them. Then the pain went and the pauses between contractions became longer. I emerged out of the sleep and could communicate and have eye contact with people again.'

Michel Odent describes how, towards the end of labour, there is a sudden shift in the mother's hormonal balance as the birth approaches. He call this a 'hormonal storm'. This may happen before, soon after or at the time of full dilation of the cervix – commonly known as 'transition'. High oxytocin levels produce the long, intense contractions with only brief intervals between them, which are typical of the end of labour. At this point a high level or rush of adrenaline is released, which now, paradoxically, has the dramatic effect of stimulating contractions instead of slowing them down as would have happened earlier. As a result of this, we might notice a new restlessness in the mother in contrast to the relative passivity of late labour. A surge of energy may result in an urge to move and use her muscles, to be upright and to hold onto or grasp something. Combined with the mechanical pressure from the baby's descending head on the pudendal nerves deep inside the pelvis – the rush of adrenaline coursing through the mother's blood at this point has the effect of stimulating the rapid birth of the baby.

Michel Odent calls this response the 'foetus ejection reflex', a term originally coined by the American scientist Niles Newton in connection with her observation of the behaviour of mice during birth. Odent likens the adrenaline-led birth reflex to male ejaculation – called the 'sperm ejection reflex'. In his observations of labouring women, he has noted that the onset of the foetus ejection reflex is often heralded by physiological effects that are indicative of fear, such as shivering and shallow breathing. Often the mother will mention death. She may have a dry mouth and feel very thirsty, the pupils of her eyes may be fully dilated. Such signs are due to the rush of adrenaline that from this point takes over the birth process.

This makes perfect sense if we take our minds back to the example of an animal giving birth in the wild, when at the end of labour the presence of adrenaline can be beneficial. The baby is ready to be born and it is now safer for the mother to deliver her baby quickly, with maximum alertness. An energetic and wide-awake mother would be better able to protect her newborn infant against attack from predators. Interestingly, some doctors and midwives mention the strategy of saying something frightening to a labouring woman at the end of the first stage whose labour is not progressing, as a way of unknowingly triggering this rush of adrenaline.

The birth reflex

When a woman experiences a true foetus ejection reflex and remains undisturbed and able to follow her own instincts, she will spontaneously adopt the optimal position for giving birth. She will usually want to be upright or leaning forward over a piece of furniture or edge of the birthing pool. Alternatively, she may want to kneel or squat supported by her partner. Such positions maximize the space within the pelvis and utilize the help of gravity to make the descent and birth of the baby as easy as possible.

> *'My body took over and I felt like a spawning fish! The midwife had to sometimes remind me about breathing though, when I started panicking – the breathing then became stronger until it transformed into huge groans – and I felt myself start pushing – it was involuntary, like throwing up – I'm sure it was invaluable that I was weightless – I can't imagine doing it outside of water – it would be so much harder to completely let go.'*

Odent notes that the foetus ejection reflex doesn't occur in all labours. In particular, when there is too much well-meaning 'support' for the mother, the necessary primal anxiety is suppressed. Instead of experiencing the involuntary powerful final contractions that propel the baby out, she may need to consciously make the efforts to 'push' the baby down the birth canal. It is interesting that we have the possibility of either letting go to the involuntary reflex or, in the absence of such a reflex, we can also consciously use our muscles to work with the efforts of the uterus. My own view is that nature gives us a dual possibility during this critical time, to ensure that one way or another the baby is born safely. We can help to make the birth as easy as possible for mother and baby by minimizing disturbances to increase the possibility of a spontaneous foetus ejection reflex.

> 'It was dark and silent. I felt myself retreating into the zone you go into for the "push". I had a few more contractions and the need to push became totally overwhelming. She was born into the water literally minutes later.'

After the birth

As mother and baby gaze in wonder at each other when they meet face to face and skin to skin for the first time, deep and lasting bonds are forged that lay the foundations for the relationship to come. Both of them are alert and wide eyed – another beneficial effect of adrenaline. It takes about an hour for the high level of hormones to begin to be eliminated after the birth. For this reason it is important to keep the room very warm, even overheated, in the first hour after birth and to continue to maintain deep privacy so that the mother is not distracted in any way from giving her full attention to her baby. Many women leave the pool before the placenta is delivered.

The time between the birth of the baby and the expulsion of the placenta is a time when the level of oxytocin reaches a peak in the mother. The baby's first contact with the breast or first sucking stimulates more oxytocin secretion, as do all the interactions that happen between mother and baby at this time. This results in the massive contractions that ensure the delivery of the placenta, the retraction of the uterus and the sealing of the blood vessels at the placental site. So we can see how these final strong contractions prevent haemorrhage and ensure the safety of mother and baby.

'We had a really relaxed atmosphere, cosy and intimate. I think the baby must have sensed it as she was very quiet and cuddly in my arms after her birth and still is now. We spent ages just looking at her. Then she went to the breast and suckled continuously. Eventually I stood up to deliver the placenta.'

The environment for birth

Setting the scene for the use of a birth pool, it is essential to first consider the atmosphere in the birthing room. We have seen how the need for privacy is crucial to creating the right conditions for a birth – whether on dry land or on water – that is led by a woman's natural hormones and instinctive behaviour.

This is true for all mammals, who have an instinctive tendency to withdraw into a safe, darkened space to give birth – where they will be undisturbed and hormone secretion will be optimal. For example, as she nears the end of her pregnancy, a female cat will search for the most secluded part of the house and will change locations if she finds it is disturbed. Herd animals such as horses separate themselves from the rest before giving birth and generally give birth in the dead of night. There are obvious reasons for this behaviour. An animal in labour is at its most vulnerable and the need for safety and seclusion is paramount. There is no reason to suppose that we are any different in our basic instincts.

'I really wanted to be on my own, left alone. The pool was a retreat and private.'

It is clearly visible in our hospitals that when a woman labours in an over-exposed, over-public place, she is more likely to be distracted or stressed and her labour will be less effective. Therefore it's not difficult to understand why a high proportion of women today have babies without releasing their own hormones and need the assistance of oxytocic drugs to stimulate or induce labour, an epidural to block the pain, and/or an instrumental birth or a caesarean section to deliver the baby.

Sometimes intervention in the birth process is more subtle. If even engaging the labouring woman in conversation or making her feel observed can disturb the progress of labour, we need to question the value and necessity for all routines, protocols and procedures, including the presence of strangers in the room. Odent feels that the number of people in the room during labour should be severely limited and is even ambivalent about the presence of the partner.

All women have a need to feel secure in labour. My experience is that while some women want and need to be alone with a trusted helper nearby who can be easily summoned, having a calm and sympathetic loved one present in the room can be crucial for others. What is privacy for one woman may be isolation to another. Sometimes the presence of a trained labour companion or doula can be invaluable, and for most women the motherly presence of a sensitive midwife is essential.

'I entered my own little world and completely let my body take over – with no conscious control.'

Every birth is different, and every woman is an individual with her own needs, but the need for privacy and a calm, intimate atmosphere at a birth is universal and paramount to all mammals including humans. Looking at the birth from the hormonal perspective, we can see how, throughout the whole process, the mother's consciousness is altered from that of her everyday life. Her behaviour is spontaneous and uninhibited, dominated by her involuntary primitive instincts, rather than controlled by her mind. Any occurrence – gross or subtle – that disturbs her or pulls her away from her natural withdrawal into her body is likely to interfere with the natural course of events and disturb the highly sensitive balance of hormones. Once this is understood as the underlying context for any birth, we can begin to think about how water can play a useful and important role in a natural labour and birth.

How water can help you in labour

'The water looked very inviting and I was delighted with it when I got in. I had a fire burning and the room was candle lit, with soft music and lavender oil in a burner.'

The change in how a woman feels and behaves soon after entering a birth pool in a quiet darkened room can be remarkable. It seems to alter her state of consciousness and her concentration – sometimes dramatically – so that she very soon relaxes and sinks more deeply into herself and is able to let herself surrender to the involuntary rhythms of her labour. It's as if she becomes sleepy, even dreaming.

In the *Birth and the Family Journal* (Vol. 8) Michel Odent writes:

> *'The reason why kneeling or immersion in water during labour is
> so helpful is mysterious. What is clear is that water is often the
> way to reduce inhibitions...we observe that during such immersion
> in warm water, semi-darkness is the best way to reach a high level
> of relaxation. Water may be a good way to reduce adrenergic
> secretion. Immersion in warm water with semi-darkness may also
> be a way to reach alpha brainwave rhythms. Water may be a
> symbol of mother, of comfort, regression to childlike needs and
> behaviour. Whatever way we want to talk about the effect of water
> during labour, one thing is sure. The contractions become more
> efficient and less painful at the same time, so that sometimes the
> labour is very quick. Many women do not want to leave the pool
> because it is so comfortable. As a result sometimes the baby
> comes while the mother is in the pool.'*

The benefits of water immersion, or hydrotherapy, in labour have been studied and assessed by many experienced midwives, researchers and doctors all
over the world. It is clear from common findings that including a pool of
warm water in the birthing room adds a whole new dimension to the experience of childbirth. A recent study of 1,300 waterbirths found that the use of a
birth pool is rated very highly by women, whether having their first or subsequent baby, and their enthusiasm is shared by midwives.[3]

This echoes the findings of thousands of women and their midwives all
over the world. There are some women who have had several water labours
or births and have had such satisfactory experiences that they cannot imagine giving birth in any other way. But just as every labour is unique, no two

3 E. Burns, 'Waterbirth', *MIDIRS Midwifery Digest*, 11 (suppl. 2), S10–S13, 2001

women will use a birthing pool in quite the same way. Moreover, a minority of women who try the pool do not find it helpful. Many women, however, are very keen to get into the pool at the earliest possible moment (although we will see later that it is not wise to get in too early) and some are so comfortable that they want to stay in the water for the whole of the remaining labour and birth. Others find the pool helpful for pain relief during labour, but feel the need to be on dry land for the birth itself. A further group may labour and give birth on land but use the pool for relaxation after the birth. In a long slow labour, episodes in the pool can be useful for resting. The message is that water can be of benefit in a variety of ways.

> 'My labour was very short and intense. Near the end I wanted to get my head down to slow the pain. When I went into the pool I found that I couldn't get my head down lower than my hips as I had been doing out of the water, so I felt the contractions more strongly than ever. I got out because I missed the presence of my husband to cling to and overall felt very isolated in the pool.'

> 'I had a long labour (60 hours), especially the latent phase, so I was very tired and the pool helped me to cope with the pain much better – I was in and out twice.'

> 'I found the water helped incredibly all through labour but I got out of the pool as the second stage was beginning as I didn't want to give birth in the water. I wanted to be "earthed".'

Privacy and non-intervention

One of the benefits of labouring in a pool is the sense of privacy that most women experience. Enclosed in her private space, protected by the gentle barrier of the water, a woman can feel secure from unwanted contact and more in control of her body. She is free to turn her attention inwards and focus on the rhythms of her labour and what she needs to do to ride the powerful sensation of the contractions. Although it is essential that regular foetal monitoring is carried out periodically while the mother remains in the pool, in practice there are fewer internal examinations and other procedures than in most labours on land. And, significantly, this 'hands-off' approach seems to have no adverse effect on mother or baby as was noted in a study of 2,000 women in a hospital in Switzerland where waterbirth is offered as an option to every woman.[4]

> '*I was glad not to need any stronger pain relief (I had an epidural for the birth of my first baby) and to give birth naturally feeling in total control in the pool and in my own home. I liked the fact that being in the pool meant the midwives keep a hands-off approach and leave it up to you with no internal examinations and no breaking of the waters. It was so different from my first experience.*'

Midwives who attend waterbirths often have to develop different ways of assessing progress in labour. Instead of routine vaginal examinations to check dilation, the midwife relies on more subtle indicators, such as the woman's breathing, vocalizations and movements. In fact, many midwives feel that attending labours and births in water has added an extra dimension to their midwifery skills, including an extra sensitivity to changes in the mother without the need for manual confirmation.

---

4   V. Geissbuhler, J. Eberhard, 'Waterbirths: A Comparative Study. A prospective study on more than 2000 waterbirths', *Fetal Diagnosis and Therapy*, 15, 291–300, 2000

Pain relief through water

> 'The pool helped the labour to progress rapidly...I was very eager
> to get in the water and found it a huge relief when I entered...the
> pool was very useful in coping with the pain, helping to focus me
> so I could concentrate on making the pain useful and positive.'

One of the main reasons women choose to use water during their labour is for the relief of pain. There is no doubt among midwives experienced in its use that immersion in water can provide dramatic relief of discomfort for a high proportion of women. Various studies have confirmed this finding.

For example, a clinical audit of waterbirths carried out in five birthing units in England 'supported the proposition that waterbirth is effective as a method of pain relief'.[5]

In hospital birthing units that have a long-standing commitment to the provision of pool facilities and support from birth attendants who feel at ease with using water in this way, there has been a dramatic reduction in the use of analgesic drugs such as pethidine (meperidine in the US). The study cited above found that only 3 per cent of women who used water in labour used pethidine as well, compared to 60 per cent of women who laboured on land. A reduction in the use of such narcotic drugs is welcomed by all concerned, as it is now widely recognized that they can have a depressive effect on both mother and baby's central nervous system, especially in repeated or large doses (see Chapter 9).

> 'I don't think being in the pool reduced the pain but it relaxed me
> so I felt the pain less.'

5   Dianne Garland, Keith Jones, *MIDIRS Midwifery Digest*, vol. 10, no. 3, September 2000

A systematic review of three randomized control trials exploring immersion in water in labour only (not birth) found that there was a significant decrease in the use of medical pain relief in the women who used a birth pool in labour – indicating that for some women the use of a birth pool provides an effective alternative route to epidural anaesthesia[6] (see also Chapter 4). Epidurals have become very sophisticated. They generally provide effective relief from pain and can be used very positively in some circumstances. You need to be aware that using a birth pool will not eradicate the pain in the same way as an epidural. Rather, it works indirectly by making it significantly easier for you to tolerate and manage the pain yourself. (For more detailed information about epidurals, see Chapter 9).

A study at Southampton General Hospital looked at the effect of labouring in water during the first stage. It focused on first-time mothers who were making very slow progress. This study is particularly interesting because slow progress in labour is common among first-time mothers, and often leads to unnecessarily early intervention.

This is the first study to look at the use of a birth pool as a strategy for long, slow labours, and one of the few randomized, controlled trials involving waterbirths. The study involved 99 women with dystocia (dilating less than 1 centimetre per hour). It revealed that those who were given the chance to use a birth pool progressed better than those getting standard care (rupture of membranes and induction with an intravenous drip). Less than half (47 per cent) of the birth-pool group needed an epidural compared with 66 per cent in the group who did not use a birth pool. Immersion in water for up to four hours seemed to reduce the need for augmentation (induction) of labour, reduce pain and increase satisfaction, without increasing the overall length of labour or the operative delivery rate.

6　V. C. Nikodem, 'Immersion in water during pregnancy, labour and birth', *Cochrane Review*, The Cochrane Library, Issue 3, 1999

The study suggests that labouring in water, by aiding relaxation and pain relief, may reduce anxiety and pain in women having a long labour and thus prevent the stress response which could lead to reduced uterine activity and dystocia. The authors suggest that water immersion may be an alternative option to early augmentation of labour. They point out that 'augmentation of labour, in particular oxytocin administration, is associated with hyperstimulation and decreased maternal satisfaction' (see Chapter 9, page 249, 'induction'). The study concludes that 'Labouring in water under midwifery care may be an option for slow progress in labour, reducing the need for obstetric intervention and offering an alternative pain management strategy.'[7]

What causes pain in labour?

'I expected the pain to disappear which, of course, it did not. I wouldn't say the labour was wildly painful while I was in the pool. It felt purposeful rather than painful.'

It is well known that every woman experiences the pain of labour differently. This is because many different factors can affect the perception of pain, including excessive fear, tension and emotional issues. For some women the sensations themselves may not be as strong as for others. Some people naturally have a higher tolerance of pain – or pain threshold. Women who usually have a low pain threshold may be willing to go the extra mile in labour for the benefits of a drug-free labour to the baby, or because they welcome the challenge and want to experience it. Others may need more help than a birth pool can offer; it's important to recognize and accept this and still make the most of the experience of giving birth. It's best not to have an inflexible agenda about this (even though you may have a strong intention to have a waterbirth). Keep all your options open, since what will happen during birth is always unpredictable.

7 Elizabeth R. Cluett, Ruth M. Pickering, Kathryn Getliffe, Nigel James St George Saunders, 'Randomized controlled trial of labouring in water compared with standard of augmentation for management of dystocia in first stage of labour', Southampton General Hospital, January 2004

To appreciate how water can relieve pain in labour it may be helpful first to examine how pain signals are transmitted and perceived. When a woman goes into established labour, she experiences increasingly intense contractions of the uterus. As the muscle fibres of the uterus contract strongly, they send pain signals to the nerve fibres embedded in the muscle. Just as you might feel pain in your leg muscles after running up a steep flight of stairs, so this strenuous and unfamiliar internal muscular activity causes you to feel waves of pain around the lower abdomen and/or possibly also in the lower back. Pain may also arise from the stretching and thinning of the cervix at the base of the uterus, as in menstruation, and it does feel similar. Or pain may originate from the stretching of the pelvic ligaments, and later the stretching of the soft tissues of the birth canal and perineum or may be caused by pressure on the pelvic bones and joints as the baby's head descends. Signals picked up by the receptors at the site of the pain are transmitted by nerve fibres to the spinal cord and then to the brain where they are 'translated' as the sensation of pain.

Pain sensations may be modified by other stimuli that interrupt the transmission of the signals to the brain. This explanation of pain modification, known as the 'Gate Control' theory, was first proposed by Wall and Melzak[8] in the 1960s. In simple terms, according to this theory, pain signals are transmitted along 'slow' nerve fibres to the spinal cord. Competing signals from 'fast' fibres that carry sensations of touch (such as massage or stimulation from a TENS machine) and/or heat (from the warmth of water on the skin) can interrupt or modify pain signals so that the perception of pain in the brain is reduced. An example of this mechanism in action is when you rub an injured part of the body to relieve pain. In labour, the pleasurable sensation of the warm, enveloping contact with warm water on the skin surface may 'close the gate' at least partially to the pain signals arising from the contractions, so that pain perception is reduced or limited.

8   Ronald Melzack and British physiologist Patrick Wall, 'Pain Mechanisms: A New Theory', *Science:* 150, 171–179, 1965

How does your body help you to cope with pain?

Most importantly, your body has its own natural responses to labour pain. When we experience pain, chemicals known as endorphins are released in the brain. These attach to special receptor sites in the brain, and have the effect of reducing the sensation of pain. The receptor sites endorphins occupy are the same ones used by narcotic painkilling drugs such as morphine and pethidine. For this reason endorphins are often termed natural painkillers or opiates. We all release endorphins during physical exertion such as exercise or dancing, and you may be familiar with how these activities produce feelings of wellbeing or even euphoria.

Endorphins play an important role in labour, helping you to feel better and to cope with increasing levels of pain. These chemicals also interact with oxytocin, the hormone that causes contractions. When levels of endorphins are high, indicating high levels of pain, oxytocin levels may drop. This may be nature's way of regulating labour to a level that you can cope with and can explain why an especially strong contraction can often be followed by a few milder ones.

Your endorphin level will rise to match the increase in pain as contractions intensify, building up to a peak or endorphin 'high' by the end of your labour. Through the placental circulation, these endorphins will be shared by your baby and result in both of you having a high level coursing through the bloodstream in the hours after the birth. This is an important part of bonding as this sort of opiate encourages dependency and attachment. One can only marvel at the wisdom of mother nature!

So how does immersion in water help to relieve the pain of contractions? There are several interrelated beneficial effects that might significantly reduce pain.

Improved relaxation

'In between contractions I sank into a somnolent state and it was incredibly relaxing. I found this to be the main benefit of the pool so I could get through the pains better when they came on.'

It is not hard to imagine how immersing your heavily pregnant body in an extra deep warm bath, could be relaxing. As long as it is deep enough, the buoyancy of the water supports your weight enabling your body to relax. The warmth of the water also has a relaxing effect on the muscle fibres, helping to dispel tension throughout your body.

Often there is a feeling of sleepiness as tension melts away. This deep relaxation reduces levels of catecholamines (stress hormones) and provides the conditions necessary for oxytocin to do its work. A study by Boulvain and Wesel[9] showed that stress hormone levels were reduced in labouring women who spent time in water during the first stage of labour compared with those who did not.

After more than 20 years of trying and researching different ways to help women relax in labour, I find the use of a birth pool to be the strategy *par excellence* for most women. It requires very little or no preparation and can be easily achieved by the majority of women (although practices such as yoga or self-hypnosis in pregnancy can make this effect even more powerful and may also help you if using water turns out to be inappropriate).

9   M. Boulvain and S. Wesel, 'Neurobiochemistry of Immersion in Warm Water During labour: the secretion of endorphins, cortisol and prolactin', *Prenatal and perinatal psychology and Medicine*, New York, Parthenon, 1988

Reduced anxiety

'I was very trepidacious about labour. The water helped by making me so relaxed that it took the edge off the panic when it threatened to consume me and I stayed in control.'

It is well known that fear and anxiety can increase the perception of pain. In labour one of the main causes of stress can be the sense of loss of power and autonomy, or being overwhelmed and intimidated. Undue fear and anxiety can be avoided by preparing well for your birth. This involves becoming well informed and doing some form of physical preparation such as pregnancy yoga that will help you to develop a sense of trust in your body and confidence in your ability to give birth. Learning to relax, switch off your mind and focus on the natural rhythm of your breathing can help hugely in being able to tolerate pain. You can use this skill in early labour and later when you are in the pool (see also page 109).

Becoming familiar and comfortable with the place of birth and establishing a good relationship with your birth attendants will help to allay anxiety. Forming a relationship with the midwife or midwives who will attend your birth is ideal. For this reason some women opt to hire an independent midwife or seek a home birth, a birth centre or a one-to-one midwife scheme. If this is not possible for you, it will be helpful to meet the midwife who is the labour suite supervisor ahead of time to discuss your wishes for your birth.

Many women report feeling a huge sense of relief when they enter the birthing pool. Being in your own womb-like space can increase your privacy and make you feel more secure and less anxious. It can be much easier to let go of worries, inhibitions and mental activity and to surrender to the involuntary instinctual process – letting your body take over.

'My birth experience was wonderful overall. Helped by excellent
midwives who "managed" the situation very well. I was relaxed
and confident in the pool, and up to the last ten or so contraction,
I felt totally happy and in control...Having the pool gave me my
own space and enabled me to decide who I wanted physical
contact with and when...The water helped enormously with the
pain, mainly due to the ease with which I could move about
during contractions and the support it gave me while resting...
Combined with music, aromatherapy oils, and homeopathic
remedies (Arnica, Gelsemium and Phytolacca), the water created
a calm environment and a beautiful birth – for a beautiful baby.'

The supportive effect of buoyancy

The composition of the human body allows it in normal circumstances to
float in water, provided the water is of sufficient depth. The physical law of
buoyancy states that an object will float once it has displaced the weight of
water equivalent to its own weight. Birthing pools are designed to hold sufficient water to provide buoyancy for a pregnant woman. An average bathtub is
not big or deep enough to do this. When you enter the pool the buoyancy will
support you comfortably and effortlessly in whatever position you choose,
providing a feeling of weightlessness. Since you are freed from the effort of
supporting your body weight, the buoyancy also helps you to conserve energy
so that you are less likely to become exhausted.

Many women who hire our pools comment on the comfort they feel while
resting between contractions. The support of the water allows total relaxation
at this time, which can be blissful and restorative. This enhances the value of
the breaks, which can be as ecstatic as the pain is intense during contrac-

tions. Labour is very much a polarity of intense opposites and that is what makes it bearable – pain comes and goes and pleasure can equal pain if you can let go and relax!

> 'I got in the pool at about 5 cm dilated. The relaxation through my body was immediate and the "floating" weightlessness was lovely. The water made it very easy for me to change positions at the start of a contraction. The contractions were stronger, which was a bit of a shock, but I could feel and visualize my cervix dilating much more easily.'

> 'The sense of weightlessness in water gave me enormous relief. My birth was a fantastic experience and I don't think I would have coped so well without the pool.'

Mobility and upright positions

With increasing understanding of the concept of an active birth, it is now more widely accepted that for most women, a variety of upright or semi-upright 'active' positions are the most comfortable and of greatest benefit in labour and while giving birth. This utilizes the help of gravity to ease the descent of the baby through the birth canal. In most cases a woman responding to her own instincts will move intuitively into the best position for her and her baby at any given time. A woman in labour needs to be able to respond to these instincts, moving her body spontaneously as necessary to release tension in rhythm with the contractions.[10]

In water, mobility is much easier to achieve and involves much less effort. As buoyancy supports your weight, you will be much freer to find the

10 Janet Balaskas, *New Active Birth*, HarperCollins, 1989

positions that alleviate pain, whether lying, floating or kneeling leaning forwards. Whereas the full squatting position can be very uncomfortable, tiring or even impossible on land for most Western women, it is much easier to adopt in a birth pool during labour or as a birthing position. In water there is no weight or compression on the mother's lower back. All these factors help to open the pelvis and increase the pelvic diameters – making more space for the baby to descend and to be born more easily.

> 'It was such a relief to enter the pool...I felt so weightless in the water – I was able to sway from side to side ... and felt so much more relaxed.'

> 'I found the pool very comfortable. It was very good for taking the weight off my legs while making upright positions much easier to adopt. I did lots of squatting rocking back and forth. Overall it was a very happy experience which I will enjoy looking back on.'

> 'While out of the pool there was only one position that seemed bearable, whereas in the pool much greater mobility was possible... The pool made a lot of difference to the ability to deal with the pain, but it didn't necessarily reduce the pain.'

Easing a 'backache' labour

The optimal and most usual position for the baby as it descends into the birth canal is head down (cephalic) with its face towards the mother's back and spine in the curve of her belly. This presentation is known as occiput anterior and allows the easiest passage down the birth canal.

A variation on the head down presentation is occiput posterior, in which the baby is facing forwards, spine against the mother's spine, and this may not necessarily present any problem. However, this sometimes makes for a longer, more difficult labour as the baby may try to rotate into the more favourable anterior position for birth. Pain is most usually felt in the lower back caused by pressure from the baby's head. Sometimes the use of a birth pool can be very helpful in this case – reducing pressure on the back and making it easier for the baby to turn, while making the mother more comfortable.

> '*I had horrendous backache before entering the pool which I was no longer aware of once in the water. I could naturally make noises and breathe through contractions more easily once in the water.*'

> '*When established labour was confirmed, I went into the pool. Immediate bliss! My backache went and progress was very rapid. I felt almost ecstatic at times and powerfully free and in control. It kind of made me feel like I knew what I was doing on a very natural instinctive level.*'

> '*This birth was more painful than my first, but much quicker – I think the pool eased pain by allowing me to move freely but may have increased the strength of the contractions...My baby was in a posterior position so contractions became painful in my back and the ability to move my hips in the water helped. I was surprised by the speed and strength of labour and was amazed when I could feel my baby's head! As she was born I turned to scoop her up and had a great sense of involvement as I held her.*'

Reduction in the length of labour

'I think it relaxed me and made contractions more intense. I went from 5 cm to fully dilated in less than one hour in the pool.'

One of the acknowledged benefits of the use of a birthing pool is the effect it may have on the duration of labour. Some, but not all, studies have shown a reduction in the average length of labour in women who have used water for at least part of their labour. In one study[11] the labour was shown to be 90 minutes shorter for women who had spent a large part of their labour in water compared with those who had laboured on land. However, the benefit of water immersion in terms of the duration of labour is not straightforward; much depends on the environment, the way the pool is used, when the woman enters the pool and the quality of care.

The timing of when the mother enters the pool can be a key factor in the length of labour. Over the years it has been universally noted that labour is likely to slow down if the woman enters the pool too early. In 1997 Michel Odent published a paper[12] in which he describes how the physiological effects of immersion can either boost or inhibit the effectiveness of contractions, depending on the length of time spent in the pool. A review of his observations and those of attendants at numerous waterbirths showed that a relatively high proportion of women who entered the birthing pool at an early stage of labour (say 3 cm dilation) made rapid progress to about 7 cm. After this time, however, many then experienced a decrease in the effectiveness of contractions to the point where they needed to get out of the water and, in some cases, needed intravenous Syntocinon (Pitocin) to restart labour. By contrast, women who entered the pool when labour was more established (say at approximately 5 to 6 cm dilation) were likely to

11 Otigbah, Dhanjal, Harmsworth, et al
12 M. Odent, 'Can Water Immersion Stop Labour?' *Journal of Nurse-Midwifery*, Vol. 42, No. 5, Sept/Oct 1997

reach full dilation within an hour or two. When we started our pool hire company we used to recommend that the woman enter the pool at around 4 cm dilation. Several years ago I changed the recommendation to 5 to 6 cm (the start of what is known as active labour). I notice consistently from the feedback I received, that when the woman enters the pool later rather than sooner (but not too late!) the benefits seem to be optimized and a waterbirth within one to four hours is likely to be the end result.

'I got into the pool at 5 cm dilated after approximately 4–5 hours of early labour at home, having used lots of movement and upright positions. Getting into the pool made me feel very comfortable and much more mobile and seemed to speed up labour. The contractions were very effective and I was fully dilated and ready to push after about two hours in the water. Our lovely daughter was delivered into the water after about 40 minutes' pushing and seemed very happy about the whole experience.'

The 'oxytocin wave'

Odent has suggested that this phenomenon may be the result of the effect of water immersion on hormone secretion. Putting together the research findings of physiologists on this topic outside the domain of childbirth, and the common findings of midwives, he concludes that when a woman first enters the water there is an immediate reduction in catecholamines (stress hormones) and endorphins. This and other complex physiological responses stimulate higher levels of oxytocin secretion and stronger contractions. After about two hours the effect of immersion on the circulation and on the pituitary gland may result in a reduction in oxytocin secretion, hence the slowing down of labour. So he proposes the water acts as a powerful but short-lived stimulus to labour, with a wave-like effect that builds to a peak and then tails off – which I will refer to as the 'oxytocin wave'. Entering the pool in the active phase of labour, it is more likely that the wave will carry the mother to the point of no return, where birth is imminent. Awareness of these responses among midwives and birth attendants helps them guide the woman in how best to use the water to promote labour and to avoid the risk of it becoming protracted.

> *'At first labour was quite intense but once I got into the birth pool I found the contractions easier to manage, even though they seemed stronger and I couldn't believe how quickly I felt the urge to push!'*

Reduced blood pressure

A reduction in blood pressure has been noted when women labour in water. At a conference in 1987, Dr Serge Weisel presented his findings from a study of Belgian women labouring in warm water.[13] He stated that women with high blood pressure experienced a drop in blood pressure between 10 to 15 minutes after entering a warm bath. This effect may be due in part to dilation of the peripheral blood vessels in response to immersion in warm water. Blood pressure is also reduced because water immersion inhibits the release of vasopressin, a pituitary hormone similar to oxytocin that usually suppresses urine production. The inhibition of vasopressin results in an increase in urine production and slightly lowered blood pressure. So make sure that you have a glass of water next to the pool and take frequent sips in labour to avoid the dehydrating effect of more frequent urination (a bendy straw is helpful!).

13 The Pre and Perinatal Psychology Association of North America.

While labouring in water is generally recommended only for low-risk mothers, women who have mild pre-eclampsia or mild pregnancy-induced hypertension (raised blood pressure) could benefit from using a birth pool as an alternative to drug therapy, with careful and regular monitoring. Women with low blood pressure do not generally experience discomfort in a birth pool, but if faintness or dizziness is experienced, it is best to leave the pool.

Support for women with reduced mobility, skeletal pain or spinal problems

Heavier women or those who have a disability that limits mobility may especially appreciate the supportive qualities of water during labour. In water it's much easier to have an active labour and to adopt a variety of positions that feel natural and ease the discomfort of contractions. If you have spinal problems, being in water reduces weight and pressure on your back and also provides an alternative to an epidural for pain relief, if that is not recommended. You will need to discuss the advisability of a waterbirth with your midwife. Much will depend on the nature of your disability, and there may be concerns about the ease with which you can expect to get in and out of the pool. Many practical problems can be resolved with a little thought, such as the provision of a suitable stool to assist you getting in and out of the pool, taking it really slow, sitting on the edge first while a helper then gently supports you and helps you to bring both legs over the rim.

> *'I don't think I could have got through labour without the pool. I have arthritis and found it difficult to change positions and to take weight on my hands and knees. So using the pool meant that I*

could be much more mobile and try positions that would have been too painful out of water.'

'I'd had problems with bursitis of both hips and pelvic pain, which were greatly helped by the water. The birth went very well and it was wonderfully calm and relaxed.'

'I suffer from chronic fatigue syndrome and my birth required very careful planning to make it as easy as possible. A waterbirth paid off with a seven hour labour and my little girl popping out of her own accord with no intervention.'

Birth in water – the dive reflex

'The two hours I spent in the pool were wonderful. The buoyancy of the water and privacy of the pool provided such freedom. I was able to focus entirely on what my body was doing and was so aware of my son's decent. I even felt the instinctive need to turn onto all fours when I felt him slide backwards inside me. He soon recentred and I pushed him out slowly and with natural control. All in all a fabulous experience.'

With the accumulated experience of thousands of births in water worldwide, there is no doubt that most women who give birth in water generally rate the experience very highly. They find the supportive properties of the water very helpful in easing pain and making it much easier and less exhausting to use upright positions. However, when labouring and giving birth in water first started to become popular, many in the medical establishment raised concerns that the baby might inhale the water or drown. Waterbirth is a new and revolutionary idea and it is understandable that doctors, midwives and parents have reservations about the safety of the practice. It is now commonly understood that babies born in water have inbuilt physiological reflexes that prevent inhalation of the water during a waterbirth.

This was first discovered by the waterbirth pioneer Igor Tjarkovsky (see page 7) and later named and identified as the 'dive reflex' of the newborn. However, it is important that the right conditions be maintained to support this reflex and to prevent premature stimulation of the breathing response.

In 1996 Paul Johnson, neonatal physiologist at the John Radcliffe Hospital, Oxford, published an important paper on the mechanisms that trigger breathing in the newborn.[14] As part of his detailed research into 'practice breathing' by the foetus, he found that while the baby is in the uterus there are powerful mechanisms that prevent the inspiration of amniotic fluid into the lungs. These include:

💧 The presence of high levels of the hormone prostaglandin and the warmth of the uterine environment. Johnson noted that levels of prostaglandins rise in the 48 hours before the onset of labour, 'thus an intact placenta and umbilical circulation continues to inhibit breathing even after birth into water'.

💧 The temperature of the environment into which the baby is born. Paul Johnson says, 'It is...the environmental temperature which is the main determinant of the arousal threshold of the foetus and, with it, the effectiveness of breathing....' His paper explains that exposure, particularly of the baby's cheeks, nose and mouth, to air that is at least 1°C cooler than body temperature is the main stimulant to breathing in the newborn. Thus,

14 Paul Johnson, 'Birth Under Water – to breathe or not to breathe', *British Journal of Obstetrics*, 1996

provided the water temperature is maintained at about body temperature, there is little risk that the baby will accidentally start to breathe while still under water.

◊ A highly tuned sense of taste. This additional protective mechnism triggers closing of the larynx when the baby tastes fresh water among other fluids. This reflex is designed primarily to prevent inhalation of fluids while feeding, but also serves to prevent inspiration in an underwater birth.

There is one main factor in utero that could override the dive reflex in the newborn. If the baby is short of oxygen in the womb for any reason, this will manifest as foetal distress. A distressed baby is likely to gasp on emergence into the outside world. In the event of a severe oxygen shortage, this reflex can be strong enough to override the inhibitions to breathing outlined above. This is the reason why birth in water is not safe when there is evidence of foetal distress. In such a situation you will be asked to stand up or leave the water to give birth. It also the reason why diligent monitoring of the foetal heart during a water labour and birth is so important (see Chapter 7, page 170, 'listening in to your baby'). This can continue up until the very end, when the baby is close to birth and so low down in the pelvis that foetal monitoring is no longer possible. This is called the point of no return. If there has been no sign of foetal distress up until then, the chances of a last minute hypoxia or shortage of oxygen developing are very slim indeed. However, this remains the primary risk involved in a waterbirth (and there is no way of birth that excludes all elements of risk). As with the potential risks of any procedure used during the birth of your baby, it is important that you are aware of this if you decide to have a waterbirth, although with skilled care this is likely to be a very rare occurrence indeed.

The baby may also start to breathe if stimulated by too much contact during the delivery. Midwives who attend waterbirths need to be aware of the need for a 'hands-off' approach at this critical time and ideally only handle the baby as they bring it gently to the surface where breathing can start safely and naturally (see Chapter 8).

In the light of this information, birth underwater is considered safe for the baby if the conditions and management of the birth respect the natural physiological triggers for breathing. In practical terms, observation of the following guidelines during a birth underwater protect your baby from inhaling until safely in the air:

💧 Maintenance of the pool temperature at about 37°C during the second stage.
💧 Minimal handling of the baby by the midwife during the delivery.
💧 Bringing the baby to the surface within 7–10 seconds of birth. This is a surprisingly long time and allows for a slow and gentle delivery so that the baby's face is above the water surface in time for the first breath.

Perineal benefits

A variety of factors other than the use of a birth pool may influence the incidence of perineal tears. Certainly when the mother is undisturbed and free to follow her own urges and timing when giving birth, the spontaneous stretching and release of the perineal tissues happens involuntarily and tearing is less likely. Both formal studies and informal observations indicate that the use of water in labour reduces the frequency and severity of perineal tears. While first and second degree tears may occur in waterbirths as well as land births, more severe third and fourth degree tears are a rare occurrence in water.

A collaborative audit of waterbirths in four birth units in the UK in 1998[15] found that 57 per cent of first-time mothers having a waterbirth suffered no perineal trauma compared with 51 per cent on land. For mothers giving birth for a second or subsequent time, the comparative figures were 57 per cent and 36 per cent respectively. In their paper 'A retrospective comparison of water births and conventional vaginal deliveries', Otigbah, Dhanjal, Harmsworth, et al concluded that waterbirth mothers had significantly fewer episiotomies.[16]

These findings are probably due to a large part to the softening effect of the warm water on the tissues. It is also true that when the birth takes place in water, the upward pressure of the water provides gentle support for the baby as he or she is emerging, so there is less stress on the perineum. A further factor is probably the fact that when giving birth in water, a woman is more likely to spontaneously adopt a beneficial, protective position and to be more relaxed as she gives birth. The majority of tears that occur in waterbirth mothers are minor and those that involve skin and not muscle may not require stitches.

> '*I used pools for the birth of my second and third babies, who were 11lb 6oz and 10lb 5oz, and had no tears or grazes. I feel that this was because I was able to get into positions where nothing blocked the baby's arrival.*'

> '*I felt the actual birth itself was much less traumatic (no tearing) and the baby eased out of me and just floated into the water.*'

15 D. Garland, K. Jones, *MIDIRS Midwifery Digest*, Vol. 10, No. 3, Sept 2000
16 Otigbah, Dhanjal, Harmsworth, et al, 'A retrospective comparison of water births and conventional vaginal deliveries'

A gentler birth for the baby

A more comfortable mother will herself experience greater ease during labour and birth. This, along with the other benefits listed so far, will be conveyed to the baby. Parents and midwives often comment that babies born in water seem calmer and less stressed at birth and more settled and contented as babies. There are no statistics for this remarkable and common finding. However, the benefits to each baby born this way and the long-term significance of more babies having a gentle and sensitive entry into the world is one of the broader cultural benefits of waterbirth.

> *'I don't know whether it was due to the way he was delivered but our baby is a very placid, peaceful and contented child.'*

However, not every waterbirth is easy or gentle and it's important not to be too idealistic in your expectations. Like any birth, the last phase of a waterbirth can be quite a struggle (although when this is the case it's usually best to stand up or leave the pool). Occasionally a waterbirth can happen very fast, and this can be quite shocking for mother and baby. However, waterbirths generally take place after a labour in which progress has been good. In these circumstances the potential for an easier and more efficient birth is increased and the majority of women give birth normally.

> *'My daughter was very calm and contented after the birth and has continued to be a settled baby, which I put down to such a relaxed birth.'*

We can only imagine what it is like for a baby to be born from the waters of the womb through warm water into the world. Watching a waterbirth once, I saw the baby uncurl like a sea anemone, unfurling in slow motion from the foetal position as her body opened and expanded gently in the warm water. At the same time her eyes opened under water and she seemed to smile up at her mother as she was gently lifted up and into her arms. The mother held her newborn daughter to her heart and then tears of joy ran down her face. All this, in about ten seconds, seemed to happen in slow motion. It was one of the most moving sights I have ever seen.

> *'The baby's head only was out, face down, and we waited for him to slowly turn; then I pushed his whole body out and he was calmly lifted out of the water. I am sure a birth through water makes them very relaxed and happy.'*

Summary of benefits of labouring or giving birth in water

Common findings are that using a birth pool:

- Increases privacy

- Provides significant pain relief

- Reduces the need for drugs and interventions

- Encourages a woman's sense of control in labour

- Facilitates mobility and enables the woman to adopt optimal positions for an active birth

- Speeds up labour

- Promotes relaxation and conserves energy

- Helps to reduce tears

- Is rated highly by mothers and midwives

- Encourages an easier birth for the mother and a gentler welcome for the baby

chapter four

Choosing a waterbirth

Giving birth is likely to be one of the most momentous experiences of your life. The hours of labour that you share with your baby represent a major rite of passage for you both as you begin your life as a mother and your baby is born into the world. For fathers who are present, being at the birth of your baby is a hugely meaningful milestone in the journey of parenting your child.

How and where you choose to give birth is one of the important decisions you will be making to give your new baby the best possible start in life and to enhance your personal experience of this life-transforming event. Setting the scene for a hormone-led labour and birth is a powerful way to increase the possibility of a natural birth and to enhance your bond with your baby. Using a birth pool can play an important role in this, and the possibility of having this choice is very positive and exciting.

Keeping an open mind

Labouring or giving birth in water is an option open to women who have a healthy pregnancy and are generally defined as 'low risk'. In a sympathetic environment, most labours progress well without complications, and there is no reason not to be confident and optimistic as you approach your birth. It is natural to look forward to labouring in a birth pool and to the possibility of your baby being born in water. Even though it will inevitably include pain and times that are profoundly challenging, labour and birth can also be a deeply ecstatic experience. Having a birth pool at your disposal is very reassuring, and rightly so, given the great benefits it can bring to your birth.

However, what will actually happen at the time is unknown. It's important to keep an open mind when you are considering using a birth pool, coupled with a strong intention as to how you would ideally like to give birth to your baby. You need a strong vision and intention to realize your dreams, but equally you need the flexibility to accept a complete change of agenda and adapt to the unexpected if it arises, keeping the most important priorities in view.

> *'Premature rupture of the membranes meant that my baby was induced and a waterbirth was no longer an option. I was encouraged all along to have an open mind about what might happen on the day so I wasn't disappointed for long. My baby boy is more than I could have dreamed of.'*

Is a waterbirth for you?

The UK's Royal College of Midwives' position paper on waterbirths (October 2000) outlines the following criteria for the use of water during labour:

◆ This must be the woman's informed choice

◆ The pregnancy should be of normal full term at 37+ weeks

◆ There must be a singleton foetus (only one baby) with cephalic (head down) presentation

◆ No systematic sedation (tranquillizers or other drugs)

◆ Spontaneous rupture of membranes less than 24 hours (ie if more than 24 hours have passed since membranes ruptured and labour has not yet started, a water labour may not be recommended)

These criteria refer mainly to labour. Whether or not the baby is born in water depends very much on how things progress, how your baby is coping with labour and how you feel at the time.

There are many reasons why labour in water may be appealing. Many people experience the presence of water as a soothing and healing force and are naturally attracted to the idea. This may be especially true if you enjoy being in or near water, are a keen swimmer or have used hydrotherapy in other contexts. However, sometimes the strength of the attraction to being in water during labour can come as a complete surprise to a woman who was not especially drawn to the idea. You may be mainly interested in using the pool to help you to relax or for pain relief during labour and prefer to think of giving birth on land. This is a very valid reason in itself to use a birth pool. Yet you may or may not feel the same way once you are in labour. Equally, women who think they definitely want a water labour may prefer to stay on dry land at the time.

> 'I had a strong feeling to get out of the pool when I needed to push. I moved onto my knees leaning forward onto the coffee table. I pushed for 15 minutes and baby was delivered. She was immediately passed through my legs into my arms. I felt the whole experience was really hard work, but I felt in control at all times. Overall I feel very positive and proud of myself and my husband.'

If you are attending antenatal classes that promote active birth, where you may be encouraged to use a variety of instinctive positions to ease discomfort and promote effective labour, you may see the main benefit of a birth pool as a way of making such mobility easier.

A big incentive for some parents in choosing a waterbirth is to provide a gentle transition for the baby from the environment of the womb to that of the outside world. Building on the ideas of Frederick Leboyer in the 1970s (see Chapter 1, page 2) a gentle and sensitive welcome for the baby through warm water is an ideal to which many parents are attracted. Certainly this is a wonderful way for a baby to be born and is worth aiming for.

However, if this is not how things turn out, bear in mind that there are many ways that babies can have a safe and loving birth. Sometimes interventions are needed to help make the birth gentler and less traumatic for the baby. Even when a high degree of medical intervention is used, birth can be a positive and sensitive experience for all concerned. Love can be present in any situation.

You cannot know in advance whether, at the time, a waterbirth will be appropriate for you or your baby. I always remind parents at my waterbirth workshops that the birth is not as important as the baby. While a waterbirth may be the end result, it's wise not to lose sight of the bigger picture and get too attached to a preconceived idea. It will happen if it's right for you and your baby and meant to be! In this chapter we will be looking at the issues that arise around the possibility of choosing to labour and/or give birth in water.

'I had not planned on actually giving birth in the pool but now I am really glad I did. It didn't occur to me to get out or move at the time and I forgot where I was. I didn't realize I had a waterbirth until it was over!'

When waterbirth may not be the right choice

While it is clear that water can offer hugely valuable support for most women in labour, it is not the right choice for everyone. Some women, for example, are very certain from the outset that they want an epidural and/or other form of medical pain relief. This being said, there are instances of women who have been encouraged to use a birthing pool for temporary relief while waiting for the anaesthetist to arrive; they have found the water so surprisingly soothing and supportive that they have forgotten about the epidural and gone on to have their baby without drugs of any kind. The message is that it is impossible to know what you want until you get there, though you may have a strong idea of your preferences for now. Therefore you should inform yourself of the pros and cons of a wide variety of options and choices for your labour, including the complementary therapies and pain relief described in Chapter 6 as well as a variety of medical interventions described in Chapter 9.

Medical contraindications

There are a few important medical contraindications to the use of water in labour or for birth. You may be aware of some of these in advance, while others may only manifest at the time. Because the use of a birth pool is for low-risk mothers, the primary birth attendants who are responsible for your care are midwives. Waterbirths essentially involve 'midwife-led' care. Obstetricians are usually only involved when there is a pre-existing problem or difficulties occur during labour and intervention may be needed. (There are, however, a few obstetricians who are waterbirth enthusiasts and essentially act as midwives at the birth or work with a team of midwives.)

Each hospital, birth centre or local midwife group will have its own detailed guidelines for the use of water in labour. These are usually put together by the midwives concerned, in collaboration with their colleagues and other professionals who care for women in labour including obstetricians, paediatricians and hospital technicians. They all follow general midwifery recommendations, but policies and protocols will vary from place to place. Confidence comes with experience. If the team are new to waterbirth, they may be understandably more cautious in their approach with more restrictive protocols. Most waterbirth units in the UK have been inspired and initiated by the enthusiasm of the midwifery supervisor or team of midwives, and they are the best people to help you explore whether the use of a birth pool is right for you.

Some of the most common reasons why a woman would be asked not to labour in water are as follows:

- The baby is not lying in the head-down position (cephalic presentation) in the womb
- Labour is not well established
- The baby is considered to be at risk for any reason
- Narcotic analgesics (eg pethidine/meperidine) have been administered within the past four hours
- There is evidence of foetal distress, for example meconium has been observed or the baby's heartbeat patterns are unusual
- The mother has a raised temperature or significantly raised blood pressure
- There is bleeding that is not just a 'show'
- The mother is known to be HIV positive

The baby's position at full term

If your baby's position or presentation before the onset or at the start of labour is found to be unusual, you will need to give careful consideration to your options and the suitability of using a birth pool for labour only or for labour and birth. Much will depend on the type of position and the size of the baby relative to your pelvic opening as well as the progress during labour when the baby may rotate or move. Typically, a baby lying 'posterior' (baby's spine facing your spine) may rotate during labour to the more favourable 'anterior' position (baby's spine facing your belly – possibly to the left side). A posterior labour can be lengthy and is usually felt mainly in the back. In such cases a birth pool can be very helpful in relieving fatigue, easing discomfort and making movement more possible. A further factor will be the willingness of the midwife to support you in trying for a vaginal delivery in water if possible. The guidelines of most hospitals and birth units may exclude some women who have an unusual presentation from using a birth pool.

In about three per cent of labours, the baby is in a breech position in which the head is uppermost and the baby's bottom or feet emerge first from the birth canal. There is potential increased risk at some breech births and therefore obstetricians these days generally strongly recommend a caesarean section for all breech births. In reality a high percentage of breech births could potentially progress vaginally without complications, as they did many years ago. But with the prevalent attitude, the skills and experience of delivering breech babies are no longer available to most midwives. Doctors and midwives who do have experience of delivering breech babies normally, will sometimes support a mother who wants to try for a vaginal birth. However, most practitioners agree that it's best not to use a birth pool in labour or for the birth. This is because the decision about whether to go ahead with a vaginal birth depends on the progress of labour and it's considered best not to influence the labour in any way. Michel Odent, who has delivered large numbers of breech babies, advocates a 'high-gravity' birth on land for breech births, and does not recommend the use of water in labour. Nevertheless, there are a few experienced waterbirth practitioners who, under favourable conditions (for example, a frank breech[1] with really good progress in labour, possibly a previous good birth, etc), might occasionally consider the use of a birth pool as an exception. Since the art of a safe breech birth is not to touch or stimulate the baby at all as it is being born – the 'hands off' approach of a waterbirth (see Chapter 7), it has been suggested the warmth of the water at body temperature could be a positive advantage in a favourable breech birth. This is, however, largely unexplored and therefore unresearched territory, and generally water labour and birth are contraindicated for breech babies.

It's worth exploring ways of encouraging a baby to turn in late pregnancy with acupuncture, homeopathy and exercises. Some obstetricians offer to perform an internal cephalic version. This is a way to turn a baby by manipulating it through the abdomen from the outside. It can be successful but involves some discomfort and risk and should be discussed in detail with your obstetrician first.

Whatever your situation, it is important that you feel an active participant in the decisions you make for the birth of your baby and that you make them with your baby's wellbeing as a priority. Be as well informed as possible and consider the professional advice you receive with an open mind. While it's natural to feel disappointed for a short while, there should be no sense of failure if you have to abandon your original birth plan for a more high-tech

---

1　A frank breech is the most common breech position, in which both hips are flexed, and the legs extended with the feet close to the baby's head. This is the most favourable position for a breech birth.

birth if this is in your baby's best interests. In this case focus your attention on finding ways of making your birth incorporate some of the most important aspects of a natural one. For example, you can try to ensure that you are able to hold your baby 'skin to skin' as soon after the birth as possible and have an hour of privacy so that you still share the benefits of those intimate first moments.

> '*I planned a home waterbirth and ended up with an emergency caesarean in hospital. One hour later I was breastfeeding my beautiful baby in bed. I couldn't believe the enormous feelings of love and gratitude that poured from my heart. Even though it didn't go to plan at all, my son's birth was a wonderful experience and the best day of my life.*'

Previous caesarean section

> '*I had a caesarean for my first birth. When my contractions were very strong I was shivering. I got into the pool and felt better right away in the warm water – I got back the control I was beginning to lose – my husband massaging my back at the end of each contraction. After 50 minutes I felt as though everything was dropping out down below – I was checked – I was fully dilated. The policy of the hospital does not allow a water delivery after a previous caesarean so I got out.*'

Attitudes about the use of water by mothers who have had a previous caesarean section can vary greatly. Some obstetricians take a very hard line approach, recommending that all subsequent births should also be by caesarean. This attitude is more common in the US than in the UK, where a vaginal birth after caesarean is generally encouraged these days wherever possible. (VBAC means 'Vaginal Birth After Caesarean' or 'Very Beautiful And Courageous' a term coined in the US protesters to the hard-line approach.)

Although there is some increase in risk after a previous caesarean, the chances of a problem occurring are very slim, provided labour progresses well and is properly monitored. There are also some risks to performing a further caesarean, so the odds need to be weighed up carefully.

While some practitioners consider a previous caesarean to be a non-negotiable contraindication for the use of water at all, others hold a more moderate view, allowing the mother to labour in water, but perhaps requiring her to get out of the pool for the birth itself.

There are also many practitioners who will consider the birth itself taking place in water, when there are no problems and progress continues to be consistently good throughout labour. The US waterbirth pioneer Dr Michael Rosenthal enabled hundreds of women who had previous caesarean sections to have a waterbirth, with no notable problems. While the general view is that such a birth should take place in a hospital where facilities are at hand in the event of a problem, there are also independent midwives who will consider a water labour/birth at home for women who have had a previous caesarean. One view that seems logical is that the water minimizes pressure in the uterus from the descending baby, protecting the uterus from trauma, and thereby reducing the unlikely risk of a scar rupture.

> 'The birth was fantastic, even more so as my first child was born by emergency caesarean. To go on and have a vaginal delivery at home in water feels like a huge achievement.'

There are quite widely divergent attitudes on this topic and it is a good idea to explore what options are open to you within reasonable range of your home. Although you will be subject to the policies of your birth attendants on this issue, the fact that you have had a previous caesarean section need not necessarily be a reason to exclude the use of water in labour. If the hospital protocol excludes all previous caesarean mothers from waterbirth, you may be able to argue the case for making an individual assessment of the risks for you in particular and negotiate a compromise. Much depends on the reason for the caesarean and whether the problem that necessitated the operation is likely to recur in the current pregnancy. For example, if you have an unusually small pelvic brim or narrow pelvis, this may remain a problem in all your pregnancies, although in many cases this cannot be certain until the woman has a trial of labour. I know several women with unusual or small pelvises who managed to give birth vaginally after one caesarean (generally with the help of squatting to maximize the pelvic diameter) – and in at least two cases, to several more babies! Other reasons for a previous caesarean might include a difficult presentation, placenta praevia, foetal distress or exceptionally high blood pressure. These conditions would not necessarily happen in subsequent pregnancies and need not necessarily be a barrier to a vaginal birth or a water labour or birth *per se*.

If you have had a previous caesarean you will need to discuss your situation in depth with your midwife and obstetrician and clarify what the concerns are in your case. It may be that you can reach an agreement whereby you are able to use water in a hospital setting, where the facilities are on hand in case of the need for medical intervention. It can be confusing and upsetting to face limitations to your plans that you do not feel are justified. I recommend some quiet time breathing and meditating as a way to help you find your own inner guidance. This will help you to connect with your baby and somehow work out what is best for both of you in the circumstances, so you can approach these discussions with a clear understanding of your own convictions. While it is important to take professional guidance seriously, especially if there is a medical concern, this is your baby's birth and it's important that your wishes are respected and taken into account as much as possible. In the UK, this attitude is consistent with the general recommendations of the health authority for maternity care.

'I had a very traumatic birth experience with my first baby – an emergency caesarean at 36 weeks for fulminating pre-eclampsia. This time there were no complications and my baby was born in hospital in water. Thinking about it in retrospect I do not know how I would have coped with the strong sensations at pushing stage if I had not used a birthing pool. The whole experience was healing and helped me to connect the pregnancy to the actual baby as one continuum.'

Where to give birth

Most women start to consider the type of birth they would like almost as soon as they know they are pregnant. Even if you don't know what the full range of options are at first, you will be asked to make your first decisions as soon as you register for antenatal care with your family doctor, hospital obstetrician and/or midwife. It is important that you bear in mind that such decisions can be changed later, if you come to feel they are not right for you. You have options and the right to change your mind at any point – even the day before labour starts. It's a good idea to do quite a bit of research and to interview or meet the people who will be helping you bring your baby into the world. Try to visit several birth places near you to see how they feel before you make your choice.

Your partner is an important part of these decisions, so make sure you both attend any exploratory meetings and have plenty of time to discuss how you both feel. Taking your partner to a good workshop or course about what is involved in the birth will help to provide more information to guide these choices.

If you attend a pregnancy yoga or antenatal class you are likely to hear about other possibilities for your birth you may not have known about. Among most mammals, the choice of birth place does not occur until late pregnancy or early labour and is driven by a powerful nesting instinct. This is no different in humans, so if you are unsure about where to give birth, keep exploring, visit other places, ask questions and talk to midwives. Give yourself permission to choose what is right for you, especially at the last minute. Above all trust your intuition and your gut feelings – they will lead you to the right decisions. Once you have made your choice you can make your birth work in any supportive environment.

In many forward-thinking birthing units in the UK, the option of using a birth pool is not seen as a separate or special choice, any more than making provision for medical pain relief: it is seen as just one of the strategies that may be considered as the labour progresses. As such, a birthing pool is ideally available for all births as long as there are no overriding medical contraindications (see page 80).

In basic terms, the first choice is whether to have a home or hospital birth or perhaps to choose a birthing centre with a low-tech approach if there is one within reach of your home. What is most important is that you have a sense of trust in the people who will attend both your pregnancy and your birth, to be there for you in the way that you want and to give you good guidance. You need to have the feeling that they will be on your side and support and encourage you as much as possible to have the birth you want – while also being able to respond appropriately if there is a problem.

Hospitals offer medical support for all births and provide backup for home births and birth centres, which will have pre-arranged systems of communication and support in place 'just in case'. A small percentage of women (less than 10 per cent) who plan to give birth at home or in a birth centre do need to transfer to hospital in labour. It's reassuring to know that we have such reliable life-saving technology readily available to support all births if the need arises. The bottom line is that thanks to modern medical care, you can afford to be much less anxious about your safety or your baby's safety, no matter where you decide to give birth.

> 'All women should be offered information on the option of using water for labour and birth. There are no grounds for seeing this option as particularly suitable for, and acceptable to, certain groups of women on the basis of non-clinical criteria.'[2]

Giving birth at home

> 'I am very happy I chose to have my first baby at home. I felt
> in control, relaxed, and enjoyed the home comforts and privacy,
> especially being able to get into my own bed with my baby and
> fall asleep! It was a very powerful, positive experience and I would
> recommend it to any woman who felt deep down that it was what
> she wanted but "wasn't sure". My husband was very sceptical and

2   Royal College of Midwives, Position Paper No 1a, *The Use of Water in Labour and Birth*, October 2000

scared that something would go wrong, but I was totally committed to having as "natural" an experience as possible. He is now converted and pleased I was stubborn. We would definitely choose the same birth plan next time round!'

A home birth can be a great choice for those who are at low risk of complications and have good local midwifery support. If you are healthy and having a normal pregnancy this is an option worth looking at if you want to have optimal control over your birth. Researchers have demonstrated that it's a myth that hospital is necessarily the safest place to give birth – even for first babies. Bear in mind that about 95 per cent of births are potentially uncomplicated and that the familiar environment of your own home can help to ensure the smooth progress of labour (see Chapter 3).

The big plus is that you can create the birth environment in exactly the way you want it. It can be intimate and secure and it's up to you who's present. At home you can arrange to have the personal, supportive care you need and all the attention will be focused on you. It is easiest to guarantee privacy at home and to avoid unwanted interventions.

These days increasing numbers of midwives have experience in attending waterbirths, and your birth choice may affect who is the right person to take care of you. You will need to discuss your preferences with your midwife or team of midwives. It is very important that you feel confident the person who will be looking after you is fully in sympathy with your preferences and is also knowledgeable about using water in labour and in underwater delivery. In the UK the local health authority is under an obligation to provide an appropriately trained midwife to support you in the type of birth you have chosen. This ideal does not always manifest so easily in reality, especially in areas where there is a shortage of midwives. While a water labour or birth does not alter the midwife's practice greatly, some basic training and experience is necessary. Usually two midwives are provided at a waterbirth, one of whom is experienced in the use of birth pools and the other to support her and learn. By law, however, only one midwife needs to be in attendance. You can request that only one midwife is with you in the room during labour. If possible provide another room for the midwives to rest and relax.

Women requesting a home waterbirth do sometimes meet with ambivalence, and it's not uncommon to be told there is no midwife available who is trained in waterbirths. In this case you may need to put your request in writing to the local supervisor of midwives.

If the local health authority cannot provide a waterbirth-trained midwife, you may want to consider employing an independent midwife. Organizations that can put you in touch with a waterbirth-trained independent midwife in the UK, USA and Australia are listed in the Resources section. This is an option for which you will need to pay, but is sometimes the only way to have a more personal relationship with your midwife. In some areas of the UK, midwives working for the National Health Service make great efforts to provide this kind of individual care to all women.

'What I loved about being at home was the fact that I had to dig deeper inside myself to get through it all than I knew was possible. There wasn't an epidural nearby so I had to draw on every reserve I had. I gripped my partner's hands really tight and stared into his eyes through the worst of it and that kept me going. I think that if I was in a hospital I would have been tempted to ask for help. Instead I surprised myself at what I could do and I feel great about it now.'

For a waterbirth at home you will need to hire a birth pool. Make preliminary enquiries as early as possible. Take the time to research the different pools available and find out what the hire arrangements are. This can be done easily through catalogues and websites and by calling the pool-hire company to ask any questions you may have.

You also need to be sure that the room you are planning to use is suitable for a home waterbirth. Make sure you take into account the requirements of the pool. Most importantly, you will need to consider the following: the dimensions of the pool and the size of the room; the pool's weight when filled with water and you, and therefore the strength of the floor; and water supply and drainage.

You need to site the pool where access to water is possible, and once the pool is filled you cannot move it. However, the hoses supplied with most hire pools are long and can extend to link a water supply with most rooms in an average house or apartment. Drainage needs to be through an outside drain or bath, as the emptying pump works very fast and a sink or basin will overflow. You will also need a good supply of hot water; this is an issue you should discuss with the pool-hire company who will have the experience and expertise to advise you. With a small boiler it can take several hours to fill the pool so be sure to allow enough time.

When selecting the room for your birth, it's best to choose a part of the house in which you feel cosy and secure. Ideally, the pool should be situated in a place where semi-darkness, privacy, intimacy and seclusion can be ensured. It's helpful to have a toilet nearby. The room should be large enough so there is enough space around the pool for you to give birth on land beside the pool, if necessary or preferred. You also need to be sure that the floor is strong enough to support the weight of up to 200 gallons of water. If in any doubt, you can get advice from a structural engineer. The strongest parts of most floors are in the corners or over a load-bearing wall on the floor below. The pool should be situated either below or at least on the same level as the water supply.

> 'It was the most intense, amazing and empowering experience of my life. I feel very proud of myself and my body. My decision to have a home birth was definitely the right one for me. The care and attention I received definitely contributed to my confidence and ability to trust that I could do this without any fear or complications. Being at home after the birth has helped us to relax more easily into parenthood.'

Choosing a hospital birth

> 'I felt safest having my first baby in hospital. I can't praise the staff enough and the midwives were so encouraging. They did their best to give us exactly the birth we wanted and even reminded me that I didn't want any pain relief.'

You may feel most confident about having your baby in a hospital, where hi-tech specialist treatment is available on site for yourself and your baby should it be required. A hospital birth is usually advised for anyone who has had previous problems in labour that may recur, or who has experienced problems with the current pregnancy or is at risk for any other reason.

If you are going to be giving birth in a hospital where the use of water in labour is standard practice, you won't have very much arranging to do. You will need to visit the birth unit and familiarize yourself with the hospital setup. Take your partner with you, talk to the midwives and be sure to ask any questions you want to. You might want to write down a short list of things you would like for your birth and have a copy attached to your notes for easy reference at the time by the midwives on duty, whom you may not have met. It's important for you to feel at ease, relaxed and familiar with the environment where you will be in labour.

In recent years many hospitals have been taking on board the lessons of the past few decades about the benefits of an active birth and a calm and quiet environment. You may well find that even though large hospitals tend to be busy public places, efforts are being made to provide a less clinical and more homelike and private atmosphere in the labour rooms. You can arrange to visit the hospital and check out the labour rooms and the general feel of the place. It is important to reassure yourself that the environment feels as secure and intimate as possible. The best-designed delivery rooms have a toilet within the room for ease of access and privacy. Look out for features such as effective curtains or blinds and dimmer switches for the lights. Remember that low lighting is important for creating the right feeling of privacy that will promote the optimum release of oxytocin. There may be a birthing stool provided, and some hospitals these days may have homeopathic remedies, aromatherapy oils for massage and/or vaporization and TENS machines (see Chapter 6). Also look at the environment around the pool and check out whether a floor mat, birth ball or beanbag is provided. These are basic comfort aids you can bring in yourself, if not provided by the hospital. Find out about whether there is a waterproof, hand-held Doptone foetal heart monitor available as this will be the least disruptive way of checking your baby's heartbeat from time to time (see Chapter 7, page 170). Start dreaming about how you can make the labour room your own special place and what you can take with you to personalize the space.

> *'Our boy was born into water at our local hospital after one and*
> *a half hours of intensive labour. I was in the pool at 9 cm dilated*
> *– it made a huge difference and the whole experience as*
> *pleasurable as I was hoping.'*

More than 150 hospitals in the UK now have birthing pools and birth attendants trained to use them. Provision varies in different areas and you may
need to shop around a bit to find the hospital that can best provide for your
needs. The fact that a hospital has a birth pool does not necessarily mean
that it is being well or fully utilized. Although in the UK the Royal College of
Midwives has recommended that all maternity units and midwives should
develop expertise in attending waterbirths, a possible problem in some hospitals is that there are too few staff who have experience and/or training in
waterbirths. It is therefore important to ask the hospital about the training
and experience of their midwives in relation to waterbirth, and also about the
numbers of water labours and births that occur there. In hospitals that are
truly committed to the practice, a significant percentage of women will be
using water at some stage in their labour. If around 25–30 per cent of these
women give birth in water then the pool is being well utilized.

If use of the pool is becoming very popular, availability of the pool is something you need to consider to avoid disappointment. If there is only one pool
in the birth unit you may be warned ahead of time that it could be in use by
somebody else on the day of your birth. It can be upsetting to have such
uncertainty about the availability of the pool if you are planning and looking
forward to using it. Though it makes sense for hospitals to keep a spare
portable pool for such situations, very few have this facility. Some hospitals
have two or three installed pools, and this helps to provide most women who
want one with a pool. Others may have a large bath that can be used instead.

*'I took a pool into hospital with me as they didn't have one. The
water really helped with the pain and the second stage was very
short with only five push urges before my baby was born. His
waters were still intact and not broken until he was fully born. I
did not tear and the birth was very calm and controlled. The water
birth was a first for the hospital and we caused quite a stir with
lots of staff coming in for a look!'*

Bringing a hired portable pool into the hospital yourself may be the best way
of guaranteeing that you have the opportunity to use water during your
labour, although not all hospitals will allow this. This may be because hard-
pressed busy midwives do not have time to assemble and dismantle a birth
pool – but if you arrange for your partner or someone else to do this they may
be more willing to accommodate you. Look for a portable pool that is easy to
transport and assemble. Most hospitals have a continuous supply of hot
water so the pool can be filled quite quickly.

If you encounter a negative response you can consult an organization such
as AIMS (see Resources) to find out about your rights and the best way to
proceed if this happens. There may be no room for a pool and in this case
you may want to reconsider your options. If you start these enquiries early,
you give yourself time to change your mind if you come to feel that your original choice of birthing unit is unsympathetic, or in a more extreme case, you
come up against a 'brick wall'. More hospitals, however, are installing pools
and in many cases are positively encouraging women to use them.

*'There came a point where pain relief in the pool was not enough
after hours of painful contractions. I was very pleased that I was in
a hospital and could ask for an epidural. I was exhausted and it*

was a huge relief. I slept for a while and then managed to push my baby out normally.'

Birth Centres

'I wanted to know help was there if I needed it and a home birth was not for me. The new birth centre in my local hospital was a great solution. The pool room was very peaceful and the midwives were totally confident. I felt very much at home and had a fantastic experience.'

Birth centres are generally much smaller and more intimate than hospital units and offer a compromise between the qualities of a home and hospital birth that is ideal for some women. This is a good choice if you don't want to give birth at home, but nevertheless want to have a low-intervention birth. The care is midwife-led and the atmosphere is usually welcoming and informal. Family members can accompany you, and kitchen facilities for light refreshments and a TV room or lounge may be available. In a birth centre you will get more individual attention than is usually possible in a hospital, and you are likely to be encouraged to have an active birth. Birth centres tend to specialize in waterbirths and may be well-equipped with pools and midwives who are especially trained to use them. A birth centre may be independent and linked with one or two hospitals for backup or may be within or adjacent to a hospital.

'We had a wonderful, cosy room in the birth centre. The midwives were really pro 'natural'. I felt confident and supported, and my partner and toddler were always welcome so we felt like a family at all times. I was sad to go home at first.'

While birth centres have been a popular option in the US and Australia for some years, there were very few in the UK until fairly recently, as the trend has been to close down smaller birth units in favour of larger consultant units in hospitals. An example of a successful birth centre is the Edgware Birth Centre, London, which has become one of the most forward-thinking of the UK's maternity units, with several birth pools on site and their use actively encouraged (see also Chapter 1, page 13). Thanks to the success of this venture, new birth centres are currently opening within or attached to larger hospitals with a philosophy of minimal intervention and at least one installed birth pool.

However, this option is designed for low-risk mothers only and most birth centres have to adhere to strict acceptance criteria. This may mean that if the birth occurs slightly early or significantly later than at full term, or another minor variation or problem occurs, the birth may have to take place in hospital, since there are no facilities on site for medical intervention.

If a birth centre appeals to you, you can start by asking your doctor if there is one in your area. Provided you can get there fairly easily, birth centres often accept women who do not live locally.

> *'The birth centre was a home from home and had three birth pools so*
> *we did not have to worry about the pool being used. Although I had*
> *not met her before, the midwife understood exactly what I wanted and*
> *kept reminding me to relax and trust my body. There was a wonderful*
> *atmosphere with lots of privacy and we just got on with it.'*

Choosing a doula

A doula is a birth professional whose primary role is to provide continuous support to the mother before during and after childbirth. The word 'doula' comes from the ancient Greek and refers to an experienced woman who helps the birthing mother. During labour she would stay by your side or nearby throughout and provide emotional support, physical comfort measures and assistance in getting information you may need for making decisions. She works alongside your birth attendants, essentially in the role of your companion, and also supports your partner. Research has demonstrated that the presence of a doula is associated with less medication for pain relief, fewer instrumental births, fewer caesarean sections and better condition of the newborn.

A doula can provide continuous care and keep her focus entirely on you, providing a calm and objective support person whom you know and have already formed a trusting relationship with. This can be very useful additional support for your birth wherever you chose to have your baby. Doulas are trained to understand normal birth physiology and the emotional needs of a woman in labour. They are increasingly accepted in maternity care with the growing recognition of the benefits to mothers' emotional wellbeing in labour and better birth outcomes. There are several training schemes for doulas and organizations where you can find out more about them and obtain local contacts (see Resources).

Hiring a birth pool

There are a variety of portable birth pools available for hire in different countries that will suit most circumstances and budgets. Key features to look out for are as follows:

- Size and depth. You need sufficient length to be able to stretch out comfortably, and sufficient width to allow you to move freely and for access by your birth attendant. The pool should also not be too large, so that you can press your feet against the firm surface of the opposite wall if you need to. It should be deep enough to allow for the water to cover your belly and reach the level of your breasts when you are seated in the pool (a depth of about 55 cm/22 inches).

- Rigid sides with wide rounded edges. For secure and comfortable support when squatting and kneeling you need a pool with firm sides. This allows your birth attendant to sit on or lean over the edge for monitoring and examinations. Your partner may need to sit on the rim to support you. For safety reasons rigid sides that will bear your weight when sitting are important, so inflatable pools are not ideal.

- Hygiene precautions. To eliminate the risk of infection, choose a pool that is supplied with a new disposable liner and new filling hoses for each customer. Recirculating water systems or Jacuzzis are not a good idea as they may harbour bacteria in the pipes.

Booking your pool

You will need to have booked your birthing pool, well in advance. Bearing in mind that it is not uncommon for labour to start two weeks either side of your official due date, ask to have it delivered approximately two weeks before that time. It is a good investment to order a spare disposable liner for use in 'practice runs' (see page 128). When your pool is delivered, take time as soon as possible to check that all the components are there, and do a practice 'dry' setup without the inner liner so that any problems with the equipment can be resolved in time for the birth. Check all the hoses and tap adapters to be sure that they fit or are long enough. A good pool hire company will respond quickly to any concerns you may have.

Other accessories and equipment

Most of the following suggestions are for a waterbirth at home, but some of the items will also be useful for hospital-based waterbirths as they are not necessarily provided. Check with your midwife to confirm what equipment you will need to bring with you to the hospital.

- A new waterproof digital thermometer, if not supplied with your pool.
- Some plastic sheeting to protect the floor around the pool as you get in and out. Be careful not to double this or it will be very slippery.
- A large non-slip bath mat. It is possible that you will want or need to leave the pool from time to time or possibly to give birth on land. Therefore you will need a comfortable and secure surface for you to stand, squat or kneel on.
- A birth ball and mat beside the pool for your support and comfort when labouring on land. The ball is also a very useful pool-side seat as it is higher than a chair or a stool.
- A powerful room heater that can rapidly raise the temperature of the room when the baby is born. Remember that any electricity supply needs to be kept well away from the possibility of contact with water.
- Plenty of large towels and an extra one kept warm for the baby.
- A large plastic strainer or sieve for removing debris from the water.
- One or more low stools for the midwife and your partner. One of these should be strong and stable enough to serve as a step to help you get in and out of the pool. Cheap plastic ones are easy to find.
- Plastic inflatable pillows or plastic-covered ordinary pillows for head support while relaxing in the pool. You can also use a large folded towel.
- A comfortable chair and a beanbag or selection of large cushions, tapes or CDs and the equipment to play them, an essential oil burner, lamps or candles to provide soft lighting, a natural sponge, essential oils and homeopathic remedies.

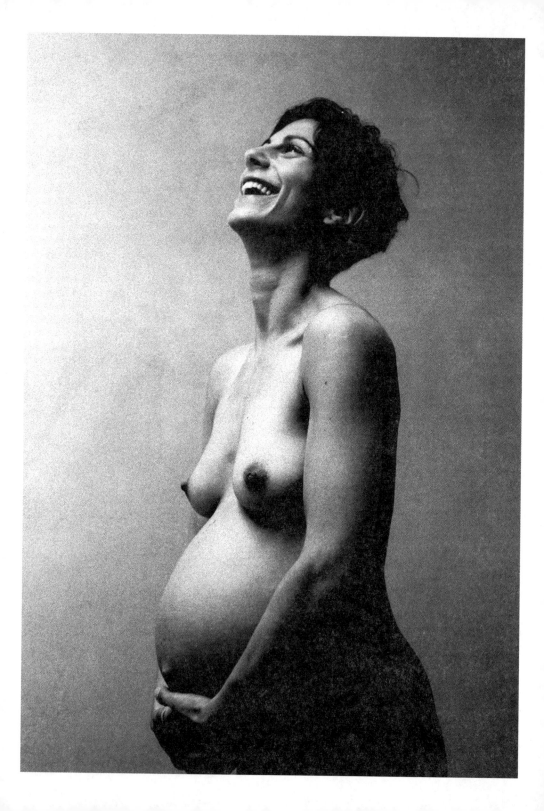

chapter five

Preparing for birth and motherhood

'Having a child is a living prayer and simply amazing grace. Our power as women to form another life within our bodies is almost too vast to comprehend. In our culture we too often forget this is a sacred miracle.'[1]

This chapter is for you – to encourage you to be aware of the miracle that is happening inside you and to make the most of the nine months of your pregnancy to prepare yourself for giving birth and mothering. While your baby is developing inside your womb, you are flowering from a woman into a mother. Your most important task is to nurture yourself and protect your growing baby. The challenge of birth lies ahead of you – but even greater than this is the life-changing transition into parenthood. You are going through a transformation. You are evolving, becoming wiser, stronger and more responsible – getting ready to be the mother of a baby and to guide your child through life. If this is your second or subsequent baby, welcoming another child to your family brings a whole set of new challenges and will expand you as a person even more.

1   Gurmukh, *Bountiful, Beautiful, Blissful,* St Martin's Press, New York, 2003

Taking care of yourself, in the most essential sense, involves living healthily and respecting your body. It means nurturing yourself emotionally, mentally and spiritually so that you feel at peace with yourself and the special people around you. Putting yourself and your own wellbeing first in pregnancy is not selfish. Out of this self-love comes the space, time and capacity to love and nurture your child, appreciate your partner and take care of your family. This doesn't start after the birth – it is happening already. Giving time and attention to yourself and your baby each day of your pregnancy is the perfect preparation for your birth and beyond. It will help you to connect to the natural forces and energies that are there to nourish you. It will lead you to discover your inner resources, power and strength as a woman.

Yoga in pregnancy

When I was pregnant with my second child I was a newly qualified childbirth educator. I was trained to offer informative birth preparation courses to couples, which were held in the final weeks of pregnancy. While these courses were helpful to a degree, I had a strong sense that they weren't nearly effective enough, that they were giving the mind lots of stimulation while totally neglecting the body and doing nothing for the spirit. By coincidence, I joined a yoga class and began to simplify and modify the yoga positions to make myself more comfortable as my baby grew. That led me to explore how to use my body most efficiently for birth and how to give birth 'actively', using instincts women have shared for thousands of years in every corner of the world. Through the yoga, my body taught me everything I needed to know about birth. I also felt amazingly well and energized compared with my first pregnancy and somehow in touch with a force greater than ourselves that helps all women bring new life into the world.

That was more than 25 years ago. Since then I have passed on the gift of practising yoga in pregnancy to thousands of women and have observed how
powerfully it can lead a woman to the knowledge and power of birthing that
is already inside her.

Practising yoga in pregnancy is much more than a method of birth preparation or a series of exercises and techniques. It becomes part of your awareness and part of your life. Yoga awakens the intelligence of your body and
puts you in touch with your intuition. It helps you to make the most of the
transformative potential of the whole of your pregnancy, to get in touch more
deeply with yourself, your feelings and your baby. After all these years, my
convictions have grown that yoga is the best way to prepare for any kind of
birth, including of course, a waterbirth.

Your body is your temple

You give birth primarily with your body. Just as no one in their right mind
would think of climbing Everest unprepared, facing the awesome and monu-
mental experience of giving birth and nurturing a baby without adequate
mental and physical preparation can be a recipe for disaster. Preparing for
your birth can make all the difference to how it turns out. This doesn't guarantee that it will be easy or that it will be a natural waterbirth – but it does
mean you will move through it with the strength and equilibrium to have a
positive and empowered start to your journey as a mother.

In our culture birth has become so medicalized that most women today have
lost connection with the ancient wisdom and birth secrets that were traditionally handed down from mother to daughter. As girls we did not learn
about birth from the older, wiser women in the community or witness active,

empowered birthing. Some of us never even saw a baby being breastfed. In addition, our lifestyle does not naturally prepare our bodies for the positions, movements and physical exertion of labour and birth. We are rarely encouraged to trust our bodies and instincts or to have faith in nature. In fact, the emphasis on medical tests and checks in pregnancy, and the general belief that we need help and intervention to give birth, can have the opposite effect and undermine our confidence. Yoga can give you an antidote to all this and a way to prepare for your birth that is truly empowering.

In this book I have not got the space to give specific guidance about yoga practice. This is available in my book *Preparing for Birth with Yoga* and other resources mentioned at the back of this book and on www.activebirthcentre.com. I recommend you join a weekly pregnancy yoga class, if you can find one in your area. It's a wonderful experience to join with other women who are going through the same life change as you are. You will learn a tremendous amount and get a lot of support and friendship from the other women, as you share your experiences and celebrate your pregnancies together.

Yoga in pregnancy needs to be gentle, soft, simple and slow with more emphasis on breathing, meditation and easy stretches than learning to adopt difficult postures. It needs to be taught by a reputable and specifically trained teacher who understands pregnancy and how to work with its changes. There are a few sensible cautions to bear in mind before embarking on a yoga programme in pregnancy:

- Never persist with a posture or movement that is painful or does not feel right for you
- Never force your body or your breathing
- Work slowly at your own pace; it is better to do one or two postures deeply than to rush through a larger number of postures more superficially

How pregnancy yoga can benefit you

Yoga is an ancient discipline that originated in India and is now practised by millions of people all over the world. While it does embrace the concept of a higher spiritual life force that pervades all of existence, which some might call God, it does not insist on conformity to any particular religion and holds universal appeal for people of all faiths. It uplifts the spirit and nourishes and heals both mind and body. It is simple and practical and can be adapted to be used by young and old, and to suit everybody.

The practice of yoga in pregnancy takes you deep inside yourself – just where you will need to go in labour! The first Yoga Sutra of Patanjali (a compilation of aphorisms from the ancient philosophical yogic texts) says:

'Yoga is the ability to direct the mind exclusively towards an object and sustain focus in that direction without any distractions.'[2]

What better guidance could be given to a woman who is approaching birth and motherhood. These words have enormous depth. Applied to labour they mean the ability to be relaxed and surrendered, to shut out the world and let go – while at the same time turning your awareness deeply within. This is how you will find the focus, the concentration and the stillness of mind to go into the heart of the experience and open yourself to its intensity.

Yoga practice helps you to start changing your priorities and learning to slow down to the same wavelength as your baby. These are some of the benefits this can bring to your life:

2 Translation from the Sanskrit from 'Reflections on the Yoga Sutras of Patanjali', TKV Desikachar Affiliated East-West Press Pvt. Ltd

- Yoga makes more space in the body, relieving the compression caused by the extra weight you are carrying. It helps you to relax and release tension, boosts energy levels and prevents tiredness
- It encourages a deeper, more conscious bond with your baby
- It helps you to access the wisdom, intuition and inner guidance to make intelligent choices
- It concentrates the mind and nourishes the body, reducing or preventing discomfort
- Yoga connects your body with gravity – the Earth's energetic force. This encourages good postural alignment, makes you feel 'grounded', calmer and more balanced
- Good posture encourages good positioning of your baby and therefore reduces the risk of malpresentation
- Learning how to work with gravity through yoga will help your labour and birth to be more efficient
- Yoga balances the glandular systems and the flow of hormones, preparing your body for the huge level of hormonal secretion during labour
- It aids all the circulatory systems of the body, improves breathing and takes more oxygen to your organs and your baby
- Your body will become stronger, less stiff and more flexible with better muscle tone
- You will feel calmer and more centred

Breathing and meditation

When you breathe well it relaxes you. Your blood is charged with oxygen, which nourishes your brain and pumps the fluid through your spinal cord. Your lungs get rid of toxins and your pituitary gland produces a plentiful stream of hormones. Your muscles and organs are nourished and your baby is protected from distress. Breathing is your best helper in labour.

The essence of yoga is awareness of the breath. In pregnancy this is not about learning breathing techniques, but about becoming relaxed and mindful of the involuntary rhythm of inhalation and exhalation. By slowing down and relaxing, the breath becomes more even and naturally deepens. The discipline is to keep the focus of your attention on the breath and to allow the mind to become quiet and still. Of course thoughts tend to come up and the mind wanders off now and then so we lose our concentration. The art of learning to meditate is to catch yourself when this happens and bring your focus back to your breathing. Cultivating this ability to concentrate the mind on the breath without distraction gives you an enormously powerful tool for getting through the painful peak of each contraction in labour. When you sink deeply into rhythm with this, it becomes easy and natural. Pain can be transformed into intensity. The unbearable can become tolerable. Fear and resistance can melt away and you can find your way through labour without help from anyone or anything. It truly is that powerful. The more you practise this in pregnancy – at least once a day for five minutes – the more effective it will be.

Try this breath awareness exercise:

Sit comfortably on the floor on a folded blanket or cushion to raise your hips. If your back feels tired in this position, try sitting against a wall so that your lower back is supported. Bend one leg, bringing the foot in towards your body and fold the other leg in front, so you are sitting in a simple cross-legged position. If you are familiar with yoga you can sit in half lotus or lotus position. Feel free to support your knees from underneath with cushions. The aim is to feel totally comfortable with a stable base in the lower body and a long, free and relaxed spine. By all means choose a different sitting or kneeling position or even sit on a chair if that is more comfortable for you.

- Now relax and close your eyes, allowing tension to melt out of your neck, shoulders and arms. Feel how your pelvis and legs are held by gravity, leaving your upper body light and free. Sense the way your spine lengthens out of the pelvis like a plant growing out of its roots towards the light. Open your chest and lengthen your trunk to make space for your baby and your breathing. Be still for a while and let your breathing slow right down into its natural rhythm.
- When you are ready, touch your sides around the lower ribs with your hands and feel the movements caused by your breathing as your ribcage expands when the lungs fill up with air on the inhalation. Then notice how the ribcage gathers inwards and contracts as the air is expelled from the lungs with the exhalation. Continue for two or three cycles of the breath.
- Notice a tiny pause at the end of each inhalation and exhalation.
- Remove your hands and place them on your abdomen so that they cradle your lower belly. This is your centre of energy, where your baby lives and grows throughout pregnancy. Notice the movements in your belly as you breathe. Like a balloon your belly inflates with the inhalation and deflates with the exhalation. Don't force the movement at all – just observe and feel

it. This is natural deep breathing. Continue for two or three cycles of the breath.

- Now place your hands on your knees and continue to focus your attention on the in and out breaths and the gentle wave-like movements they cause in the chest and in the belly. Allow each in and out breath to be fully completed and reach its natural end. You may feel your baby moving more than usual because of all the extra oxygen!
- Continue for a while, keeping your mind concentrated on breathing in and breathing out, bringing your attention back to the breath each time you realize you are thinking. But remember, you don't need to 'do' this breathing – let it happen by itself and simply observe it.

Once you have the ability to concentrate your mind like this, you can focus on a particular meditation. Here are some ideas:

- With closed eyes, feel the exhalation moving down your spine to the very tip and then sense the inhalation moving up from the tailbone towards the delicate vertebrae right at the top of the neck.
- With closed eyes, look internally at the 'third eye' spot in the centre of your forehead. Maintain this focus as you watch the breath.
- With eyes slightly open look down, towards the tip of your nose
- With eyes closed chant the sacred sound OM, pronounced 'aoum' with the exhalation. Relax and wait for the in breath to come of its own accord and then repeat the sound. Continue for a few minutes and then stop chanting the sound and keep your eyes closed and your attention on the breath a while longer.

Fitness and health

Taking care of your health in pregnancy is a priority. You need to eat a balanced diet of fresh, whole, preferably organic foods, and to drink at least eight glasses of water a day. Rest whenever you feel tired and slow down the pace of your life in order to replenish all the energy that is going to nourish your baby.

Complementary therapies can help a great deal to keep body and mind in harmony and balance your energy. Selecting a therapy that appeals to you and having a treatment regularly with a practitioner who specializes in treating pregnant women will keep you in optimal form and clear and cleanse your body, leaving all channels open and ready for the birth. Cranial osteopathy is a deep therapy that works through the cerebral spinal fluid and the nervous system to influence the whole body. Reflexology works the thousands of nerve endings in the feet and offers a proven way to prepare the body effectively for birth. Various forms of massage are beneficial in pregnancy including aromatherapy. See page 125 for more information on using essential oils safely in pregnancy. Shiatsu and Thai massage are wonderful because they release blockages along the meridians, the channels along which our 'chi' or life force flows. Homeopathy and acupuncture can provide effective alternative treatments for many ailments in pregnancy. There is more information on this topic in my book *New Natural Pregnancy*.[3]

In addition to yoga, you also need some regular aerobic or cardiovascular exercise. This increases the efficiency of the blood circulation throughout your body, making sure that plenty of oxygen and essential nutrients reach your baby and that waste products are removed. To maintain fitness, the best aerobic exercise for pregnancy is walking or swimming, and this is all you need in addition to pregnancy yoga. Your heart and lungs are working harder

3 Janet Balaskas, *New Natural Pregnancy*, Gaia Books, 1998

than usual to oxygenate and pump the increased volume of blood around your body. In some ways you are doing aerobics all the time. For this reason it's not a good idea to push yourself even more with strenuous aerobic exercises or workouts in the gym. You can walk several miles a day provided you pace yourself comfortably and do not suffer from any pelvic or back pain. Take care to keep your posture balanced while you walk and wear sensible flat shoes and a small back pack if you are carrying anything.

Practising for labour and birth

In pregnancy your body learns much more effectively than your mind. During labour you will probably forget everything you have learnt from books or courses. Your thinking brain will become passive, while your body and your hormones will become active and powerful. Everything your body has learnt in pregnancy will be available to you in labour on an instinctual level. We give birth from within. It is not something we 'do' and there are no recipes or techniques to be learnt. However, it is very helpful to awaken your body to the movements and positions that are instinctive during labour and birth. This will teach you how to make gravity work for you rather than against you. Understanding how to work in harmony with gravity is one of the chief ways to assist the progress of your labour.

Learn with your body

Whether you use a birth pool or not, you will need to know how to use your body to best effect on land before getting in the water or if you need to get out at any point. Trying out labour and birthing positions regularly while you are pregnant, or as part of your yoga practice, will make them feel familiar, comfortable and easy to do. This helps to inform your body and to counteract all the conditioning from the images of women lying on their back and gripping the bedposts that you may have seen in films and on television. Instead, this will put you in touch with the ancient birthing wisdom that has been shared by women all over the world for thousands of years. It will feel good to do this. I recommend you read Chapters 6 and 7 and start practising the active positions for labour and birth well ahead of time – including the suggestions for focusing your awareness on your breathing and on the process happening inside you. Make this a part of your daily life and you will sail into labour knowing exactly what you need to do.

Squatting

It's beneficial to practise squatting every day, even if you don't use this position during the birth. It will strengthen all the muscles that attach to the pelvis and encourage the birth canal to open wide. Your legs will become stronger and there will be more energy and strength in your lower body. All the muscles involved in the birth process are naturally exercised and conditioned by squatting. It also improves elimination and the flexibility and strength of your spine.

Caution
Avoid deep squatting if you have pubic pain, haemorrhoids, vulval varicosities, a stitch in your cervix or any bleeding – if your baby is breech or you are in the last six weeks of pregnancy, do standing half squats instead.

Deep squats

♦ Unless squatting with your heels flat is very easy for you, use a rolled up blanket, pillows or books under your heels so you can squat without straining, which would be counterproductive. Don't worry too much about having your feet completely flat if that makes you uncomfortable. It's more important for your spine to feel long and free.

- Use your hands to push into the floor to help you get up and down or hold onto something firm in front of you. Make sure that your feet are a little wider than hip-width apart and are slightly turned out so that your knees follow the angle of your feet. Practising this in a swimming pool as well will help to loosen your hip joints and make squatting easier.

Standing half squats

- If you feel any sense of strain in a full squat, listen to your body and practise standing half squats instead (you can do them in the final six weeks of pregnancy). Stand with your feet a bit wider apart, well grounded and slightly turned out. Bend your knees and lower your pelvis about halfway to the ground.
- Hold the position for a few cycles of breathing to strengthen your legs and breathe through the discomfort. You'll be pleased to know that full squatting is much easier in water!

Using a birth ball

One of the most useful aids for labour, this is a large inflatable ball, about 65 centimetres (26 inches) in diameter made from tough PVC can be bought by mail order together with a small pump (see Resources). Relatively inexpensive, it's the easiest way to transform the birthing room for active support in labour.

A birth ball is also invaluable in pregnancy, so you may as well get it early and use it now (see Resources). It's also useful as a great baby soother (sit on it holding baby and bounce gently) and for exercising after the birth.

- ♦ Use a birth ball for sitting at a table or desk instead of a chair. Because your hips are higher than your knees, your pelvis will tilt slightly more forward than on a chair and encourage optimal positioning of your baby in the womb. Reduced pressure on the hips and pelvic joints may help to prevent and alleviate aches and pains related to poor posture in pregnancy.
- ♦ Sitting on the ball, try making circular movements of the pelvis. Often a great help in labour, these natural movements gently but effectively help to tone the muscles of the pelvic floor and the internal muscles of the abdomen.
- ♦ Kneel forward over the ball for relaxation and massage.
- ♦ For the part of labour that takes place on land you can sit or kneel on the ball. During contractions the mobility of the birth ball allows you to respond to your body's signals and move according to the rhythms of your labour (see Chapter 6, page 144).
- ♦ The ball can also be used for practising supported squatting with your partner seated on the ball behind you. See Chapter 7, page 190.
- ♦ Your partner or midwife can use the ball as an elevated seat beside the pool and avoid back strain from bending over.

Emotions

Most women are amazed by the flood of emotions that surges through them in pregnancy. The hormones of pregnancy have a huge impact on your emotional life, directing your focus increasingly on your growing baby and the need to nurture and protect this new life inside you. Waves of emotions are likely to ebb and flow and may sometimes seem overwhelmingly intense. It is important to accept, acknowledge and experience all of your feelings – they are clearing the way for motherhood.

If you practise yoga and meditation in pregnancy the natural tendency for feelings to come up will be enhanced. As the body releases tension and softens, deep feelings that are held inside may be released as well. This is the perfect time to let go of them. You may find yourself crying a lot more than usual.

Having a baby is a profound life change – it gives you an opportunity to grow, to heal, and to discover yourself on a deeper level. There is no better time to heal your own past history or to find out about your unconscious attitudes about sexuality, pregnancy, birth and parenting. Find out about what your mother experienced when she was pregnant with you, how she felt about it, what happened at your own birth and when you were a baby. All of these can colour what you are feeling now.

Work with the truth

Our emotional life is a mixture of warm, joyful, positive, loving, peaceful and ecstatic feelings and the darker spaces of the more painful emotions such as grief, fear, anger, hate and resentment. Some of our feelings belong with what is happening at the present time in our lives and others relate to past experiences. Often it's a bit of both – as if the past is also part of the present. It's important not to be too analytical. Just be with your feelings when they come up and understanding and insight may follow.

You are also likely to have a mixture of feelings about your pregnancy and impending motherhood, both positive and so-called negative. When we hold back or hide our feelings we limit our growth and nothing changes. On the other hand, when we express exactly what we feel – good and bad – life moves on and the way we feel changes, opening the way for love. So I'd like to encourage you to be with the truth. This will give you power. Accept, express and flow with all of your feelings when they come up. It's very helpful to share your feelings with someone whom you feel can listen and understand, without offering advice or being judgemental. This could be your partner, a friend or relative. Your yoga teacher, midwife or antenatal teacher may also be a good person to talk to. If your feelings relate particularly to the birth, it's very important to share them with your midwife or birth attendants to assist them to be sensitive to your needs. Other ways to release feelings, especially anger, are to write a letter expressing fully and freely how you feel (and don't post it) or tear up an old telephone book.

Feeling rough

If you are having a particularly emotional day – and pregnant women do from time to time – take the day off and cuddle up in bed with a big box of tissues until you feel less vulnerable. Sometimes anxieties come up as feeling jittery, nauseous or exhausted. Flowing with your feelings as they arise is the key to a successful passage from woman to mother. Pregnancy has its dark times – embrace them if you can and they will pass.

Facing your fears

Fear comes up in all kinds of ways in pregnancy – it's hardly surprising given the momentous changes you are going through and the big challenges you are facing. Change is scary. Although fear feels very unpleasant when we expe- rience it, when it passes there is generally a feeling of relief and a release of tension. Fear helps to prepare us for what lies ahead. You may have specific fears about using water during labour, even if you are in theory attracted by the idea. Some people have a very specific fear of drowning or that the baby might drown. The best approach is to try some of the suggestions for getting comfortable in water in the section that follows and to attend courses or work-shops about waterbirth. When I ask the women in my yoga class what they are afraid of, these are some of the most common things that come up.

- ♦ Will my baby be healthy and normal?
- ♦ Will I be able to cope with the pain of labour?
- ♦ Will I love my baby and be a good mother?
- ♦ Will my partner still love me and find me attractive?

It may be a good idea to write down some of your own fears. You can add to the list as they come up. Mostly we feel fear in our bodies without knowing exactly what it's about. Stay with these feelings and breathe through them – they pass.

Healing

All of us bring our personal history with us into pregnancy including old wounds, loss of loved ones, hurt, betrayal and guilt. Previous experiences of pregnancy such as abortion or miscarriage or the death of a child may come up at times in this pregnancy. It may be that you have experienced sexual abuse in the past, which makes you especially sensitive and vulnerable. These memories can be painful, and going through this pain now can bring you great rewards.

Acknowledge that these experiences have helped to make you who you are today, then you may find that you can leave them behind you and move on. Don't beat yourself up. By accepting that life has its dark, painful and nega-tive side – and each one of us experiences this at times – you can find for-giveness and inner peace. Everything that has happened to you was meant to be – you have learned and grown from it. Love and accept yourself. Having a baby can be a wonderfully healing experience that helps you to let go of negativity associated with the past and to open up to new perspectives.

If you feel stuck with emotional issues, this can manifest as a feeling of low energy and depression or a physical ache or pain. You may find that a friendly ear is not enough to deal with the issues and feelings that are coming up for you. If this is the case, professional counselling or therapy can be very helpful. Some women choose to work with a psychotherapist, hypnotherapist or rebirther in pregnancy in order to clear and heal the past and leave the way free for the baby.

Relationships

Pregnancy changes relationships. If you are with a partner, the quality of your relationship is more important than ever as you are now creating a family and becoming parents together. Love doesn't just happen or necessarily last forever – we have to work at it. There are two ways you can do this. Firstly work on yourself and your own feelings so you don't need to project them onto your partner. Secondly develop good habits of communication. This means making sure you have the time to talk and listen to each other on a regular basis. Each of you will be having your own unique experience of the pregnancy and will have different issues and concerns. It's a great gift to be there for your partner as a listener – and to have a reciprocal exchange. You are there to love, nurture, trust and respect each other.

There will be times when either one or both of you 'loses the plot' and there is poor communication or a conflict. A good remedy is to talk about it, speaking and listening in turn and making sure that you let each other know at least three things you really like and appreciate about each other first. It's important to approach your birth with no major unresolved issues between you, in a loving, clear space.

Feelings about sexuality may change and it's helpful to talk openly about the intimate side of your relationship and to broaden your perspective about sex and sensuality. There are many ways to express affection and love which may feel more comfortable than intercourse at times. Touch and massage are especially enjoyable in pregnancy and may be helpful in labour too.

Expectations

'I obviously didn't have the birth I had planned – despite the fact that I had a caesarean, I still managed to stay calm and focused throughout and it was a positive birth!')

Hearing or reading all the positive accounts of waterbirth, it's easy to have very high expectations that may not turn out to be what happens in reality. It's especially important when planning to use a pool that your emotional preparation for the birth involves keeping an open mind. With all the support and help available today, most women can look forward to the most important outcome – a healthy live baby. So be sure to think about your expectations and to discuss this issue with your partner. That way you should be able to accept the inevitable and feel positive about the way your baby is born, even if the birth you would ideally like is not possible at the time.

'I was very keen to give birth in the pool, for me and the baby, but in the end had to have a ventouse delivery which was very disappointing but necessary as I had run out of energy after 25

hours. Although I was initially disappointed not to have the "ideal" fully non-interventionist waterbirth I had hoped for, I am left feeling as though I did my very best. I feel proud of myself that I produced the exquisite bundle that is my daughter, vaginally and without the use of drugs for pain relief.'

Using water in pregnancy

In the first chapter of his book *Watsu – Freeing the Body in Water* [4] Harold Dull, the founder of this wonderful water therapy, says:

> *'Warm water is the ideal medium for freeing the body. Let yourself be floated in someone's arms in water that gently lifts each time you breathe in, its warmth penetrating, melt the tension in your body. Drift into deeper and deeper levels of relaxation as your body is stretched freer and freer. Flow into states of consciousness to which stored tension or trauma otherwise deny access. Flow onto a level of being where there is such joy, peace and wholeness, the causes of that tension and trauma can no longer overwhelm you.'*

Watsu is an original form of 'water shiatsu' devised in Harbin Hot Springs, California. It is fast becoming the basis of the most effective and innovative pregnancy exercise programmes in water. I was invited to try a session after speaking at a waterbirth conference in Switzerland some years ago, which I did just before getting the plane home. I felt amazing afterwards. All the exhaustion from the conference disappeared and I was left with a remarkable feeling of relaxed exhilaration. Watsu is becoming more widely available and is well worth searching for – this is the future for birth preparation in water. If you hear of a watsu-based

---

4   Harold Dull, *Watsu – Freeing the Body in Water*, Worldwide Aquatic Bodywork Assn.,1997

pregnancy class or workshop be sure to try it. Combined with yoga on land, this is the ultimate preparation for a waterbirth.

The simplest moves can be learnt by anyone and are wonderful for developing deep relaxation and trust in water. It's the most nurturing form of partner work, building intimacy and love, helping to overcome fear and release emotion. You can try this with a partner in a swimming pool and it's a blissful experience for parents-to-be to do this together. Giving is as good as receiving in this heart-warming exercise – great preparation both for nurturing and for letting go in labour.

Partner

- Stand securely, feet apart, knees slightly bent in shoulder-height warm water. While she floats belly up, hold the pregnant mother close to your body in your arms, level with your heart, her head resting on your shoulder, her hips and lower back supported by your opposite arm so she can float freely close to the surface but under the water. Pay attention to your breathing and let your own body and arms and shoulders relax – sinking down a little as you exhale, lifted gently by the water as you breathe in.

- As you relax together more and more, tiny wave-like movements rock your partner in the water like a deep slow dance. Enjoy the feeling of connectedness to your partner and her baby. Relax into the stillness together. Once she is totally relaxed, softly and very slowly move her body with the water to enhance her relaxation. Give her a feeling of complete safety and freedom. Be sure to make these movements very soft and gentle, in slow motion. Remember this is about 'being' not 'doing' – just be with her, hold her, support her. This is wonderful practice for labour!

- When she is ready, allow her to lower her legs until she is firmly on her feet. Support her until she is back on the planet!

Pregnant mother

◊ Close your eyes and relax completely in your partner's arms. Let your
breathing slow down and become calm and easy. Relax throughout your
whole body, letting go completely to the continuous support of your partner
and the water. Sense the pleasure of being gently moved and held. Let go of
control, trust your partner and flow with the waves of movement, releasing
and surrendering more and more deeply like a baby in its mother's arms.

◊ Be with whatever is happening and trust the process. Each time you do this it
will be different. The oneness and bonding you will feel with your baby and
your partner in the water is a powerful and healing meditation. Think of it as
a safe space to release and let go in.

◊ To come out of this slowly, lower your feet to the bottom of the pool. Still
supported by your partner, take your time to open your eyes and come back
to the world before leaving the pool – you will have been very deeply relaxed.

There are many other enjoyable ways to relax and exercise in water, starting
with your own bathtub at home, which will help you to feel more familiar and
confident about being in water when you are in labour.

Caution: Your baby's body temperature is one degree warmer than yours while
in the womb. Since your baby has no independent means of temperature regulation, if you become overheated, so will your baby. That's why it is unsafe to
bathe in very hot water in pregnancy or to use spas, saunas and steam rooms.
Warm water at around body temperature is ideal and cold showers are very
invigorating. In a swimming pool where you may be exerting yourself more, a
cooler temperature is fine so long as you don't feel cold once you get going.

Bathing

Bathing is one of the most pleasurable personal rituals of the day. Make the most of it by lighting a few candles in the room and adding a few drops of fragrant essential oil to the water. This is a wonderful way to restore your energy, soothe away tensions and give yourself some respite from the extra weight you are carrying. Bathing softens and cleanses your skin and relaxes your muscles. It stimulates circulation, improves sleep and refreshes body and soul.

The bath is a place to unwind. The relaxing and protective qualities of water seem to encourage us to turn our awareness inwards. In the bath we can be alone, let the body go and free the mind to wander as we enjoy the sensual pleasure of the water. In this environment it's easy to make the transition from everyday thinking to a deeper state of relaxation.

Using essential oils

Aromatherapy involves the use of highly concentrated plant oils known as essential oils, which enter your bloodstream through your skin and lungs. When added to the bath water they permeate the skin and their aromatic fragrances are inhaled. The olfactory receptors in the nose transmit the sensations to the part of the brain known as the limbic system. This in turn connects with other parts of the brain that affect many of our vital functions including the nervous system and the centres that control the release of hormones. Essential oils can have remarkably powerful and beneficial effects, both physically and emotionally. They can help to soothe and relax, relieve tension and depression, stimulate energy flow, enhance sleep, discourage bacterial infection, stimulate cell renewal, aid digestion, improve circulation, reduce congestion and stimulate sexual response.

Essential oils are highly concentrated and should never be used undiluted. They can be added in the recommended proportions to your bath water or to a plain base massage oil. In pregnancy some essential oils should be avoided. As the effects can be very powerful, don't experiment with them without the expert guidance of a trained aromatherapist. It's also important that you find the smells agreeable – so try a drop on a tissue before adding it to your bath. It's best to buy organically or wild-grown essential oils.

Lavender, rose, chamomile, jasmine, rose geranium, ylang ylang, or oils from the citrus family such as mandarin, neroli and tangerine, can be safely used in pregnancy.

For an aromatherapy bath, place a total of four to six drops of your chosen oil or a combination of two or three oils (lavender, rose geranium and mandarin is a lovely combination) in a little milk and add to the bath when it is filled. Swish the water to distribute the oil. As the oils are extremely volatile, get into the bath as soon as possible for maximum benefit.

Once in the bath, relax and enjoy the fragrance. You can also give yourself a soothing underwater massage. Gently massage your breasts with stroking movements towards the nipples and with circular movements around their circumference. Move on to massage your upper chest, working outwards along the collarbones towards the shoulders. Then massage your belly with smooth circular movements under water. Try to be conscious of and sensitive to the presence of your baby as you do this. Massaging your arms, legs and feet is also beneficial. A massage of your neck, shoulders and back by a friend or partner can give a wonderful boost to your entire nervous system.

If you prefer, you can have a massage out of the bath using a home-made aromatherapy massage oil. Add 8 to 12 drops of essential oil to 6 to 8 teaspoons of a carrier oil such as sweet almond, grapeseed or wheatgerm oil. The latter is a very rich, nourishing oil that is ideal for the skin in pregnancy. You can blend carrier oils to achieve the consistency you like. Alternatively you can buy a ready-blended organic aromatherapy massage oil for pregnancy (see Resources).

Relaxation and meditation in water

▲ Choose a time of day when you will be undisturbed and free to relax for up to an hour, whether in the morning, afternoon or before going to bed. You need to feel able to immerse yourself totally in the experience. Fill the bath as deeply as possible so that your belly is also covered by the water, if possible. This will maximize the support that the buoyancy of the water will give you. The temperature of the water is important. It should be comfortably warm, but not too hot.

▲ When you are ready, get into the bath and allow yourself to float comfortably.

▲ Once you are feeling at ease in the water, close your eyes and become aware of the sensations on your skin surface. Experience the feeling of buoyancy and weightlessness in the water. Relax and let go of every muscle in your body until you feel you are floating softly.

▲ Place your hands on your lower belly, over your womb. Be aware of the presence of your baby. You are both in the water together, which is a lovely feeling.

▲ Keep your eyes closed and breathe slowly in and out through your nose. Do not try to control the rate or depth of your breathing, simply observe it.

▲ When you exhale, your hands will feel your belly moving inwards as the air is expelled from your lungs, so that the air seems to empty from the centre.

Notice the pause at the end of the out breath that creates an empty, still space.

💧 At the end of this still space, be aware of the arrival of the in breath, which expands and fills your lungs and belly.

💧 Continue to observe your breathing in this way. Acknowledge and then let go of other thoughts that may arise, allowing your focus to return to your breathing.

Trying out your birth pool

If you are having a home birth, it's well worth the expense of an extra liner to have a trial run of filling your birth pool. This will help you to check all the plumbing connections and will give you an idea of how long it will take to fill when it is really needed. If you are going to take the trouble to fill the pool, it is worthwhile making the extra effort to get the water temperature right (see Chapter 6, page 155) and getting in to see how it feels. This will give you the opportunity to become familiar with this new environment and get an idea of how relaxing the water will feel when you are in labour.

You can use your practice time in the pool to try different positions that you think might be useful in labour. You can build your confidence in moving around the pool freely or you can simply luxuriate. The night before I went into labour with my youngest child, Theo, I spent an hour or so in the pool with the full Moon shining through the window and it was memorable and very relaxing! When I went into labour the next evening the calming feeling of being in the water the night before was still present during the early stages until I was ready to get in for real.

For safety, you may want to have someone to help you in and out of the pool. Because special hygienic precautions are not required until your baby is about to be born, you can fill and empty the pool as often as you like in the days and weeks before the birth. The water stays fresh for 24 hours before you need to empty it. After pumping the water out you can dry the liner with a large towel and reuse it. However do keep a new unopened liner in its package ready for when labour really starts.

Swimming

Swimming is a great way to exercise your body in pregnancy. If you are lucky enough to live in a warm climate near the sea or a lake, bathing regularly outdoors in pregnancy is wonderful. Otherwise your nearest swimming pool offers you a perfect resource for getting familiar with water. It's considered best to avoid breaststroke in pregnancy, as the kick can sometimes cause pain in the pubic area. If you swim a lot you may be interested in making sure that your technique is correct, in order to gain the most benefit from the time you spend in the pool. The Shaw Method of swimming combines the postural awareness of the Alexander Technique with swimming and is excellent for pregnancy and beyond (see Resources). It makes swimming feel graceful and effortless and develops a feeling of trust, safety and relaxation in water.

Lap swimming is a great warm-up and provides an all-over aerobic work out. Choose the stroke that is most comfortable for you and swim at a leisurely pace so that you breathe steadily without effort. Rest between lengths when you need to.

While you are in the pool you can experiment with some of the labour and birth positions in the shallow end, such as standing and circling your hips or squatting holding onto the hand rail. Because of the buoyancy of the water, this is an ideal way to work on increasing mobility of your joints without strain. Try combining this with some deep breathing – in through the nose and out through the mouth – and imagine breathing through a contraction in water during your labour. Explore the movements you can make in water in these positions and also practise resting and relaxing on the rim of the pool as you will do in labour between contractions. Try immersing your head in the water for a while and blowing bubbles. At the end spend some time relaxing and drifting in the water using some floats or the help of a partner to keep you buoyant.

Water exercise

Many local swimming pools offer 'aqua-natal' classes, which tend to be like water aerobics and are geared specifically to pregnancy. The guidance of an experienced teacher will help you to practise movements that are of particular value during pregnancy and to avoid those that are inadvisable.

Tips for exercising in water:

- Ideally you should exercise in shoulder-high water. The greater the depth, the greater the buoyancy and therefore the support for your weight. But if you are nervous in water, exercise in waist-high water until you feel more confident.
- Wear a well-fitting maternity swimsuit that provides support for your breasts.
- Use floatation devices such as rubber rings or polystyrene kick boards to give you extra buoyancy, if needed.
- Don't be discouraged if you are a non-swimmer. You can do lots of valuable exercises within your depth, using the pool edge for support when needed.
- Experiment with yoga positions under water.
- Jogging gently in the pool while supported by the water is another way of building some aerobic exercise into your water exercise routine. Jogging on

land is not suitable for pregnancy, but in water the buoyancy prevents jarring or strain.

- Walking through the water is toning and strengthening for your legs. The deeper the water the greater the resistance from the water and the challenge provided by the exercise.
- Have fun. Don't make your water exercise too serious. Allow yourself time just to play in the water. You can dive like a dolphin, float like a mermaid, dive with a snorkel or do whatever movements occur to you. Enjoy experimenting and becoming at ease in this wonderful element.

Safety precautions

Be sure to check with your doctor or midwife before starting any form of exercise in pregnancy, especially if you have a current medical problem or your pregnancy is not straightforward for any other reason. Do not swim alone. Join a class, swim with your partner or a friend or in a pool that is supervised by a lifeguard. Never persist with any form of exercise that is causing discomfort.

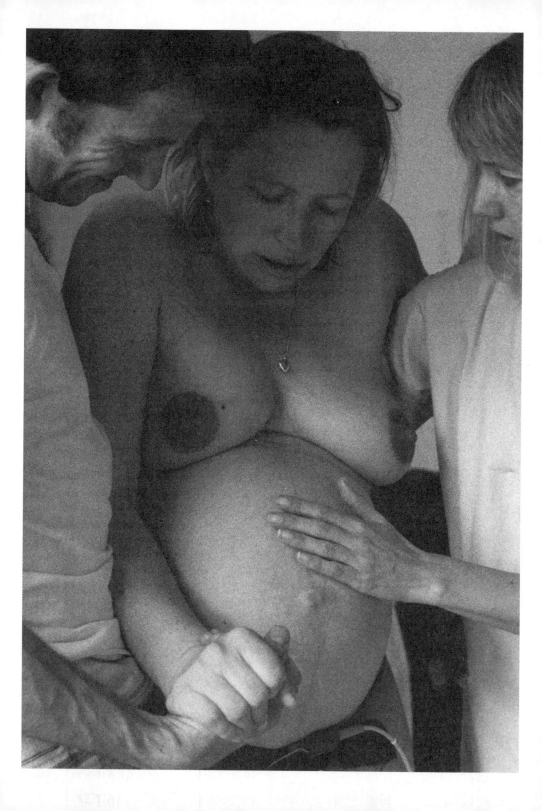

chapter six

Starting labour

In the weeks and days before labour begins, your body gradually prepares for birth and you may also notice a difference in the way you feel. There is likely to be a strong 'nesting' instinct as you prepare for life with your new baby and a need to focus your attention on taking care of yourself. Hormonal secretions increase at this time to initiate the first physical changes in your body and to prepare you emotionally for the intensity of the birth experience (see Chapter 3, page 36).

Waves of energy may alternate with a need to rest and sleep. Try to surrender to these rhythms and to go along with what your body tells you. You will make the transition into labour more easily if you simplify your daily activities and rest whenever you need to. Allow yourself to 'space out' and get onto the same wavelength as your baby.

When you feel like being active, carry on with basic household tasks, spending some time every day in the open air, practising some simple yoga, meditation and breathing, or having a relaxing massage. Getting into a swimming pool will relieve you from the heaviness of the weight you are carrying and help you to sleep better. If you are having a home birth, you might enjoy a trial run of setting up and filling your pool, and relaxing in the water for a while (see Chapter 5, page 128) or spend more time relaxing and meditating in the bath.

> 'It was wonderful to use the pool in the last days of my pregnancy, not only because it made the 'bump' less heavy, but also because it gave me relief from the hot weather we were experiencing at the time.'

Don't worry if your sleep patterns become very erratic and unusual – it's good practice for night-time parenting. Your dreams may also be more vivid. As long as you are resting a lot and getting some gentle exercise, your body will make sure that you sleep when you need to. If you have an active toddler or other children to look after, this is an important time to be together before the arrival of the new baby. It's wise to arrange some daily childcare too, so you can also have enough time alone to rest and relax.

You may feel a range of different emotions from excitement to terror. At times you may feel vulnerable and experience some anxiety about what is about to happen to you. In this case taking the homeopathic remedy aconite may be helpful. You may also feel blissfully contented and peaceful. Some women positively glow with radiant energy as the pregnancy reaches full bloom.

This is a good time to consider taking a supplement of evening primrose oil, which is said to be helpful in ripening the cervix (see below). You can take one 500mg capsule three times a day from 36 weeks until birth. You can also drink three cups of organic raspberry leaf tea daily throughout this period.

This is a mild uterine tonic and stimulant with proven beneficial effects on the uterus. These supplements to your diet, in addition to really slowing down the pace of your life and getting into harmony with your baby, will support your body's natural preparation for birth and help to ensure that labour starts on time.

Pre-labour

Runs of frequent or mild contractions, which usually feel a bit like period pains, may stop and start over several days. Unusual lower back pain or a feeling of being disconnected or extra sensitive are also possible. The build up to labour begins long before it actually starts. You may or may not notice the subtle changes that are happening. Diarrhoea is common as the bowel empties in readiness for birth, as is increased mucous discharge from the vagina. The practice contractions you will have felt throughout pregnancy will now increase in frequency and intensity. These contractions do the important work of preparing the cervix for dilation. This is the ring of muscular tissue at the base of the uterus that forms the opening to the womb. Situated at the top of the vagina, the cervix is closed in pregnancy and sealed with a plug of thick mucus.

During the final weeks of pregnancy, hormones secreted within the cervix itself cause it to soften – or 'ripen' – in readiness to open during labour (see Chapter 3, page 38). The action from the contractions gradually draws up the muscular fibres of the cervix so that it 'effaces' or becomes much thinner. By the time labour starts, it will thin from its normal thickness of about 3 cm to the thinness of a sheet of paper. It may even open a centimetre or two – but this is not yet established labour. The cervix is usually tucked quite far back in the pelvic cavity and it will move forward to the centre of the lower uterus during this phase. These crucial changes of pre-labour generally go unnoticed. However, some women are very sensitive to pre-labour contractions. Although they are quite mild in intensity, they can keep you awake at night. If this happens, resting and sleeping whenever activity stops or slows down is important to conserve your energy. Alternatively, it can be comfortable to lie resting forwards in a kneeling position supported on a beanbag or on a big pile of cushions on the bed. Make sure that you eat small, easily digestible meals at frequent intervals and drink plenty of clear fluids.

The huge increase in hormones at this time also further softens the ligaments that bind the pelvic joints, preparing the bony passage to open to its widest for your baby to descend and pass through during the birth. Across the base of the pelvis, the pelvic floor muscles form a 'hammock' through which the urethra, vagina and anus open. These ligaments are also softened by hormones to allow them to stretch and open as the baby passes through during birth.

The show

As pre-labour contractions thin the cervix, the jelly-like mucous plug that seals the cervix may be expelled. This is called having a 'show'. This may appear blood-stained and red, pink or brown and may be quite thick and glue-like in texture or thinner and more liquid. It can come away gradually a little at a time, or all at once. A show may occur some time in the week or so before labour starts, immediately before established labour begins or further on in the labour. Don't panic if you see a show – there is probably some time to go before you are really in labour.

Waters breaking

Inside the uterus your baby floats in the amniotic fluid, surrounded by the strong double membrane of the amniotic sac. In about 20 per cent of pregnancies, the first sign that labour is imminent is the natural rupture of these membranes. This releases part or most of the amniotic fluid and is called breaking of the waters. More amniotic fluid is produced throughout labour – so this does not mean a 'dry' labour. The sudden drop in pressure within the uterus may trigger the onset of labour contractions immediately or within an hour or so. The waters can also break much later, once labour has already started. Frequently this happens just before or even as the baby is being born. Occasionally the membranes remain intact and the baby is born 'in a caul'. In this case the midwife will rupture the membranes as the baby emerges.

However, it's also common for membranes to rupture a day or two before labour starts. This marginally increases the risk of infection, since the protective barrier formed by the membranes is gone. While infection is actually highly unlikely, you may come under considerable pressure to induce labour if your membranes rupture early. The risk of infection does marginally increase over time and how long you are able to wait is something you need to discuss with your midwife. However, labour will usually start spontaneously within 48 hours, and most practitioners can be persuaded to wait that long. Beyond this, most midwifery guidelines will rule out a water labour and birth or a home birth and induction is likely to be recommended. Common-sense precautions to prevent infection are to stay close to home where you are naturally immune to the household bacteria, to avoid intercourse or introducing anything into the vagina, to avoid lying in the bath or the birth pool and to wash yourself after emptying bladder or bowel. If there is no sign of contractions after 24 hours, it may also be helpful to take a high dose vitamin C supplement once a day and garlic capsules three times a day to help prevent infection. In the very unlikely event of an infection you would notice an unpleasant odour and would probably have a temperature. In this case a caesarean would be necessary.

Your baby before birth

While your body prepares itself for labour, your baby is getting ready to leave the womb. In the final weeks before the birth, the journey downwards begins as the baby's head 'engages', or enters the pelvic brim. In some pregnancies, especially second or subsequent ones, engagement may not happen until labour starts.

As described in Chapter 3, page 38, when your baby is ready to breathe independently, hormonal secretions from the baby's lungs will initiate labour. This stimulus combines with that created by an increase in pressure on the base of the uterus from the baby's head as it descends deeper into the pelvis to initiate the start of labour. Some babies remain active throughout pre-labour while others seem to move much less, as though they are having a big rest or sleep, getting ready for the birth.

Approaching your due date

Sometimes nothing much unusual seems to be happening as the due date comes and goes, and you may well be wondering if pre-labour is ever going to start.

Jacqueline Vincent Priya, in her book *Birth Traditions and Modern Pregnancy Care*, says:

'When I talked to pregnant women from traditional societies, their happy vagueness about when the birth was likely to take place always amused me. After my own experiences with modern doctors who provided a specific "B-day" and started to worry if the baby hadn't arrived by that date, the relaxed attitude of these women was a tonic. They usually knew within a month or so as to when the baby might arrive and trusted their own internal knowledge and experience of the pregnancy as to when the birth would take place.'[1]

She goes on to describe some of the special rituals used traditionally to ensure that the mother goes into labour relaxed and confident. This seems a very long way indeed from the experiences of pregnant women who are under pressure to start labour 'on time' in our culture. Pressure, anxiety and worry are counterproductive to the hormone secretion everyone is waiting for – so try to keep up your faith in your body and trust its wisdom.

The tyranny of the due date

The EDD (estimated due date) has probably been in your mind since your first antenatal check-up. It can be very disappointing and frustrating to find that you are still pregnant a week or more beyond this date, even more so if you are told that using a birth pool is no longer a possibility and the hospital is talking about booking a date to induce labour. Unnecessary inductions are the cause of many complications in labour. Since most women go beyond their due date, this is an issue that comes up for many women who are planning to use a birth pool. The information in Chapter 9 will help to guide you if you find yourself 'overdue'. Since there are many variables involved, you may not be genuinely overdue at all. Unless there is an urgent medical

1   Jacqueline Vincent Priya, *Birth Traditions and Modern Pregnancy Care*, Element, 1992

problem, you can take your time to assess the situation and explore your options. Be sure to get some gentle exercise such as walking, swimming (unless your waters have broken) or doing yoga. Meditate and relax every day to stay in tune with your baby and your inner guidance. Ask yourself if there is anything unresolved, upsetting or bothering you which you need to deal with before labour starts – an emotional block can hold back labour. This is a great time to indulge in a special pampering treat like a wonderful massage. Keep yourself entertained but don't overdo it!

'I valued using the pool prior to labour as it really eased the aches and pains of late pregnancy and helped me to relax and prepare mentally for the birth.'

Inducing labour naturally

If you are past your due date and worried that you may need to have an medical induction, try some of the following suggestions:

- Acupuncture, reflexology or shiatsu combined with homeopathy can be very effective in helping to get labour started. A cranial osteopathy session can also do the trick. It's best to consult a specialized practitioner with experience in this area.
- Wait as long as possible and then try a glass or two (no more!) of good organic red wine one evening.
- Provided your membranes haven't broken you could try making love. This will stimulate the release of oxytocin. There are natural prostglandins in semen which soften the cervix, the hormone that makes the uterus contract. Nipple stimulation may also help to release oxytocin.
- Encouraging the bowel to empty can sometimes trigger the onset of labour.

This can be done by eating a good quality vegetarian curry or by the old-fashioned (but effective) way of taking a 50 ml dose of castor oil mixed with squeezed orange juice and sweetened with sugar. Have another glass of fresh orange juice at hand to rinse your mouth with. Spit out to take away the oily taste and then drink the rest. This may make you feel a little uncomfortable and cause the bowel to empty within about three hours. Then luxuriate in a nice warm bath and have someone gently flush the warm water over your belly to help you to relax.

- Your midwife could do a 'cervical sweep' – a massage around the cervical opening. This may stimulate the secretion of natural prostaglandins which soften and 'ripen' the cervix and help to start labour. This may be a bit uncomfortable, but has been shown by research to be effective.

Continue drinking three cups of organic raspberry leaf tea per day and taking evening primrose oil supplements.

> 'After supposedly being overdue according to scan dates by nearly two weeks, we decided to accept a cervical sweep rather than give up on a waterbirth. It was more painful than I expected but luckily labour started the next day. When my baby was born it was clear she was not overdue.'

Early labour

Eventually contractions will intensify and become more regular. You will know you are in established labour when you have to breathe with your complete attention through every contraction and lying down becomes impossible. You will feel your energy centre in your womb as the sensations you experience become much more powerful. To use a birth pool most effectively, it's usually best to stay out of the pool until you are 5 to 6 cm dilated and to avoid medical pain relief if you can. The following information offers suggestions for using your body's natural resources most effectively. There are also guidelines for harmless options for pain relief and complementary therapies that you can use during this early or 'latent' phase of labour.

Labour is like a sea of contractions that ebb and flow like the tide. Caused by pulses of oxytocin (see Chapter 3, page 37), they become more frequent and intense as your body opens ready for your baby to be born. Each contraction begins at the top (fundus) of your uterus and then spreads downwards like a wave towards the cervix. At the peak of the contraction, or crest of the wave, the entire uterine muscle is contracted to draw the cervix upwards. As the contraction subsides, the fibres relax. Then there is a gap before the next contraction or 'wave'.

Each labour has its own rhythm. There are times in most labours when contractions seem to slow down or may even stop for a while, rather like reaching a plateau when climbing a mountain. In an intense, fast labour the breaks between contractions may be short from the outset and birth often occurs within a few hours of the onset of regular contractions. In a long labour, which may last up to a couple of days and occasionally more, the intervals between contractions may be longer. A first birth sometimes tends to be longer than subsequent labours.

You will feel each contraction begin as a rush of energy that reaches full intensity at its peak and then slowly dissipates. Between contractions there is an 'expansion' or resting period before the next contraction begins. Labour continues in this way, contractions becoming more intense and closer together until the cervix is fully open or dilated.

During the resting phases between contractions, the blood flow to the uterus and placenta, which slows down during contractions, is restored. This ensures that the muscles have the energy to continue to work and that the baby receives sufficient oxygen and nutrients during labour. The rhythmic pulsation of the contractions also massage your baby's body, stimulating the nerve endings in the skin, which in turn stimulate the baby's internal organs in readiness for the birth.

Turning within

Labour is a deep inner journey. Like a spiral, it draws you inwards towards your centre, where you will find the power to let your body open to give birth. During early labour, as your uterus begins to open beyond 2 cm, your baby moves downwards deeper into the pelvis. The weight of the baby exerts pressure on the dilating cervix, which gradually pulls up over the baby's descending head. By the end of labour the cervix will be around the baby's ears with most of the head entering into the birth canal formed by the distended vagina aligned for birth.

When labour starts, wait as long as possible and carry on with life as usual before you start to do anything special. It's probably a good idea to contain your excitement and avoid telling anyone other than your partner that you are in labour. The last thing you need is to attract a lot of attention or anxiety from well-meaning friends and relatives. The start of labour is a sensitive time when you need your privacy to get into a rhythm with the contractions and to allow your hormones to build up without distractions (see Chapter 3, page 40). Many women like to be alone at this time and may leave their partner to sleep while they quietly get into labour late at night or in the early hours of the morning.

Staying upright

> *'I spent the pre-hospital part of labour, when contractions were every 3–5 minutes, draped over my birth ball – rotating my hips while groaning audibly.'*

When the contractions get so strong that you have to move and breathe with them, that's the time to start thinking of using upright positions. This will allow gravity to assist this process and will result in stronger, more efficient contractions.

Try out a variety of positions using simple props like a birth ball, beanbag, chair or low stool and plenty of pillows. A soft but firm surface on the floor for kneeling on is essential. An exercise mat or a thick yoga mat is ideal. Make sure you are warm and draw the curtains or turn down the lights. Have something that you feel like to eat and drink as well: a small light meal, some pasta or soup, or even tea and a few bites of toast are ideal. Wear cosy socks and something loose and comfy that's easy to take off, unless you prefer to be naked.

The following suggestions for upright positions may be helpful.

- Stand or walk, leaning forward onto a wall, a partner or a piece of furniture during contractions.
- During contractions or while resting in between, sit on a birth ball, a chair or low stool, legs apart and leaning forward onto some pillows. Alternatively, kneel upright on something tall and secure keeping your body fairly vertical – a pile of large cushions, two beanbags, the rim of the birth pool, even the ironing board with a pillow on top will do. In the kneeling position put a pillow in the space under your ankles so that you feel secure in the kneeling positions.

◦ Kneel on the floor over a birth ball, beanbag or a pile of cushions on the sofa. Put a pillow under your ankles. In this position your body is more horizontal which may help to reduce the intensity of strong contractions.

◦ Squat on a stool. This will increase the intensity of the contractions. Alternatively you can squat on the stool to rest in between contractions and stand up when they come on. There may be a birth stool for squatting available in some hospitals or birth centres. Don't try to do full squats without support or you will get very tired.

When in these positions move your body freely, leaning forwards, rotating, rocking or swinging your hips. Do what feels most comfortable. This helps to dissipate the pain and assists the descent of your baby. Try them out ahead of time and imagine going through a contraction while making these movements and focusing your concentration on your breathing. While working hard in labour, most women breathe in through the nose and out through the mouth during contractions. As labour progresses it's usual to become more vocal and to express the way you feel with sounds or words as you exhale. These will become more expressive as labour progresses – groans, moans, wails, cries and curses are normal sounds of the birthing mother and are a way to release the pain while exhaling. Although others may find these sounds disturbing, the woman making them gains considerable relief. The following ways of keeping your focus on the breath may be helpful.

◦ Concentrate on the exhalations, breathing the pain away into the ground through whichever part of your body is in contact with the floor. Stay relaxed each time you breathe in.

◦ Visualize what is happening in your body. Think of the cervix softening and opening around your baby's descending head. Keep your mouth relaxed with soft lips and a loose jaw. Usually the mouth reflects what is happening to the cervix — so by feeling the softness of your lips with your fingers you can get a sense of the opening of the cervix.

♦ Imagine diving under or over a wave or climbing over a mountain as you go through the contraction.

♦ Leave each contraction behind you, and rather than thinking of what lies ahead, be in the moment.

♦ Each contraction should last for four to six cycles of the breath. Some women find it helpful to count the exhalations and to know when they are halfway there.

> 'The most helpful thing I learnt was to focus on my breathing and visualize what was happening inside my body. With each exhalation I "breathed" the pain away and let my body relax and open.'

The value of pain in labour

Labour pain comes and goes and is felt most intensely at the peak of contractions, ebbing away completely in between them. Most challenging life experiences involve a combination of pain and pleasure, and giving birth is no exception. There is a tendency in our culture to want to run away from pain, yet the pain of labour is natural and has a purpose. It can be transformed by using your body and your mind positively.

Try to view the pain as one of your most valuable helpers. The way you breathe and move in reaction to it keeps your blood well oxygenated. This helps your muscles to do their work and your baby to move downwards through the birth canal, stimulating more efficient contractions.

The body's response to pain is to produce endorphins, which result in a feeling of blissful rest during the breaks, alternating with the work of getting through the pain at the peak of contractions. Learning to ride these alternating waves of pain and ecstasy is the key to a good labour. Turning inwards and going into the heart of the pain rather than fearing it or running away from it can transform labour pain from an overwhelmingly negative experience to something you can tolerate and accept.

Freedom of movement and of expression through your vocalizations is very helpful, but most beneficial is quiet concentration. Go deep inside yourself and focus on the rhythm of your breathing through the peak of the contractions, then relax completely between them. Going through the pain of childbirth is an opportunity to discover that you are more powerful and courageous that you knew. This can give you the strength you will need to get through the many challenges that lie ahead of you as a mother.

> 'After 24 hours of trying everything, I was so tired that I finally realized that the answer was inside myself. My helpers fell asleep, and in the quiet space of being alone I found my breathing and learnt how to cope with the pain. From then on it wasn't a problem – it was just pain.'

Using complementary therapies during labour

The use of complementary therapies is very compatible with a water labour and can help greatly to support your journey through the birth. Such therapies do not clash with conventional medication should you need it, but are alternative options that may help significantly to enhance relaxation, reduce pain and ease labour. They tend to work in a subtle, gentle way that supports and stimulates the natural process, and there are no harmful side effects.

As the effects are cumulative, complementary therapies can be used from early in the labour when it is too soon to get into the pool, to use drugs or to have an epidural for pain relief. They can help you to get off to a good start as labour is becoming established. Generally at this time you will begin to find the pain of contractions much more challenging and need to start focusing deeply on your breathing and using movements, upright positions or visualizations. At the same time you can begin to take some homeopathic remedies, use some essential oils or apply a TENS machine.

Many complementary therapies can be helpful in labour. I have selected from those that the women I work with have found especially useful over the years and that can be used safely and easily simultaneously in labour, without the presence of a practitioner. The recommendations that follow are very general and can be followed by anyone. If you prefer, you can go more deeply into the subject and have a session with a qualified practitioner for more specialized individual guidance.

Homeopathy

Homeopathic remedies are generally acknowledged by both conventional doctors and alternative therapists to be perfectly safe. While some scientists may doubt their usefulness, there is plenty of anecdotal evidence among users of homeopathy to support their effectiveness. Homeopathy works best when remedies are tailored for an individual, taking account of her specific 'picture' and physiological type. For this reason it is best to consult a trained homeopath for advice on remedies to take during pregnancy, labour and the postnatal period. However, there are several standard remedies that can be taken at this time without risk. They do not interfere with other treatments or therapies. You can order remedies by telephone, and some homeopathic pharmacies supply a kit of remedies with instructions especially for use before, during and after childbirth (see Resources).

The remedies below are classically recommended for labour. It is a good idea to brief your partner or birth assistant on which remedies should be offered to you for the alleviation of different physical and emotional signs, since you will need to concentrate on your labour and will not be able to prescribe for yourself at the time. It may be helpful to label the containers according to their use, for example 'backache' or 'weepiness', and I have suggested a label in brackets for each remedy below. Your partner can then observe carefully what you are expressing and offer the most relevant remedy if necessary.

How to take homeopathic remedies

Because labour is such an intense experience, remedies can be taken every 30 minutes as required, although the interval may be longer or shorter according to the severity of symptoms. If you need more than one remedy at a particular time, for example if you are in pain and exhausted, make sure you allow 10 minutes between taking each different remedy. The pills should be handled as little as possible. Tip one pill into the lid of the container and then put it into the hand of the person taking it, who should suck and swallow it at once. It is helpful to ask for fast-dissolving remedies for labour as these can be simply slipped under the tongue where they will be easily and quickly absorbed into the system. The figure 200 in the list below refers to the potency and is the strength commonly recommended for labour where the body burns up remedies very fast. Don't expect a dramatic effect as when taking a strong pharmacological drug. The effect is subtle and builds up over time to stimulate the work your body does naturally, rather than giving an instant result. For this reason it's good to start taking these remedies in early labour, once contractions are properly established.

- Arnica 200 (pain 1): This remedy is known as the number one trauma remedy and is beneficial to nearly all women in labour. It can be administered regularly throughout labour to help the muscles and tissues to soften, and to reduce exhaustion and pain.
- Aconite 200 (fearful): Reduces fear, anxiety and panic. It is very helpful where labour is too fast, the woman is fearful and where contractions are over-whelming. It can also be taken before labour where there is fear or anxiety about the birth.
- Bellis Perrenis 200 (pain 2): Useful for deep abdominal pain where Arnica is not working.
- Caullophyllum 200 (ineffectual contractions 1): Used to promote strong productive contractions in early labour. It is useful where contractions are ineffectual, sharp, painful and short, often concentrated in the lower abdomen and groin. It is also good for weak contractions due to exhaustion in a long labour. Take once and do not use this remedy routinely throughout labour.
- Gelsemium 200 (ineffectual contractions 2): This remedy is the next best choice if Caullophyllum doesn't help with weak contractions. The woman may feel especially 'heavy', with heavy eyes and limbs. There may also be weakness leading to trembling, chilliness and the 'stage fright' of transition.
- Kali Carb 200 (back pain): Especially useful for backache labours or a posterior presentation (see Chapter 3). It is also indicated for chilliness after a contraction.
- Kali Phos 200 (exhaustion): For exhaustion or low energy at any time in labour.

🌢 Pulsatilla 200 (weepiness): Useful if the woman is weepy, clingy or pleading for help. The contractions may be short, weak or have stopped entirely.

Massage and aromatherapy

'When labour became much more intense, I used yoga breathing and inhaled clary sage oil for pain relief until contractions became overwhelming. I began to push and before long I had my daughter in my arms!'

For some women, being massaged in labour, particularly around the lower back, provides comfort and relief from the pain of contractions, both before getting into the pool and while in the water. This can be the most effective form of non-medical pain relief. Other women find physical contact of this kind during labour unhelpful or even irritating. It may feel like an unwanted distraction from the instinctive process of withdrawing inside yourself that is often the key to an effective labour. The best approach is a 'try it and see' one, and your partner should be prepared for you to reject this contact without any sense of disappointment. If you like massage, the oriental techniques that work pressure points along the meridians such as shiatsu, acupressure or Thai massage can be particularly useful and least distracting. Simple techniques can be learnt that may be very helpful in labour and it would be well worth a visit to a practitioner who can teach your partner the basics.

If you find massage helpful during your labour, you may find that its effects are enhanced by the use of essential oils diluted in a carrier oil (see Chapter 5, page 125). Essential oils can also be diluted and added to a cold water spray or evaporated in a vaporizer. In a hospital where candles and electric appliances are sometimes not allowed, the ceramic ring burners that fit onto a light bulb may be useful. When burning oils, your partner or midwife should add a little water and ensure the burner never runs on empty – a nasty burnt toffee smell may have the opposite to your desired effect! Making warm aromatherapy compresses when you need them may be a much better idea. A simple compress can be made with a wash cloth soaked in hot water to which a few drops of essential oil have been added and then wrung out. It's bliss to be handed a fresh fragrant compress in the pool to place on your chest, upper back or shoulders or to bury your face in.

Many essential oils can be useful in labour, but as they are very concentrated and powerful they can easily be misused. Unless you know a lot about aromatherapy, avoid making up your own blends or buy a ready blended labour relief oil for massage (see Resources). The three oils below are most commonly used in labour and can be used by most people. Your own reaction to the smell is the best guide as to whether the oil is beneficial for you or not. Do not use an oil you find disagreeable.

- Lavender: Relaxing and soothing. Many women find this oil very helpful for pain relief or to reduce nausea, boost energy or calm emotions. Ideal for general use in the labour room.
- Marjoram: Relieves muscle pains such as backache. It also calms the mind and helps to shift the energy in labour. Makes a welcome change from lavender if you have been using it for a while.
- Clary sage: Known as 'natural gas and air' this is a great oil to produce when the going gets tough. This uterine tonic and relaxant is warming, relaxing and reduces panic. It is euphoric, uplifting, encourages labour and stimulates contractions. It is useful when contractions are weak, progress is slow and hard going or labour stops. Do not use this oil before labour starts (unless you are overdue) as it can stimulate the onset of contractions. You can burn

it in the room, put 10 drops on a natural sponge or tissue and inhale it, make a compress, or simply take the lid off the bottle inhale deeply once or twice.

> "I used clary sage in my bath and this seemed to speed up the contractions greatly and may have expedited the delivery!"

TENS (Transcutaneous electrical nerve stimulation)

> 'I used a TENS machine for the early stages of labour and found it effective. I was keen to hold off using the pool to the later stages when the greatest benefit could be gained. Combined with lavender in the oil burner and relaxing music, it was a very positive experience.'

This method of pain relief is widely used by physiotherapists for the relief of chronic pain for a variety of conditions. It has also been found to be effective for relieving the discomfort of contractions in labour. TENS works by placing electrodes on the lower back on either side of the spine by means of sticky pads. These are connected through wires to a battery-operated handset that transmits minute electrical pulses through the skin to the deeper nerve fibres. When using this method of pain relief you can control the strength and frequency of the pulses yourself by choosing a setting and then simply pressing a button during the contractions. The buzzy sensations caused by the pulses are transmitted to the brain via the same route along the spinal cord as the pain signals arising from the uterus. It is thought that the competing signals from the pulses moderate the brain's interpretation of the pain signals and therefore reduce the perception of the pain (see also Chapter 3, page 53). TENS may also increase the production of endorphins in the brain.

'I used a TENS machine until I was 7 cm dilated, then the midwives arrived and I jumped into the pool; Using the TENS machine in early labour dramatically reduced the pain level so that I could cope. It was part of the 'getting through each contraction' ritual, but I couldn't really relax until I was in the water.'

Because it involves the use of electricity, TENS cannot be used when you are in the pool. However, many women find it very useful in early labour (at less than 5 cm dilation) when it's generally recommended that you do not yet get into the pool. It can also be used while you are in transit in the car on the way to hospital. Some women do not find TENS helpful or may be irritated by it. In this case it is easy to stop using it and remove the electrodes.

TENS does not have a dramatic effect, but over time the cumulative effect helps to moderate pain in some women. You can hire a TENS machine for a reasonable sum and have it available as an option to help you through the first stage of your labour. Most women find that getting into the pool is more deeply effective, but I have met one or two women who preferred to continue using the TENS machine throughout labour, finding it more helpful than the pool. TENS does not interfere with any other medical treatment you may need during labour and has no lasting effects. It is also easy to use in any upright position of your choice and does not restrict movement in any way.

'The change from the TENS machine to the pool gave me the boost I needed just as the contractions got pretty unbearable.'

Pain relief options for early labour – 2–5 cms

- Start focusing on your labour as late as possible when you really need to concentrate on the contractions.
- Stay on land and out of bed once strong labour is established.
- Use upright positions, movements and focus on your breathing, especially the out breaths.
- Use homeopathy, aromatherapy, massage and/or TENS.

Setting up and filling the pool

Once labour is established it is time to prepare the pool for you to get into later on. Birthing pools hold far more water than an average bath and may take some time to fill, so it's worth starting to fill your pool as soon as labour starts. If you've done a trial run, you'll know how much time you will need to allow. Some hospital birthing units and birth centres start to fill the pool as soon as they are notified that a woman in labour is on her way there. This way the pool is full and ready for use when you need it. At a home birth, start with hot water and keep the heat-retaining cover on the pool while it is filling. The water will only lose one degree per hour with the cover in place. You may need to allow for the boiler to fill and reheat several times. Add the cold water once you have about 30 to 45 cm (12 to 18 in) of hot water in the pool. The water stays fresh for 24 hours – so if labour is longer than this, the water will need to be changed.

The water temperature

Maintaining the right temperature of the water is very important. Babies in the womb are dependent on the mother's temperature regulation mechanisms and are unable to make their own adjustments. It is also the case that their body temperature is maintained at a slightly higher level than the normal adult body temperature of just under 37°C (98.4°F). An excessive rise in the baby's temperature may adversely affect its oxygen supply, possibly leading to foetal distress.[2] Although there is no need to be fanatically precise, most waterbirth practitioners agree that the water temperature should be maintained between 32 and 36°C during labour. The most important factor is that the mother feels comfortably warm and not hot or flushed. This would indicate that the water is too warm. The water temperature for birth in water should be slightly higher at 36 to 37°C so that the baby emerges into water at body temperature. The midwife will check the temperature of the water at regular intervals throughout labour and extra hot or cold water can be added as necessary. This can be done easily with an installed pool by simply emptying some of the water while running the tap. With a portable pool you need to empty a large bucket of water from the pool before adding another of hot water. Take care to pour in the hot water at a safe distance from the mother. Checking the water temperature is also a job that can be done by your partner. Make sure that you place the thermometer in the centre of the pool as the water closer to the surface will be cooler.

Depth of the water

This is easy to measure. If the mother kneels upright in the pool sitting back on her heels, the water should cover her belly and reach up to just below her breasts. Then sitting down in the water, her breasts will be covered as well.

2   Catherine Charles, 'Foetal hyperthermia risk from warm water immersion', *British Journal of Midwifery*, March 1998, vol. 6, No. 3

Having her shoulders exposed will allow her to lose heat. Bear in mind that if a partner gets into the pool, some water will need to be removed first.

Comfort

Make sure that the room is well ventilated and not overheated. Provide a large jug of water so that everyone can keep drinking, as a birth pool can make the atmosphere very dehydrating. Take care to put away hoses after use and that there is a non-slip area to get in and out of the pool. A warm towelling bath robe is a good idea for when the mother leaves the pool. Pool accessories like a rubber swimming ring, a polystyrene 'woggle' and a snorkel have been known to be helpful!

> 'I waited for the midwife before I got into the pool. I'm sure I was coping so well only because I knew I would be able to get into the pool soon and I was confident that it was going to be a wonderful relief when I did.'

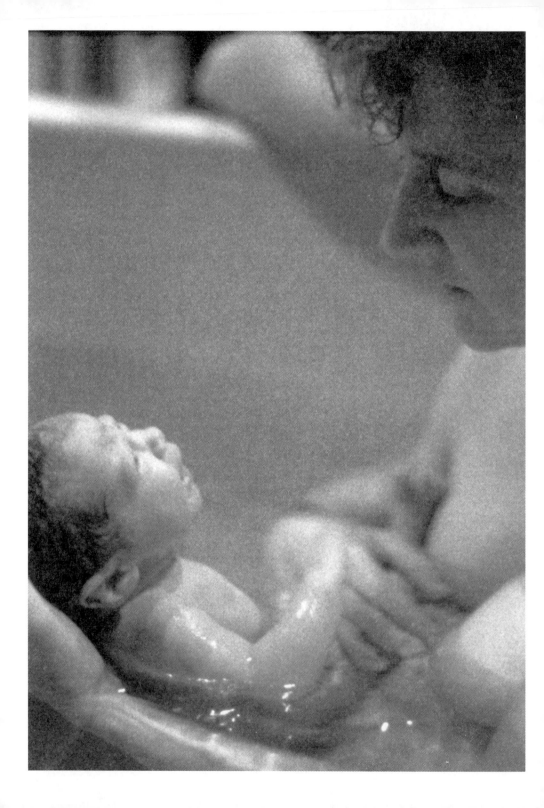

chapter seven

Labour and birth

After you have been in established labour for some time, there will come a point where the quality of the experience deepens. Inhibitions disappear as the powerful muscular activity of the uterus predominates, opening your body at its very core. Contractions seem longer, much more intense and closer together. Involuntary movements and primal sounds come naturally as your behaviour becomes unthinking and instinctual. Now is the time when it is easier to lose all conscious thought, to surrender to something bigger than yourself and to trust your body. Pain at the peak of the contractions becomes greater and more profound than any you have experienced before. Try to surrender to this intensity rather than resist or fight against it, and your perception of the pain may change. Such intensity can be terrifying, yet the pain is completely different to that of an injury or an illness. It invites you to dive right into the heart of it – to let go of fear, resistance and control. This surrender is the key to transforming the pain into the energy that opens your body for birth.

By contrast, the resting spaces between the contractions become increasingly blissful, and these moments of profound peace can seem infinite. Returning to this peaceful place after every contraction when the pain disappears holds and sustains you and creates an overall feeling of high energy that precedes the birth of a baby.

When to enter the pool

> *'Getting into the pool was fantastic. Sinking into the warm water at that depth was bliss! It was surprisingly deep and very supportive.'*

Shared experience from all over the world confirms that the optimum time to enter the pool is about halfway through labour at around 5 to 6 cm dilation. Women use a birthing pool in different ways and there are few absolute rules. However, there is increasing evidence to suggest that this is the best time to get into the pool to enhance relaxation, relieve pain and boost the effectiveness of contractions. An exception to this may be a very long and slow labour (see Chapter 3, page 52).

A study carried out in Sweden, published in 1997,[1] observed 200 women who spent their labour in water. One group entered the pool at an early stage – before 5 cm dilation – and the other group after that stage. The results showed that the women who got into water early had a longer labour than those who waited until later. Moreover, a higher proportion of the early bath group were later judged to need Syntocinon (Pitocin) to boost contractions or had an epidural.

You will need your midwife's help to decide when you are ready to get into

---

1   M. Eriksson, L-A Mattsson and L. Ladfors, 'Early or Late Bath during the First Stage of Labour: a randomised study of 200 women', *Midwifery* (1197) 13, 146–148

the pool. An experienced midwife can usually assess this from observation of changes in your behaviour and the quality, power, length and frequency of contractions. Approaching mid-labour, it is common for some women to feel nauseous. This is generally relieved by retching and is a positive sign that labour is intensifying and your body is releasing deeply, preparing to evacuate your baby. Another sign might be the appearance of a 'show' if it has not already been discharged. (see Chapter 6, page 136).

'In some ways, what midwives learn from their experience of waterbirths shows how to give better help to women in all labours.' [2]

Before you enter the pool, some waterbirth protocols require a complete assessment of the progress of labour and your own and your baby's vital signs. This will include a vaginal examination, a check of your temperature, pulse and blood pressure and also a check on the baby's heartbeat and position. While the need for a vaginal examination to assess dilation is debatable, monitoring the baby's heartbeat before entering the pool is essential and will need to be repeated every half hour to hour while you are in the pool.

Waiting until labour is well established before entering the pool will enable you to gain maximum benefit from the oxytocin-boosting effect of the water (see Chapter 3, page 63). Most commonly, though not in every case, entering the pool has the effect of intensifying contractions and increasing their power and effectiveness. Then, within an hour or two, when the oxytocin wave reaches its peak, you will probably be so close to the birth of your baby that nothing can stop or slow the momentum of the process.

'For each of my labours, I was in the pool for no more than an hour or two, after reaching 5 cm dilation, as it intensified the whole labour. I can't imagine giving birth in any other way.'

Another way of knowing that you have reached 5 to 6cm is that you may begin to feel you need something more to help you cope with the increasing intensity of the pain. This is the ideal time to have the possibility to enter the pool – a completely new environment in which you will probably feel very different. The pain-relieving effects of the water, as well as the increased comfort from the buoyancy, will probably give you an immense and immediate sense of relief.

Many women vividly recall the difference in how they felt when first entering the pool.

'I could not wait to be surrounded by the warm water – it was blissful. It made the pain more manageable immediately...I had a feeling of being enveloped and hugged by the warm water...as if the water was receiving me in her arms and looking after me...'

'Contractions seemed stronger in the pool, which was intimidating at first. But there was a definite feeling of security in the pool. Psychologically, I felt that we were on the home stretch – which felt good.'

Other options for pain relief

While the majority of women feel immediate benefits when entering the water, it does sometimes happen that the relief from being in the pool is disappointing.

After trying the pool, some women prefer to get out to labour on land or to continue using a TENS machine, or may wish to opt for some medical pain relief. I recommend that you stay in the water for at least half an hour if you can, before you decide to get out. Sometimes a bit of time is needed to get used to such a dramatic change in labour. You may find that once you relax it feels very soothing. It's wise to view the use of medical pain relief as a last resort – but equally not to deny yourself this help if you need it. At around 5 cm dilation, when you are entering the active part of your labour, is a good time to review your pain relief options. Since it's easy to change your mind, you could try getting into the birth pool first.

> 'The water was very comfortable, although I found I had to change the way I had coped with contractions on land. I had to let go and "allow". This was frightening at first until I got used to it.'

> 'The nature of contractions changed when I got in the pool from three every ten minutes to one super intense one per ten minutes. The change was stunning and I didn't know how to deal with the first couple of very intense contractions in the pool. Between contractions was great though the pool water was just lovely.'

> 'I was disappointed in the pain relief in the pool. After a while it was just too much and I asked for an epidural. For me that was the right choice.'

Pain relief options in strong labour

These guidelines may help you in making choices and decisions about pain relief. If you opt for medical pain relief, the timing and dosage are important considerations to gain the most benefit and avoid side effects. There is more detailed information about this in Chapter 9.

Active labour – 5–7 cm

- Enter the birth pool and try it for at least half an hour. Relax and focus on your breathing.
- Continue with homeopathy, aromatherapy and massage. Try changing the homeopathic remedy and/or using a different essential oil.
- Leave the pool and use movement, breathing and upright positions as previously, and continue using a TENS machine if you wish.
- Medical pain relief options you may consider at this time are an epidural or a minimal dose of pethidine.

Approaching birth – 7–10 cm

- Continue with the above. It's generally best to avoid having an epidural or taking pethidine at this stage, since you are close to the birth of your baby.
- Try putting 10 drops of clary sage on a wash cloth or natural sponge and breathe in the aroma.
- If you need medical pain relief, use minimal amounts of gas and air (see Chapter 9).

Labouring in the pool

Soon after entering the pool you are likely to feel relaxed, comfortably spaced out and even a bit sleepy. Amazingly, you can doze off between contractions yet remain alert enough to meet them and work through them. This is not really sleep, but a profoundly relaxed state that allows you to shut out the world, go deeper into your labour and conserve your energy. In this state of consciousness you will be able to stop thinking and accept the energetic waves of sensation and intensity with greater ease so that the power of your body can take over.

Privacy

The sense of privacy, of having one's own womb-like space, is one of the most important benefits of using a birth pool for most women. It offers protection from unnecessary disturbances and a greater feeling of being in control. It's much more difficult for anyone to touch you and impossible to check or examine you without first gaining your co-operation.

> *'The "cocoon like" feeling in the pool made an enormous difference to my sense of privacy, safety and relaxation. I could keep people at arm's length by being in the pool and it was soothing and calming.'*

It's a good idea to plan with your partner and attendants to keep the atmosphere in the room very calm and quiet with dimmed light and nothing to distract you. In the privacy of your own space in the pool, you are free to explore the possibilities. You can move around and adopt whatever positions feel right for you in the water. You may find that kneeling and leaning forwards onto the rim of the pool with your head resting on folded arms is most comfortable. Use a large, soft folded towel for comfort when resting on the rim (it doesn't matter if one side of it gets wet).

> *'I was on my knees facing the wall of the pool holding onto the rim, and in the same position but sitting back on my heels between contractions.'*

Alternative positions include floating on your back or side, sitting or squatting, either supporting yourself or supported by your partner (see page 176). It's much easier to squat in the water than on land. You can squat with your back against the side of the pool or face the other way and hold onto the rim with your hands. You may change positions during contractions and when resting in the intervals between them – or stay more or less in one preferred position.

> *'I remember being very active – on all fours rocking backwards and forwards, kneeling and squatting holding onto the sides or hanging with my arms over the rim in a squat during contractions and resting with my back to the pool side during the breaks.'*

For many women in labour, the key to releasing is rhythmic movement. You may find it soothing to kneel upright or squat, making circular or swaying movements with your body. You can roll around in the water like a dolphin, immerse your head for a while and feel free to experiment. There is no prescription about what you should do in the pool. You can't 'do' labour – you can only follow the urges of your body, let go and let it happen.

Conserving energy

Most women feel exhausted as they approach the end of labour. In some ways this is necessary and natural and will help you to let go. Though it may feel similar, this exhaustion is different to really reaching the end of your tether. The demands on your energy will depend on the length of your labour and will be affected by your overall level of fitness. Women are usually astonished at the level of endurance and exertion they are capable of in labour.

Getting into the water at the right time can help enormously to conserve energy, because it may shorten your labour and help you to relax more effectively. The water helps reduce energy expenditure as it supports your body weight at all times. Many women comment on how much easier it was to rest in between contractions in the pool. This helps to set up a rhythm of breathing and moving slowly to work through contractions, resting and dozing in the intervals between them.

> 'The use of the pool transformed my ability to cope compared to "dry land". I was exhausted after a long labour and the contractions were strong and painful. The water's buoyancy allowed much greater relaxation and rest...I used no other form of pain relief.'

You need to take frequent sips of water during labour. Most women do not want to eat in strong labour, but if you feel hungry or it is a long labour, every now and then, eat a mouthful or two of a light, energy-giving snack (like banana, pasta or toast). This will prevent dehydration and keep up your blood sugar level. Both dehydration and low blood sugar can lead to listlessness, and your contractions may slow down or become less effective. If this occurs, fruit juices such as grape or apple, which contain natural sugars, or a herb tea such as camomile or raspberry leaf sweetened with honey will help to replenish your energy and fluids. Glucose tablets can rapidly boost blood sugar if you begin to feel very depleted.

> 'During the delivery I got extremely tired. The pool then became so helpful. Having the water to float in and take away one's body weight is tremendous.'

Working with the contractions

There is no doubt that labour generally lives up to its name and is incredibly hard work. It's like being in the ocean where one wave after another is coming towards you. This is a great metaphor to work with, since each contraction itself is like a wave – mild as it begins, then building to a peak of intensity which 'breaks' and gradually diminishes as it finishes.

You can expect your emotions to ebb and flow in labour like the tides of a great ocean. You are bound to experience a range of intense feelings that may include bliss, calm, excitement, joy, fear, anger, irritability, weakness, despair, terror, confidence, passion, tenderness and even moments of humour. Releasing and expressing your feelings freely is the key to letting go. Labour is noisy, messy, wild, uninhibited and completely unladylike. You can't control it. Let yourself cry, laugh, shout, be silent, moan, complain, curse or sing – this is your time.

Like an ocean, contractions keep coming wave after wave – gentle at first, then gradually increasing in strength to become the huge tidal waves that precede the birth itself. The art of getting through them is very similar to body surfing or diving through strong, powerful waves in the ocean. If the surfer is well prepared for the wave and starts to swim just before it arrives, he or she will safely ride the wave to its completion. Otherwise it's easy to panic, get overwhelmed and bowled over. Alternatively, for some women, the idea of facing the approaching wave and diving under it to the other side works best.

'Being in water was a great relief, allowing me to move freely and diminishing feelings of panic. I made a lot of noise during

contractions during both the first and second stage – including groans, moans and grunts. Altogether the birth was all I could have hoped for and was greatly facilitated by the pool.'

Here are some tips for riding the waves of labour.

- Take it moment by moment. Stay focused on one wave or contraction at a time – don't think about the whole ocean or how much more there is to come.
- You will be able to anticipate when a contraction is coming. Be ready for it. Start your pattern of moving, breathing or vocalizing just before it arrives, so you are already working with the wave and can stay on top if it. Leave each contraction behind you – see it as another one gone. You can't know how many waves are in your ocean but each one gone brings you closer to meeting your baby.
- Keep your mental attitude positive. Replace 'I can't' with 'I can', 'I won't' with 'I will', 'no' with 'yes', and repeat it out loud if necessary. It's amazing how the mind can affect the body and transform an experience.
- Think of the feelings in your body as sexual energy, the pain as power, preparing you to open and surrender to the orgasmic release of birth. Some people find this concept hard to accept – but in reality that is exactly what this is.
- Make the most of the periods of bliss between contractions. Rest and relax your body completely.

Listening in to your baby

*'I was monitored every half an hour. It was no problem or
discomfort at all. I was happy to hear my baby was doing well.'*

While you are engrossed in your labour, your midwife will be there to encourage you and will also be aware of your baby's wellbeing throughout. As mentioned previously, your baby's heartbeat will need to be checked at regular intervals. This is important at any birth, but especially where there is the potential for a waterbirth, as the safety of a birth in water depends on regular confirmation that the baby is doing well and there is no sign of foetal distress.

Changes in the heartbeat indicate that the baby may be becoming short of oxygen. Another indicator of foetal distress is the presence of fresh meconium in the pool water. This is the dark green substance that accumulates in the baby's bowel during pregnancy and is usually excreted after the birth. A distressed baby may defecate in the womb, and this will stain the amniotic fluid so it appears greenish or brown. The midwife will be looking out for the presence of meconium in the water of the pool. If your midwife notes any sign of foetal distress, she is likely to ask you to leave the pool for further assessment. Sometimes the change of position and your movements as you leave the pool may improve foetal distress, but if it persists an emergency caesarean section may be necessary (see Chapter 9).

The onset of foetal distress rarely happens without warning. The signs of the possibility of foetal distress are predictable to the midwife and usually arise gradually. So the midwife generally has time to recommend that you leave the pool or transfer to hospital if you are at home. Your midwife will have been especially trained to recognize these signs and will be making sure it's safe for you to remain in the pool by regularly checking on your baby. If she strongly recommends that you leave the pool or go into hospital if you are at home, this is the time to trust her professional expertise and judgement. She may err on the side of caution, but this is in the best interests of your and your baby's safety.

Ask your midwives well ahead of the start of labour how they intend to monitor your baby's heartbeat. Most midwives attending waterbirths are equipped with a hand-held, foetal heart monitor that can be used with minimum disruption to you and without you having to leave the pool. There are also waterproof monitors that can be used underwater so that you do not even have to change position, keeping disturbance to a minimum. These are available for use in hospital, in a birth centre or at home. A regular hand-held monitor can be made waterproof by placing the sensor in one finger of a long surgical glove used by midwives.

An alternative way of monitoring your baby's heartbeat is with a long pinnard or stethoscope. It's relatively easy for a woman in a birth pool to float up to the surface close to the side to enable the midwife to use a pinnard, especially if her partner helps to support her hips. This choice may be preferable if you have concerns about the low-frequency ultrasound used in the monitor.

Unless there is cause for concern, you should not need to leave the pool to be monitored. This would be unnecessarily disturbing. Some midwives prefer the woman to sit up on the rim of the pool and may occasionally ask her to stand up. This would be less disturbing than getting out. However, it's best for you to stay in the pool in the position you are already in, to minimize disturbance and make it easier for you to maintain your concentration on the labour. This will also provide a more accurate reading, as the baby's heartbeat may change when you get up.

The baby's heartbeat changes or decelerates during and after a contraction, so the midwife may need to keep listening through one or two contractions to observe the whole pattern. This may be a bit uncomfortable – but try to relax and concentrate on your breathing. It's a good time to say hello to your baby inside. Hand-held monitors amplify the baby's heartbeat so you can hear it too, and most parents find this reassuring.

> 'The midwives had been checking the progress of the baby by listening to the spot where they could hear the heart, and I wasn't sure whether I was allowed to push yet, but the urge was unmistakable, and they just told me to go ahead.'

All other checks can be done while you are in the pool. This includes vaginal examinations if you float close to the side and a partner or the midwife gently supports the back of your pelvis (she can do this with one hand while examining you with the other).

> 'The midwife did a horizontal floating examination which was much less uncomfortable than any other I have received.'

This is possible because of the buoyant effect of the water and easiest if the midwife seats herself on a birth ball which provides an elevated seat. Vaginal examinations, mainly to check the progress of the dilation of the cervix, are usually carried out at four-hourly intervals. They are done in between contractions and can be uncomfortable. Because they can be perceived as intrusive, most women are keen to keep these to a minimum. If you have very sensitive feelings about this, be sure to discuss this beforehand with your midwives so that they are aware. While such examinations may sometimes be justified, most midwives who attend waterbirths develop a sensitivity to other indicators, such as the sounds you are making or your body language, and are often able to keep internal examinations to a minimum.

'I got into the pool when I was in strong labour. The warm water felt lovely and the whole atmosphere enabled me to concentrate deeply on each contraction. I had one internal check in the pool; squatting in the water, the midwife just put her arm in the pool and felt how far I was dilated. That was no discomfort at all.'

Getting out of the water

The key principle at a waterbirth is that if labour is not progressing well on land, try water, and if it slows down in water, try land. While most people agree that it's best to get into the pool at around 5 to 6 cm dilation, there are no rules for the amount of time that a woman should spend in the water. Every labour is individual and assumes its own rhythm and pattern. Provided contractions remain strong, there is good progress and you and your baby are doing well, you can stay in the pool throughout and remain there for the birth.

However, if the power of the labour seems to be diminishing after some time in the pool, this may indicate a lower level of oxytocin. In this case it's best to leave the pool and continue upright on land, where the effect of gravity will cause the weight of the baby to exert more pressure on the cervix. This will help to increase the secretion of oxytocin and in most cases this will stimulate contractions and labour will progress. See also Chapter 9.

'I had hoped to give birth in the water, but the second stage was just so much more difficult than I expected, and because of the

length of the labour, I was absolutely exhausted and didn't seem to be making much progress in the pool. So I got out and gave birth beside the pool to a calm and peaceful baby girl. I was amazed at her calm, given the primal sounds I was making. My throat was much more sore than my vagina or perineum – with all the screaming!'

If you remain in the pool when labour slows down, the result of the lower oxytocin levels may mean that the contractions become too weak to birth the baby and/or there may be problems with the delivery of the placenta. The aim is for oxytocin secretion to be as high as possible. So it's important that the main indicator as to how long you stay in the pool is the power and effectiveness of the contractions. When using a birth pool, the contrasting help of gravity and water need to be balanced. It's therefore wise to aim for an active birth, in which you can draw on the help of either or both these elements as needed.

The partner's role at a waterbirth

'As a watching father the sight of my wife delivering her own baby and watching her swim up to the surface for the first time is something I shall treasure always.'

Usually, the partner takes responsibility for looking after the pool and maintaining the water temperature (see page 155), in addition to often being the main person offering both emotional and practical support. Tending the pool to maintain temperature and depth is an important job at a waterbirth, especially at a home birth where a portable pool is used. This usually keeps the partner busy.

Your birth partner may be the baby's father, a friend, relative or a doula (see Chapter 4, page 98). In labour, it's best to have no more than one person with you at a time and also to be alone if you want to, with your supporters outside the room where they can hear you call if you need anything. Some women rely heavily on the close participation of their partner, while others need more solitude. It's important that partners realize that being available and fully attentive to you, even outside the room, without necessarily 'doing' anything is also very helpful. It's hard to quantify the comfort gained from the presence of a partner, but this has been shown by research to make women feel safer and to reduce the need for pain relief.

For some couples, the partner actually being in the pool during labour brings an intimate sense of shared experience. There may be an increased sense of safety for the woman, and feelings of protectiveness and connection with the birth process for the partner. If you feel like being held in labour, it can be amazingly comforting to lie back and relax in your partner's arms, while also having the support of the water.

On the other hand, the pool may feel like your own territory that needs to remain 'inviolate'. This can mean that whatever you planned when you and your partner discussed the birth, you do not want your partner to be in the pool at the time. Equally, your partner may not want to get in the pool.

From a hygiene point of view, there is no problem with the father entering the pool at any time during labour or for the birth itself, since you share the same bacterial environment. If it's possible, he could bathe or shower first, but this is not essential. It's generally recommended that the partner at a waterbirth have a swimsuit available to wear, just in case there is a need to enter the pool. However the mother feels about it beforehand, it might be necessary or helpful for her partner to be in the pool at the time.

> *'I felt better and more contained in the pool once my partner got in and I could lie against him. That felt incredibly safe, comfortable and supportive.'*

While some women may find any physical contact in labour distracting, for others holding, touch or massage is essential. Non-verbal communication through touch is often highly effective. When the partner notices signs of tension – for example, raised shoulders or tightly clenched hands – a warm, reassuring touch can remind you to relax. Preparing aromatherapy compresses or offering you homeopathic remedies is another way your partner could be helpful. However, the main role of the partner is to provide emotional and sometimes physical support for the woman as she labours or gives birth. As a partner, you also need to be prepared for your support to be rejected by the woman in labour, especially at the very end of labour when she is close to giving birth and may easily be irritated by any attempts to help. For the woman, the main priority is to retreat into herself, and she should rightly have no thought for your feelings or anyone else's. Her only concern is to get through labour and complete the birth in what her instincts are telling her is the best way.

In the pool, women rarely need additional physical support, although they often enjoy it and find it comforting. However, if the birth takes place on land beside the pool, the partner's support may be essential to help her give birth in a squatting position. This will encourage the opening of the pelvis and the descent of the baby down the birth canal. It's therefore useful to practise this together before the birth (see Chapter 5, page 113).

*'Sophie had a textbook natural birth. She only used a TENS
machine and the pool for pain relief and got really primal. We had
two excellent midwives present who made us both feel relaxed and
in control of what was happening. Our daughter was born in the
pool into my hands so I was able to bring her to the surface and
give her to Sophie. Perfect, lovely and wonderful!'*

Some fathers are keen to be the first person to receive the baby and pass him
or her to the mother at birth. This is often possible at a waterbirth when the
baby is born into the water and within seconds is brought to the surface
gently and in slow motion. If you would like to do this, then let your midwife
know ahead of time. She may judge it necessary to deliver the baby herself,
but if the baby is born easily in a convenient position, she may be happy to
help you to 'catch' the baby. This is most easily done with you in the water
but can also be achieved from outside, by leaning over the side. You may
also wish to cut the baby's umbilical cord after the placenta is born. This
symbolic gesture of separation from the womb and entry to the world is an
important ritual for some parents, while others are happy for the midwife to
cut the cord.

Some fathers enter the pool immediately after the baby is born, to share the
intimacy of welcoming the baby. It's also delightful to fill the pool with fresh
water the next day and get in as a family. This can include older siblings and
is a wonderful way to make the most of your pool. I've even known grandpar-
ents who gave it a try!

*'For several days the pool was very helpful in relieving afterpains
and for soothing sore nipples and swollen breasts. The baby also
enjoyed being in the pool. I found the pool useful in spending some*

"quality time" with our older child, helping him to feel part of everything and to get to know his new baby brother.'

The transition from labour to birth

'On entering the pool my contractions slowed down as I was almost fully dilated by this stage. The slowing down was a very welcome break. My friend commented that in between contractions I looked so relaxed in the pool that she thought I had gone to sleep.'

The time between the labour and birth is commonly known as 'transition'. It may be very brief, lasting just a few minutes, or it may go on for up to an hour or more. To you, this phase will seem timeless and you should not have any sense of how long it takes, unless someone draws it to your attention.

As you reach the end of labour, the contractions mount in intensity and duration. They occur very close together with brief intervals of about half a minute between them. The very high level of hormones ensures a state of consciousness that enables you to be totally absorbed by the labour (see Chapter 3). This is the peak of labour. It signals that the cervix is now fully dilated and drawn up around the baby's head, leaving the way clear for the baby to start its descent and rotation through the birth canal.

Women's experiences vary as dilation is complete or completing and the expulsive phase and the birth of the baby are beginning.

- The contractions may slow down and the resting phases may lengthen. This is a bit like the calm before the storm.
- Alternatively, there may be a phase where contractions cease altogether and

nothing seems to be happening for a while. This has been called the 'rest and be thankful' stage and may last up to an hour or so, giving you a welcome break to rest before the birth.

🌢 You may feel the bearing down sensations coming on gradually or suddenly. This is often felt as a sense of pressure on the bowel, rather like an urgent need to defecate. It is caused by pressure from the baby's head on an internal nerve centre at the base of the spine that stimulates the urge to push.

Transition can be a time of strong emotions in which you may feel fearful, exhausted, angry, despairing or irritable. Or you may feel peaceful, calm, still and centred. For some women transition is like moving through an abyss – an ocean of the unknown, sometimes experienced as darkness or confusion. You will be deeply focused within yourself as if 'on another planet'. Most likely, any attempts to comfort you with physical contact or well-meant words of encouragement will be a distraction. Absolute quiet and privacy are what is most needed. You will need to drink water – the high levels of adrenaline at this time can make you feel thirsty with a dry mouth.

> *'I thought I might shout and swear at my husband in transition but instead I told him "I love you"!! – amazing!'*

During transition you will move and position yourself spontaneously. It's helpful to know that kneeling on all fours or forward over the rim of the pool or a support will give you a sense of control over the intensity of the contractions. Not surprisingly, this is the most common position women instinctively use at this time.

If you are kneeling on all fours outside the pool, lowering your head close to the floor with your bottom up – sometimes called the 'knee-chest position' –

will slow you down if the intensity is overwhelming. This position is also useful if the final dilation is incomplete or there is an 'anterior lip', when the front rim of the cervix is still not quite dilated. The slope of your body from your hips down to your head will take the baby's head away from the cervix, thus reducing pressure and making it easier for the cervical dilation to complete.

A whiff of essential oil of clary sage (see Chapter 6, page 152) can be a good alternative to gas and air at this point.

Remember you can't *do* this, you can only let go and let it happen to you. This is birthing from within.

> *'I wanted to get in the pool when I felt I needed pain relief, which it did offer – 10 minutes of bliss. I remember saying "This is heaven". Then I changed positions – squatting up the side of the pool – "pop" my waters broke and I was blown away by an almighty contraction. It was full on from there, yes, painful and overwhelming. My body took over. I didn't even try and push, it did it itself.'*

Giving birth

Michel Odent has said that 'in any hospital where a pool is in daily use, a birth under water is bound to happen every now and then.'[3] He is making the point that actually delivering the baby in water is not the goal of labouring in water, but something that may occur as a result of it.

> *'The atmosphere was calm. The baby was born in a very relaxed way. I didn't really "push", the contractions seemed to move her*

3   M. Odent, 'Birth Under Water', *The Lancet* 1983; 2 (8355/8356): 1476—77

out rather than a conscious pushing by me. Being in the water helped me find the best position quickly and easily. She was actually born in two contractions. The first, I could feel her head starting to be born. The second followed very quickly and she came out like a torpedo. There was no pain in the second contraction, and I was very surprised to see her swimming up as I didn't realize she'd been born!'

'Contractions intensified very quickly. Within half an hour I was ready to push and needed the earth, gravity and a cooler spot. I climbed out and had a fantastic second stage – loud and as big as the universe! He was born within five minutes. I had a couple of contractions hanging from straps hung in the doorway, then pushed him out in a standing squat.'

A combination of stimuli from the mechanical pressure of the baby's head and the release of hormones (see Chapter 3, page 36) initiates the onset of the expulsive reflex of birth. You may wish to leave the water to give birth to your baby on land or you may feel completely secure in the pool and have no thought of getting out.

During the expulsive phase of labour, the release of adrenaline stimulates the reflexive contractions that push your baby down through the birth canal and out into the world. If you experience a foetus ejection reflex such as Michel Odent describes, this may take just a few contractions (see Chapter 3, page 42). In many women, however, this phase lasts for an average of an hour to an hour and a half, and occasionally longer. Your bowels are likely to open as the baby moves down. It is important to surrender to these natural reflexes as being not only normal and natural, but essential to every birth. They will help you to release your baby. This may happen in the pool and the midwife will remove any debris with a plastic sieve.

There is no risk of infection from your own body fluids entering the water the baby will be born into, since the baby shares immunity with you. In fact, since the baby is born sterile and the first bacteria to 'invade' the territory will predominate, being born into water that inevitably contains the mother's satellite bacteria may even offer protection to the baby. Once the expulsive reflex is established, and without creating any disturbance, the temperature of the water should be quietly checked and increased if necessary to about 36–37°C (97–98°F) in readiness for the emergence of the baby.

How giving birth feels

The expulsive contractions feel totally different to labour pains. When you are giving birth, it feels as if your whole body releases both physically and emotionally. Nothing is held back. As your baby presses down through the birth canal, you may feel the need to shout or roar. Free and uninhibited expression of the deep primal sounds or cries of birthing have an opening effect on the muscles inside. With the huge exhalations, the diaphragm muscle lifts up, the pelvic floor lifts and opens, and the long psoas muscles that run down the inside of the spine to the pelvis become active – tilting the pelvis forward to create a kind of internal slide for the baby.

> 'I managed to squat while giving birth to my son with the help of my partner and the pool. My perineum remained intact. I did not imagine I would make such noises. It was a totally primitive, uncontrollable, primeval experience.'

These powerful expulsive contractions are exhilarating for some women and can be experienced as pain-free and more like involuntary waves of orgasmic release. In my experience, how this stage feels varies and depends on the size, position and shape of the baby's head, whether the membranes are intact or not, the posture of the mother and other factors. Usually there is a burning, hot feeling of fullness and the head feels hard as if there is a melon inside you, stretching you to the limit. Each of my four births was different and only one could be called painless – the others were a kind of unique combination of agony and ecstasy that is characteristic of birth. As with all of labour, pain is generally felt during the contractions and not in between them. The breaks between contractions are usually longer than they were in late labour, giving you time to rest and gather your strength for the huge involuntary efforts of giving birth.

> 'The pool was very useful in coping with the pain, helping to focus concentration on making the pain useful and positive. Loud shouting also helped, especially when pushing took over. The baby came out in about five pushes (I think), one push after the head was born.'

Birthing positions in water

In cultures where active birth is the norm, women have the benefit of traditional wisdom and the expectation of giving birth in upright positions. They may have seen this or heard about it when growing up. They also have the benefit of the help of other women who have given birth or assisted at births. Giving birth is instinctive and a culturally learnt skill. If you study birth practices all over the world, it's easy to observe that different cultures seem to have their preferred upright positions and means of support, and generally a variety of standing, squatting or kneeling positions are used. In our culture, where this wisdom has been forgotten, women can benefit greatly by practising birthing positions in pregnancy to make them more familiar and easier to achieve. This is also important if you are aiming for a waterbirth, as you may need or want to give birth actively beside the pool or adapt these positions to be used in water. My book *New Active Birth*[4] is a more detailed resource for this information.

In a birth pool, upright positions are easy to use for the birth of the baby. Your instincts are likely to guide you into the best position. You may also feel the need to grab onto something for support, whether this be your partner or the side of the pool.

It's very helpful to provide your midwife with an angled mirror that can be placed on the floor of the birth pool and a torch. Then she will be able to shine the torch onto your perineum and view what is happening very clearly in the mirror as the baby emerges, even if the room is dark. Since babies are often born at night or in the early hours of the morning, this is a useful tip. The umbilical cord is usually long enough to enable the midwife to receive the baby while you are in any upright position and pass him or her to you without the need to clamp or cut the cord.

Kneeling

- Kneeling in the pool, lean forward onto the rim for support. In this position the baby is born into the water behind you. The midwife will wait for the baby to emerge and then pass him or her to you under the water between your legs. You can reach down and lift your baby up out of the water and into your arms and then sit back into the water to hold your baby.

4   J. Balaskas, *New Active Birth*, HarperCollins, 1989

- This can be varied by kneeling in a more upright position and bringing the baby up from the front, or half kneeling and half squatting with one leg up.

Squatting

- You can simply squat in the pool with your back against the side, feet turned slightly out, knees comfortably wide apart and arms resting on the rim for support. The buoyancy will support you and make this position much easier than it would be on land. The midwife can then receive the baby from the front and pass him or her to you, or you can reach down yourself and lift up your baby.

Partner squatting

A partner can support you squatting in three different ways. In each of these positions you are facing the midwife who can bring the baby up from the front and pass him or her to you. You can then sit in the water with your baby.

- Your partner can sit on a stool outside the pool and support you under the arms. Because of the help of the buoyancy, this is more for comfort than for actual support, so it's not necessary to use much strength and both you and your partner can relax.
- Your partner can sit on the rim of the pool, feet in the water. You can squat down between his legs and rest your arms on his thighs. There is no need for your partner to hold onto you.
- Your partner can sit or squat in the water in the pool behind you so that you are supported by his body.

'My waters broke in the pool and I felt a strong urge to push. After a little difficulty at first, I managed to do long and effective pushes in a squatting position holding onto the rim of the pool. I felt the head coming, and with the next contraction and four pushes the baby was born. I lifted him out of the water and we stayed in there until the cord stopped pulsating and my partner cut it.'

Standing up

It sometimes happens that the mother unexpectedly stands up out of the water in the pool as the baby is being born – or the midwife may ask you to do this to help the baby out. In this case the midwife must ensure that the baby's head remains above the water surface, as breathing may be stimulated as soon as the face comes in contact with the atmosphere. She will either receive the baby from behind and pass him or her to you, above the water surface between your legs, or receive and pass the baby to you from the front, depending on which is more convenient at the time. You can then sit down in the water, holding your baby in your arms.

'I was mainly leaning forward and squatting, holding onto the side, but also floating back between contractions and leaning back against the side. Finally I gave birth standing and leaning forward with my hands on the side of the pool.'

If there is any difficulty with the birth of the baby, the midwife may ask you to stand up and it's important that you do so. She may or may not ask you to leave the pool. This may be to assist the birth of the shoulders. The action of lifting a leg over the side of the pool is often enough to release the shoulders. If one shoulder is stuck behind the pubic bone this is known as shoulder dystocia. In this case the birth will happen on land and the midwife will call for urgent help. Midwives are trained to deal with this condition in a variety of situations by applying pressure above the pubic bone to release the shoulder.

Crowning and birth

Just before the birth, the crown of the baby's head begins to be visible at the opening of the vagina. In water the tissues of the vaginal opening and perineum are softened. This helps them to expand around the baby's head as the final contractions push the baby out. As they accommodate the widest part of the head this can cause a burning, stretching feeling that has been called the 'ring of fire'. Once you reach this point, though it can be excruciatingly uncomfortable, you know the baby's arrival is imminent. This is a signal to relax and slow down. Focus on breathing your baby out slowly rather than giving one huge push to get past the pain. This control of the final contraction may help to prevent tearing. Then the whole of the baby may emerge or there may be a pause between two contractions after the head is born, while the rest of the baby's body is still inside. A gush of warm amniotic fluid may be released with the baby.

> 'Our daughter was born in the water. She burst through her water sac right at the end and apparently shot through the water. She came floating to the top quite happily and was handed to me by her father. We sat in the pool and looked at each other in amazement.'

If only the baby's head emerges at first while the head is still under water, the 'dive reflex' suppresses the breathing response and the air passages are closed, so the baby does not inhale the water. The baby continues to be nourished by oxygen from the placenta until after the birth when lung breathing is established. The birth of the baby's head is usually a huge relief to the mother and a wonderful moment for the parents, as the baby is on the brink of being born. In a few moments the next contraction should bring the shoulders and the rest of your baby's body out. If the body does not emerge with the next contraction, the midwife will assist the baby out with her hands.

If the baby is born in water, the midwife will slowly and gently bring the baby to the surface. Sometimes the mother or father choose to lift the baby out themselves. These are the moments you have been waiting for, when at last you can hold, see and touch your baby — safely born and in your arms.

'Labour progressed steadily for five or so hours, and then my waters broke with a gush. That was when I felt I wanted to enter the pool, which made me relax completely. My baby's head was delivered five minutes later and I could see her hair floating. I then "breathed" her out and she swam into my arms. It was a wonderful experience and such a calm entrance to the world.'

Birth on land

'I called the midwives and they arrived at 3.40 p.m. to find to my amazement I was fully dilated. We were still filling the pool and the contractions weren't unbearable, and there was space between each one. Suddenly my waters broke and my baby girl was delivered seven minutes later. I was on all fours supported by my partner and friend on the living room floor with the doors open and sun streaming in — a lovely experience. We used the

> *pool for a fun bath afterwards, and again next day as a*
> *paddling pool for our two year old and her friend, who*
> *loved it!'*

Sometimes the best laid plans don't work out and the baby arrives before the pool is full. Many women choose to leave the pool at the end of labour, preferring to give birth on land. Another reason to leave the pool is because the contractions seem to have slowed down and are lacking in sufficient force. Without effective contractions, there is a risk that the birth may become prolonged or difficult and there may not be sufficient uterine power to safely deliver the placenta and prevent blood loss after the birth.

In this situation it is essential to leave the pool and use the help of gravity to stimulate contractions and the descent of the baby. This should soon get things moving. Your attendants will need to make sure that the room is very warm so you don't feel chilled and your baby emerges into a warm environment. You will need a soft mat to kneel on and a few simple props for comfort (see Chapter 4, page 101). Until the head crowns, use simple upright positions for bearing down such as kneeling or standing, making sure you have something firm to hold onto and grip such as the rim of the pool, a chair or the end of the bed.

> *'My labour was 27 hours with a day and night of pre-labour.*
> *The labour was very stop-start. I felt very active and in control*
> *throughout, even during transition, which surprised me. I broke*
> *my waters when jogging up and down in the bathroom and then*
> *gave birth on all fours on dry land. I had a completely drug-free*
> *labour and delivery. No stitches, no tears, despite the fact that*

*my baby was born with his hand on his face. A totally positive
experience; whenever I think about it I feel triumphant and joyous.'*

The following positions may be helpful for the birth:

- Kneeling on all fours on hands and knees, onto a support or upright.
- Squatting with the support of a partner. Your partner can sit on a chair or
a birth ball behind you. Facing towards the midwife, squat between your
partner's knees, resting your arms on his thighs. Do this only if you are
comfortable in a deep squatting position. You can have your feet flat on the
floor or squat on your toes if it's more comfortable. Putting something like a
rolled-up bath towel under your heels will help increase comfort.
- Standing squats are easier to do for most women. Stand with feet apart and
slightly turned out. Bend your knees and lower your pelvis halfway down into
a wide squat. You can hold onto something firm in front of you like the end
of a bed or the back of a heavy chair.
- Alternatively, your partner can stand behind you and support you under
your arms in a standing squat. There is a knack to doing this properly. It is
quite strenuous and requires practice and is not suitable for a partner with
a bad back. Ideally it should be taught in a class and practised at home.
You partner will need to stand behind you with feet apart, keep his knees
bent and lean back, supporting you against his pelvis to avoid back strain.
Placing his hands under your arms, you can then hold hands by interlinking
your fingers, your partner's hands palms up and yours on top, palms down.
Lower your hands until there is not too much pressure under your arms
and you can both relax.

'I got out of the pool to give birth. I was sort of squatting on a wide-brimmed bucket with my arms on the side of the pool. I bit the rubber during the last couple of contractions! The bucket was taken away at the last minute and my baby was born onto a soft towel between my legs on the floor.'

After your baby is born

Once your baby is born, whether in water or on land, the moments when you look into each other's eyes and see each other for the first time are magical. Your first sensual impressions of each other through skin-to-skin contact, smell, sight, touch and hearing are very vivid and come naturally as you hold your baby in your arms. You are likely to feel floods of emotion as you welcome your baby, although some women feel a bit numb and awestruck at first and loving feelings arise gradually later on.

'I couldn't believe how beautiful our new baby was, I fed her for 40 minutes while waiting for the placenta. I put some drops of the Bach Flower Remedy called "Star of Bethlehem" on her forehead and pulse points as it is very good for shock, and I took some too. The carol 'Gloria' was playing as she was born and it couldn't have been more appropriate.'

Whether you are in the pool or not, the first hour after your baby is born is a very important phase of the birth. It is not over until you have given birth to the placenta. The physiological events of this phase are stimulated by the interactions between you and your baby. It takes about 20 minutes for the placental circulation to slow down and cease. During this time your baby will start to breathe independently and then may search for the breast and begin to latch on and suck.

All of this stimulates a huge final release of oxytocin which results in very the powerful contractions known as 'afterpains'. These enable the placenta to separate from the shrinking wall of the uterus and seal off the blood vessels of the placental site to prevent bleeding. Once this has happened, further contractions will expel the placenta and membranes and then the cord can be cut. Within an hour of birth, the uterus will have contracted down to the size of a grapefruit.

When to leave the pool

If you have given birth in water, you may want to remain in the pool with your baby or you may feel ready to get out. If you have had a physiological birth, without drugs or other interventions, this will have encouraged high levels of oxytocin, and if there are strong contractions there is no reason to assume there might be a problem with the delivery of the placenta. Whether or not or how long the mother should stay in the pool after the birth is still a contentious topic. Some waterbirth practitioners, including experienced midwives and one or two obstetricians, will allow the mother to remain in the pool throughout this phase until the placenta has emerged and the cord is cut, and have done so for many years with no ill effects.

There is no evidence that remaining in water for the third stage is any more risky than being on land. However, there are two concerns, that have resulted in protocols which insist on the cord being clamped or the mother having to leave the pool very soon after the initial welcome of the baby. One is the theoretical risk of water going up into the uterus and entering the mother's bloodstream through the placental site – known as water embolism. To date there has never been a report of this happening. Some believe it is impossible because the cervix closes down after birth and is quite swollen, so water does not get into the uterine cavity. The other is a condition called polycythemia (which means the baby has too many red blood cells). An incident of this was reported some years ago following a water labour and was later thought not to have been specifically related to the use of water. (See Chapter 8 for more details on these topics.)

Certainly if bleeding appears excessive or if you are feeling faint, the midwife will want to assist you to get out of the water. If you remain in the pool, you need to be aware that the water may be quite bloody by this stage, but this is not a cause for concern. Observation and experience will tell your midwife if the blood loss is abnormal.

To err on the side of caution, the current recommendation generally is that the mother leave the pool for the delivery of the placenta, and you can discuss this with your midwife. I don't think it's worth spoiling this special time over this issue. The key point here is to minimize disturbance to what is happening between you and your baby. If this is a strict requirement that the midwife has to adhere to for her own protection, it may be best to slowly stand up holding your baby, with cord intact, step out of the pool and continue welcoming your baby beside the pool. This is preferable to clamping and cutting the cord and staying in the water, thus depriving the baby of the cord blood (see below). A soft, clean floor surface to sit on is important, as well as keeping very warm. The room temperature may need to be raised and a towelling robe or large bath towel draped over your shoulders. Your priority is to carry on bonding with your baby. When the strong contractions begin, you will feel the urge to push again to deliver the placenta. You can squat, kneel or stand to do this, or sit on a bed pan – continuing to hold your newborn baby in your arms.

> 'There was a slight panic as the midwife thought there may have been another baby! I looked at Jesse who was big (9lb 2oz) and thought "You've got to be joking!" It was in fact placenta.'

Welcoming your baby

The flow of oxytocin is maintained throughout this time by continued stimulation from physical closeness with your baby and perhaps breastfeeding. In the light of this, it is easy to understand why undisturbed first contact between mother and baby is so vitally important until the placenta has been expelled. The atmosphere of privacy is even more important now and nothing should distract you from focusing all of your attention on your baby. The room should be very warm – even overheated – to promote good hormone secretion. It's best to hold back from calling friends and relatives and to allow the birth to take its own time to complete.

> 'My wonderful baby was passed through to me as I turned over to sit down in the pool and recover. It was magical – being at home, candlelight, the pool, a brilliant midwife and fantastic partner! An amazing experience!'

The umbilical cord

Once the placenta has emerged and the uterus has had time to contract down, the umbilical cord will have stopped pulsating and will appear white or translucent and flaccid. Now is the best time to cut the cord and separate the baby from the placenta. You will need to discuss your wishes for this phase of the birth with your midwife.

It is customary to clamp the cord with a plastic clamp an inch or so from the baby's navel or it can be tied with sterile string. Waiting to do this until the placenta has been delivered has important benefits. The baby will have benefited from nature's plan to provide continued oxygen from the cord throughout the time that breathing is being established, as well as the final quota of blood from the cord, which is very rich in nutrients, hormones, immune factors and stem cells. It may be surprising to learn that up to 40 per cent of the baby's blood volume is gradually shunted down the cord after the birth, before it stops pulsating.[5]

Early clamping and cutting of the cord or inducing the third stage with an injection of an oxytocic drug as the baby is being born or soon after are common routine interventions in the birth process (see Chapter 9). These are not necessary in a physiological birth where the mother's own hormones are working well, whether on land or in water, provided blood loss is normal. There is a lot of controversy about how to 'manage' this phase of the birth and your midwife may have to work within the parameters of quite restrictive protocols. This is a topic you should discuss with your birth attendants before the birth, and you may have to negotiate for a physiological approach. Delaying the cutting of the cord allows the baby the gentlest transition from dependence on the placenta for oxygen to dependence on lung breathing.

Proponents of an approach called 'lotus birth' recommend parents to leave the cord intact throughout the early days, wrapped alongside the baby until it dries up and falls off by itself. They believe that a subtle energetic exchange

5   Beverley A. Lawrence Beech, (ed.), *Water Birth Unplugged,* Books for Midwives Press, 1996

continues through the cord during this period and that the time this takes marks the gradual transition of mother and baby into their new, separate relationship.[6] This may be going too far for most people, but there is a great deal of sense in waiting until the cord has completed its work and ceased pulsating before cutting it.

After the placenta is delivered is often the ideal time for the father to hold and enjoy the baby. Many fathers remove their shirt to have direct skin contact with the baby. This is an unrepeatable time with your baby, so make the most of it. While you are doing so, your partner can prepare herself to get into bed where the three of you can enjoy your first hours as a new family together. If you have other children you may wish to include them at this stage.

Overwhelmed by the physical and emotional effort of labour, a small percentage of mothers do not feel ready to hold their baby immediately after the birth. In such cases, the father can take the opportunity to hold the baby, while the mother takes a little time to recuperate. However, from a physiological point of view, the ideal is for initial contact to take place undisturbed between mother and baby.

> 'Our toddler was introduced to her new sister beside the pool, 20 minutes after the birth, and it felt very natural and relaxed. I'm sure their future relationship will be shaped by the happy way they first met.'

---

6   Shivam Rachana, *Lotus Birth*, Greenwood Press, Australia, 2000

Your newborn baby

'The fact that my daughter swam to me after being born will be a memory I will always treasure.'

Many parents expect their newborn baby to cry as soon as he or she is born, and indeed many babies do. However, this is not usually the case with babies born in water, who often seem much calmer than land-born babies. The transition to breathing is slower and more gentle than in a land birth, where the sudden impact of the atmosphere can make the baby gasp immediately. During the minute or so after a waterbirth, the baby is taking little gentle breaths; he or she may be moving, opening the eyes or sometimes may even smile. The baby may appear very pale or blue, or grey in the first seconds after birth, but as soon as breathing begins to be established, the normal colour will appear.

'The second midwife, at one point was edging towards the oxygen after the birth, but then reminded herself that water babies take longer to "pink up"!'

Very occasionally the midwife needs to gently remove any excess mucus or fluid from the baby's nose and throat in order to clear the airways. This is easily done by suction while you are holding your baby and, if carried out with sensitivity, should cause little discomfort to the baby.

Your baby is highly sensitive and will be experiencing light, the sounds of the environment and the feeling of air and gravity for the first time. Vision is geared to focus on your face, and beyond that distance will be blurred at first. Sounds in the proximity of your body are the main ones your baby will hear. The sense of smell is very acute and the baby will soon begin exploring your body with touch.

Babies are born with a natural instinct to find the breast. The 'rooting reflex', as it is known, leads your baby to turn towards the nipple when it touches his cheek or the side of his mouth. He is also attracted by the smell of your body and breasts. Some babies are keen to feed soon after the birth, while others are content to make contact with the breast but take a little longer to latch on. It is a good idea to encourage your baby to feed as soon as possible, since this is one of the main hormonal stimuli for the contractions that expel the placenta, prevent bleeding and retract the uterus. However, if your baby does not seem to want to feed, massaging the nipples is a good alternative and your baby will start feeding later on.

All of the above interactions usually occur without your having to think about them. Provided there is nothing to distract you, your reactions to your baby come naturally. It's an amazing symbiosis. Your posture as you sit up to hold your baby facilitates the physiological events. The high levels of hormones promote powerful feelings of love and attachment and ensure that you and your baby are alert and highly responsive to each other. Everything is designed by nature to intensify your communication on an instinctual level involving all the senses. You will be fully engrossed in the joy of holding your baby, gazing into his or her wide open eyes, marvelling at the velvety, soft feel of the skin and the beauty of this little person who has emerged from your body. Now is the time to rest and relax and to be thankful and proud of yourself for getting through such a huge experience and producing such a wonderful baby. He or she has finally arrived safely and, from the shelter of your body and the warmth of your loving welcome, begins to acclimatize to life outside the womb.

'For the first 24 hours afterwards, I had a sense of shock at the enormity and power of the pain and experience, but that has gone now and I am left with very happy memories and a deep sense of achievement and contentment, as well as the most beautiful baby boy in the whole world!'

chapter eight

Midwives and waterbirths

'It's a lovely way of looking after women.'

Waterbirth is an option that contributes a valuable resource to midwifery care. Forward-thinking midwives in many countries have been among the most important pioneers of the use of water in labour and have devised reliable guidelines for the practice of waterbirth, whether at home, in birth centres or in hospitals.

The Royal College of Midwives in the UK issued a position statement in 2000, setting out expectations and recommendations for the use of water in labour. While acknowledging that more research is needed, it states:

> *'...the available evidence does not justify discouraging women from choosing this increasingly popular option. Women*

1   Caroline Flint, 'Water Birth and the Role of the Midwife', *Water Birth Unplugged*, Books for Midwives Press, 1996.

experiencing normal pregnancy, who choose to labour or deliver in water, should be given every opportunity and assistance to do so.'

Midwives are specialists in normal pregnancy and birth. The word midwife means one who is 'with woman'. Ideally this entails not only giving antenatal care and performing the necessary checks for mother and baby before or during the birth, but also guiding and accompanying the woman emotionally throughout the experience of labour and the early days after the birth. In an ideal world, this relationship is formed during pregnancy and enables the midwife to give continuity of care and to work with each woman and her family according to their individual needs. While this sort of midwifery care is not always available, many midwives aspire to provide the essential qualities of continuity and one-to-one care.

The focus of midwifery care is generally to enable the natural processes of birth and minimize the use of obstetric interventions whenever possible. Countries where the proportion of midwife-attended births is highest also have the lowest rates of interventions such as caesarean section or instrumental deliveries. Midwifery care is associated with fewer epidurals and fewer episiotomies. This reflects the skill and professional expertise of midwives and their motivation to support women in their birth choices.

The motherly presence of a midwife at the birth is crucial to most women. Even when the midwife has little to do beside the necessary checks, her presence gives the woman the sense of safety, security and support she needs to give birth to her baby. The midwife's experience enables her to help a woman get through the normal challenges and difficulties of labour, and also to identify the small percentage of births in which complications develop and to refer those cases to an obstetrician. In most countries, women are referred to obstetricians only if they are ill or have developed a complication. The exception to this is the United States, where for historical reasons obstetricians still outnumber midwives as the primary caregivers for healthy women. However, this is gradually changing as uncomplicated births in the US are increasingly attended by midwives.

Within the general pattern of care described above, there are some midwives who work primarily within the medical model and some doctors who work primarily within the midwifery model. The degree of midwife autonomy to care for healthy women can also vary greatly in different hospitals and regions. Most midwives are women but there are also some male midwives. What most women want to support their labour and birth are attendants with whom they feel comfortable, who are sensitive to their needs, respect their choices and are enthusiastic about a natural approach to labour including the possible use of a birth pool.

The enthusiasm and confidence of the midwife in the use of water can make all the difference to the birth. Once midwives have attended a few waterbirths and have observed the benefits, they generally become very keen to learn more and to encourage more women to try this option.

'The birth of my baby was very calm and peaceful. The midwife described it as "beautiful" and what midwifery should be about. She was struck by the contrast between the atmosphere in the room and the traditional hospital birth. A midwife has the power to bring out the best of a birth – this was a very special moment for me to keep forever.'

Although a birth pool does not greatly alter the essentials of a midwife's practice, not all midwives have experience, training or enthusiasm for water labour or birth. The guidelines below are intended for both parents and midwives to read and discuss together prior to the birth. They address the main issues for midwives that are specific to labour and birth in water. A trusting relationship and good communication between mother and midwife is essential at any birth, especially at a waterbirth when your midwife has the responsibility of caring for you and your baby and assessing whether or not it is appropriate for you to be in the pool.

Midwifery guidelines for the use of a birth pool

'All you're doing is observing and supporting something that's quite natural.'

As the practice of waterbirth becomes more common, most birth units and midwife groups have developed their own guidelines and protocols for safe management. In general, these guidelines do not differ to a large degree, although some may have a more conservative emphasis on the cautions. Birth units and midwife groups with a large experience of waterbirth are usually willing to share their knowledge and expertise with those who are new to waterbirth. It is well worth making contact and finding out about the availability of workshops and courses for midwives.

The following topics address the most common concerns of midwives at a waterbirth and are not intended to replace any guidelines or protocols that are in practice. They are based on those currently observed at London's Hospital of St John and St Elizabeth, whose birthing unit, under the guidance of the pioneering obstetrician Yehudi Gordon, was one of the first to include waterbirth as a standard option in the 1980s and has provided an example for many

2   Sandra Dick, Midwife Practitioner, Birth Unit, Hospital of St John and St Elizabeth, London.

hospitals. Thanks are due to Patricia Scott, senior midwife at that hospital, for her help in compiling this information. Together with Anita O'Neill – the midwifery manager at this unit – Pat and I have shared our knowledge and study of the literature over the years and have presented workshops for midwives. These are the questions and issues that most commonly arise.

How important is the temperature and depth of the water?

Maintenance of the water temperature within an optimum range at approximately body temperature is very important, bearing in mind that the baby is generally 0.5–1°C warmer than the mother and is dependent on her for temperature regulation. What is most important is that the mother feels comfortably warm and is not looking flushed or overheated. Since women vary a lot in what temperature feels right for them, this is the main guide. There is a risk that preheated water on tap at 37°C (98°F) may be too warm for most women. Unless the pool has an inbuilt thermostat, the water temperature should be measured hourly and recorded in the mother's records, and always adjusted to the individual mother's comfort within the recommended parameters. The temperature should also be recorded at the start of the second stage and increased if necessary and if there is time. (See also Chapter 6, page 155.)

Recommended water temperature ranges are:

- During labour: 32°C–36°C
- For delivery: 36°C–37°C

Water depth plays an important part in temperature regulation. The depth of the water is best measured by asking the mother to kneel upright in the pool and sit back on her heels. In this position the water level should be just below her breasts and covering her belly. Then when she sits, the water will cover her breasts and leave her shoulders exposed so she can lose heat. Once the baby is born, it's preferable for the mother to be able to sit in the pool holding her newborn baby so that the baby's head is at the level of the breast above the water to facilitate breastfeeding, while the body is submerged to keep the baby warm. Some adjustment to the water level may be needed to achieve this or if the partner enters the pool at any point, as this will increase the depth. The room should be well ventilated and comfortably warm, but not overheated. This will assist in maintaining a normal core body temperature. If the mother leaves the pool, the room temperature needs to be raised to 'overheated' and warm towels provided. After birth the baby's thermal regulation is poor and the baby must be kept warm.

An important factor in temperature regulation is to ensure that the mother is encouraged to drink plenty of water while in the pool to avoid dehydration. Maternal temperature should be recorded regularly. Maternal hyperthermia at a water labour was a concern some years ago and this has largely been addressed by adherance to the above guidelines.

When is the best time for the mother to enter the pool?

It is recommended that the ideal time for the mother to enter the pool is when labour is well established and the cervical dilation is 5 cm or more. Getting into the pool too early may slow labour. However, a degree of flexibility is required and each woman should be reviewed individually. Some women having an intense labour may benefit from entering the pool earlier. This may help the woman relax enough to 'let go' and surrender to the birth process. Dianne Garland says,

...water is not a panacea for all evils, and just as labours can be slower or stop out of water so is true in water...Changes to the woman's body are normal in labour and each of us will tolerate different lengths of first and second stage. Just as we will all deal with different amounts of fatigue and stress, so each woman is individual, so her labour should be cared for, within the normal parameters set by ourselves as autonomous practitioners, or within the maternity units where we work.' [3]

Reviewing the questionnaires returned by women who have hired a pool from the Active Birth Centre, I have noticed that outcomes are significantly better when women enter the pool at 5–6 cm dilation. Most of them progress to full dilation in the pool within a few hours and a higher number give birth in water. It is wise to remember that the boost to oxytocin secretion is thought to be short acting and there may be a decrease after a couple of hours (see Chapter 3, page 63). In the event of a slowing of progress in labour, asking the woman to leave the pool and adopt upright positions on land usually helps to restart effective contractions. The effect of gravity and mobility on land, as well as perhaps having something to eat and drink, may help to increase the power of contractions.

How often should the baby's heart be monitored?

Diligent monitoring of the baby's heart rate for any signs of foetal distress is the most important way to help ensure the safety of a water labour or birth. Use of a waterproof foetal heart monitor makes this procedure less intrusive for the mother and should not necessitate her radically changing her position or leaving the pool. (See page 170 and Resources.)

3   Dianne Garland, *Waterbirth: An Attitude to Care*, Books for Midwives, 2000

'I was kneeling up in the pool or on all fours when the midwife listened in to the baby. It was quite comfortable and I could go on concentrating on my breathing.'

The baby's heart should be monitored and confirmed as normal according to local protocols before the woman gets into the pool. In order to exclude foetal heart decelerations, it is important to listen to the foetal heart immediately following a contraction and from time to time during a contraction, and for the midwife to be confident in CTG skills. All observations and events should be clearly noted in the mother's records.

The general recommendations for a water labour are:

💧 During the first stage of labour, the baby is monitored every 30 minutes.
💧 During the second stage of labour, the baby is monitored, if possible, after every contraction.

If you have any concern, ask the woman to leave the pool where you can commence continuous foetal heart monitoring, if necessary. If the birth is imminent, it may be wiser and safer to ask the mother to stand up in the pool for delivery above the water surface (see Chapter 7, page 186).

It should be noted that the dive reflex normally causes apnoea when a baby is born in water, so that water is swallowed rather than inhaled. The obstetrician Yehudi Gordon said in his summary of the safety issues at the International Water Birth Conference in London in 1995, 'In mild hypoxia the foetus responds with apnoea but this changes when the hypoxia is severe and prolonged ... The gasping response will override apnoea if mild hypoxia becomes severe and gasping is the mechanism involved in meconium aspiration in utero. Gasping is more dangerous after water birth than after birth on land because of the risk of inhalation of water.'[4]

He highlighted the need for diligent intrapartum monitoring and surveillance to reduce inhalation risk to a minimum. Yehudi Gordon recommends that midwives who attend waterbirths acquire advanced neonatal resuscitation skills. He has also said that the very rare occurrence of unexpected and undetected severe hypoxia at birth is, albeit very rare in the presence of skilled care, a risk factor at a waterbirth of which both midwives and parents should be aware.

Meconium stained liquor

Because of the possible association with foetal distress and the potential dangers to the baby of meconium aspiration at birth, the current recommendation is for the mother to stand up or leave the pool for continuous monitoring and suctioning, if necessary, if fresh meconium staining is observed.

> 'Contractions were coming fast – I got into the pool and almost
> immediately felt the urge to push. There were traces of meconium,
> so I stood up in the pool – but it was all happening very quickly.
> I gave birth standing up with one leg very high to relieve the
> baby's shoulders and so that the midwife could suck away any
> meconium. The baby was fine at 11lb 7oz and I had a superficial
> tear but no stitches. It was a wonderful, happy experience.'

What other observations are required?

Normal observations of maternal temperature, pulse and blood pressure should be carried out prior to the woman entering the pool and can easily be

4   Beverley A. Lawrence Beech, (ed.), *Water Birth Unplugged*, Books for Midwives Press, 1996

repeated once she is in the pool. Monitoring maternal temperature ensures that she is not overheated or chilled. Use of an ear thermometer is the easiest method of temperature-taking.

If there is a concern about the mother's blood pressure, it can be recorded between contractions with the mother either kneeling over the rim of the pool or sitting supported on its rim. It is worth noting that the mother's blood pressure is often lower during immersion in water due to the benefits of increased relaxation. This can be very helpful for a woman who has mild hypertension.

What about vaginal examinations?

Most midwives experienced in waterbirths find the need to perform vaginal examinations in a water labour is less than on land. Evidence suggests that most women entering the pool at around 5 cm will deliver within 4–5 hours (primigravidae) or 2–3 hours (multiparae).

When necessary, vaginal examinations can easily be performed in the water with the mother lying, kneeling or squatting supported by her partner. If the woman is deep in the water, the examination may not be so accurate. Depending on the indication for examination, it may be best to request that she float higher to the surface and closer to the edge. In this position it can be helpful to have a second person gently support her hips. In a few cases, if further assessment is needed, it may be necessary to ask the mother to leave the pool.

What to do if the woman feels faint

If a woman feels faint while in the pool, check her pulse and blood pressure. If these are normal, she may be overheated. Opening a window, using a fan, drinking cold water or tepid sponging may help, as may encouraging the woman to breathe slowly. A glucose sweet or energy drink may also help. It may be best if the woman leaves the pool until the faintness has passed. Rescue Remedy may be very helpful in reviving her.

It is very rare indeed for a woman to collapse at a waterbirth, and most midwives I have asked about this have not seen an occurrence. Nonetheless it is important to pre-empt the unlikely event of this happening in advance and rehearse how you will assist the woman out of the pool if necessary and how long it takes to drain an installed pool. Because of the water buoyancy, it's relatively easy to help the mother to sit on the rim by first seating her with her back against the side of the pool in the water. Then, inserting your arms under her armpits, lift her up slowly to sit on the rim of the pool against your body (keeping your knees slightly bent). Once she is securely seated, you can assist her legs over the side and lower her onto a mat beside the pool, placing her on her left side. Usually the feeling of faintness passes fairly quickly. Observations of pulse, blood pressure and foetal heart should be recorded until normal. If symptoms do not improve then call for medical help. An intravenous infusion may need to be sited to aid recovery. Sips of water with Rescue Remedy added and/or the homeopathic remedy Arnica may help, as will cool air and a spray of cool water on the face. A super caution is to procure a lifting sling to be kept handy in case of such an emergency.

The second stage in water

'By the time the midwife arrived, I was 7 cm dilated so I literally dived into the pool. Present were my midwife, my husband and mother-in-law. All commented on my relief as I entered the water – I even smiled. The second midwife arrived shortly afterwards.

> *At this stage I hadn't even opened my eyes to look at the first*
> *midwife, but just prior to baby arriving I had a moment of clarity*
> *when I opened my eyes, smiled and greeted my midwives (one of*
> *whom I had never met!).'*

Since timing is unpredictable, never leave the woman alone during this phase of the birth. Many units advocate the presence of a second midwife at the time of delivery. This is helpful not only for practical reasons, but also provides an opportunity for midwives to skill-share and observe a waterbirth. It is wise to time the entry of the second midwife into the room once transition is over and the second stage is established. Remember to check the temperature of the water when you anticipate the approach of the second stage: ideally it should be 36–37°C. While adjusting the temperature and preparing to receive the baby, try to ensure minimal disturbance of the mother who is making the highly sensitive hormonal transition from labour into birth. Maintaining deep privacy will help to encourage the onset of an effective 'foetus ejection reflex' (see Chapter 3, page 42). Vaginal examinations are best avoided at this time unless you have any concerns about progress.

> 'My husband massaged my back while the midwife was busy
> arranging all her kit around the kitchen so, apart from monitoring,
> I hardly saw her except when she was needed at the birth. This
> seemed ideal to me as I could just get on with the process without
> interruptions'.

During birth, the emphasis is on observing the normal progress and spontaneous behaviours without any intervention. Often it is best for the midwife to avoid giving any suggestions or guidance to the mother about bearing down – especially if you see that she is behaving instinctively without inhibitions and seems to be connecting well with what her body wants to do. This is likely to involve free expression of loud, animalistic, primal sounds. However, some women will appreciate and need helpful suggestions, guidance, affirmation and encouragement from the midwife.

> *'I groaned and roared as my baby was being born and I remember sounding like a beached whale. My midwife told me to focus on deep sounds and to send my energy down to the earth to help my baby out. That really helped me.'*

Maternal positions for delivery in the pool

The woman is likely to kneel, squat or sit when she is bearing down. She may change positions and even stand up in the pool. As at an active birth on land, midwives need to adapt their practice and techniques to the position the mother spontaneously adopts for the birth. Changing position to a more upright one such as squatting may be a helpful suggestion as it increases the pelvic diameters and assists the descent of the baby. Women with pubic pain need to avoid squatting for the birth and ensure that the knees are not separated more than the acceptable range. Kneeling positions with legs closer together are often best in this case. Squatting is much easier in water than on land and most women can manage it without a problem and without much support. In a sitting or squatting position the baby is brought up to the surface and handed to the mother from the front.

If she chooses to kneel, it is important to remind the mother of the importance of keeping her bottom under the water during the birth. In a kneeling position the baby emerges into the water from behind. Keeping the baby under the water surface the whole time, the midwife gently receives the baby and passes him or her 'face up' to the mother under the water and between her legs. The mother is asked to bring her hands down and hold the baby and then lift her baby up out of the water herself. This avoids the problem of the mother having to lift her leg over the cord if the baby is brought to the surface behind her.

Some women stand up out of the water at the last moment during the second stage. In this case, encourage the mother to lean forward and hold onto the rim of the pool. If the baby's head is delivered above the surface of the water, then it's essential that the delivery should be completed out of the water, as the baby is likely to start breathing once the face comes in contact with air. The baby is usually received from behind and passed to the mother face up, above the water surface and between her legs. Once the baby is in her arms, the mother can then sit down into the water with her baby. If taken by surprise and momentarily in doubt about what to do in this situation, you can hold the baby against the mother's lower back for a few seconds. Take your time and then ask her to get ready to receive the baby between her legs. Then pass the baby through to her 'face up' above the water surface and between her legs.

Some women feel the need to leave the pool in the second stage to give birth, whatever their previous intention had been. If second-stage progress is slow, leaving the pool is recommended to help the woman maximize her pushing power. Prolonging the time in the pool for the sake of a waterbirth, when power is diminishing, may result in lower oxytocin levels (weaker contractions) and increase the risk of problems in the third stage (see Chapter 3, page 63).

Delivery of the baby in water

Before assisting at a waterbirth, it's wise to read the literature about the dive reflex.[5] Understanding how newborn breathing is inhibited in warm

---

5   P. Johnson, 'Birth under water – to breathe or not to breathe', *British Journal of Obstetrics and Gynaecology*, vol. 103, no. 3, March 1996

water will increase your confidence in underwater deliveries. The natural adaptation of the baby for birth under water is a combination of the inhibition of breathing through physiological and hormonal processes and the large number of chemo receptors in the baby's larynx that enable the baby to distinguish between fluid which is swallowed and air which is inhaled.

In a waterbirth, delivery of the head is technically a 'hands off' procedure. This benefits from a good rapport between the woman and midwife. A mirror is useful for viewing the advance of the baby's head. In addition, some women like to see the head crowning and this encourages them to progress further. Placing a mirror in the pool so that the perineum is visible is especially useful if the mother is giving birth squatting, when it can be difficult to view the emergence of the baby. In a darkened room, shining a torch on the perineum will give you a good view in the mirror.

The head may crown in full view, or the midwife may use her hand to gently feel the advance of the head. This can be helpful, not to 'guard the perineum', but in order to determine if maternal efforts need to be less forceful to minimize the risk of perineal trauma and to give some direction. The head and body may emerge in one contraction. However, the head commonly emerges first and the next contraction brings out the shoulders and the body. There should be no hurry when the baby's head is born. Wait for the next contraction. Two to three minutes can pass, so remain calm. The dive reflex ensures that the baby does not inhale until brought to the surface.

As the baby is born under water, bring it to the surface in a slow gentle movement, taking five to seven seconds. Usually you will hand the baby directly to the mother, but be prepared for the mother to need a minute or two to recover before receiving her baby.

Briefly check the cord for pulsation to confirm that the baby is still receiving oxygen via the placenta but avoid unnecessary handling. This gives a good indication of the baby's condition. Often babies born in water do not cry and are very peaceful, so feeling the cord is reassuring. They tend to start breathing with smaller breaths than the gasp of a baby born directly into the atmosphere. Midwives attending their first waterbirths often comment that the initiation of breathing seems slower and may have some anxiety around this at first. If you are concerned, blowing gently in the baby's face helps to stimulate breathing.

Generally it is thought best to avoid touching the baby or the baby's head under water to avoid stimulus of the breathing reflex – however, if the shoulders and body don't emerge with the next contraction you will need to assist manually. If there is any difficulty, ask the mother to stand up and lean forward over the rim of the pool. Lifting one leg up onto the rim of the pool may help to increase pelvic diameters.

Immediately after the birth, it's best if the baby's body, apart from the head and face, is immersed in the warm water to ensure the body temperature is maintained.

> *'One midwife commented that there was a magical atmosphere and the other said that she felt honoured to be present. We had soft music on and aromatic candles – it was very peaceful and joyful – despite the pain.'*

Shoulder dystocia

Waterbirth is not recommended if there are strong risk factors for this condition such as a large for dates baby, poor progress in first stage, early second stage of labour or previous history. However, shoulder dystocia cannot always be predicted and a midwife needs to be confident of what to do if there is difficulty delivering the shoulders during a waterbirth. A well-rehearsed procedure needs to be in place for dealing with both difficulty delivering the shoulders and a true shoulder dystocia.

Dianne Garland comments 'the same principles exist in water as on dry land – rotate and tilt the mother's pelvis to facilitate rotation of the baby's shoulders'. An 'all fours' or supported squat position on land may help to release the shoulders.

In the event of a true shoulder dystocia, emergency medical aid should be called and the mother helped out of the pool. Local protocols should be observed. The McRoberts position can be used with the woman lying with her back flat and knees well drawn up to her chest as if squatting on her back. Supra-pubic pressure can be applied in this position to dislodge the shoulder. Record keeping relating to shoulder dystocia is very important.

> 'I had a very positive birth experience. It was much quicker and seemed more intense than my first. I felt in control at all times, which is very important to me, and I was safe and protected. I draped myself over the birthing ball in early labour (up to 6 cm) along with using TENS. My midwives arrived around four hours after contractions had begun (also at 6 cm) and I got into the pool. Wonderful! I immediately felt much more able to "cope" and my partner could finally stay in one place and support me. Not long after getting into the pool the contractions began to change and I really wanted to push. My baby was OP [occiput posterior]...her head was pressing on my lower back/bowel, making the pushing

urge more intense. About one hour after entering the pool I began actively pushing. My baby was active too and doing her bit! One hour later her head was born, very controlled. A few pushes later it was clear that her shoulders were stuck so the midwives got me out of the pool quickly to change the position of my pelvis, which dislodged her. The placenta was delivered 10 minutes later. My beautiful baby girl latched onto the breast immediately.'

What if the cord is tight around the baby's neck?

If the cord is so tight that it might adversely affect the baby, late decelerations of the foetal heart rate will generally be obvious in labour and the woman will be asked to leave the pool prior to the birth.

Based on this principle, some waterbirth practitioners therefore feel that it is not necessary to feel for the cord prior to the birth of the shoulders, since this may cause discomfort for the mother. If the head is born first and the baby is not born with the next contraction, some midwives recommend feeling for the cord and slipping it over the head or delivering the baby through the loop. If the cord is around the baby when it emerges, it is simple to rotate the baby's body under the water to disentangle the cord.

Never clamp and cut the cord under water as this could trigger respiration. On the rare occasion when you might need to clamp and cut the cord, make sure that the mother is standing up or has left the pool before you do so.

Care of the cord

Unit policies differ on the protocol for cutting the cord. At the Hospital of St John and St Elizabeth, the practice whether on land or in water is to wait for the cord to cease pulsating before clamping and cutting, unless there is a concern. Sometimes the placenta is delivered prior to the cord being cut. One independent midwife I know will usually wait for the placenta to emerge in the pool with the cord intact, then gently lift it into a plastic dish before inviting the father to cut the cord.

Provided there is no bleeding and there are no complications, there is no reason not to complete the third stage physiologically. You may respect the parents wishes regarding cutting of the cord or offer them the opportunity to participate in the separation of the baby from the cord. This can be a memorable ritual for them. It's wise to inform them beforehand that there are no nerves in the cord and the baby does not experience any pain when it is cut. Bear in mind that it is important to minimize any handling of the cord, as excessive 'fiddling' can cause undue bleeding.

Cord snapping

The important study of waterbirths by Gilbert and Tookey,[6] while broadly reassuring, highlighted a concern about the vulnerability of the umbilical cord to snapping in water. A few cases have been observed in this study and elsewhere, but there is no research to indicate whether this is more common at waterbirths than among those on land or whether the water was a contributing factor. Whatever position the mother is in, it's important to bear in mind the length of the cord once the baby emerges and to keep the baby close enough to the mother's body to prevent tension on the cord.

6   R. Gilbert and P. Tookey, 'Perinatal mortality and morbidity among babies delivered in water: surveillance study and postal survey', *BMJ*, Vol. 319, 21 August 1999 pp. 483–487

At any birth, the midwife observes the cord carefully. In the event of the cord snapping she is ready to attempt to catch and clamp the cord immediately, before any major blood leakage. Observance of such precautionary guidelines for the management of the cord by midwives – and in particular the avoidance of exerting any strong traction on the cord while in the water – ought to ensure that cord snapping remains a rare occurrence and the risk of the baby being compromised is minimized.

Neonatal polycythaemia

A paper published in *The Lancet* in 1997[7] recorded one instance of neonatal polycythaemia in a baby born in water. This is a condition in which there is an unusually high number of red blood cells, which may sometimes occur as a result of reduced oxygen supply. At the time, this article raised some implications for the physiological management of the third stage where there is delay in clamping the cord after the birth. In land birth the cord should vasoconstrict on contact with air, but if the cord remains in water for a prolonged period there was concern that the physiology may alter, causing polycythaemia. However, there is no evidence to suggest that the case reported was related to the birth having occurred in water. Since that time – an estimated 100,000 waterbirths have taken place and there have been no further cases reported. Therefore most practitioners have seen no reason to alter their practice.

Where to deliver the placenta

At the birth unit of the Hospital of St John and St Elizabeth, the view for many years has been that the mother can remain in the water for the delivery of the placenta if she wishes to, provided third stage is not prolonged and

7   T. Austin, N. Bridges, et al. 'Severe neonatal polycythaemia after third stage of labour under water', *The Lancet* 50: 1445–47, 1997

there are no complications. There have been no notable problems reported at this unit or among other practitioners who follow this approach.

At a waterbirth where hormone levels have been maintained with good progress throughout, the third stage generally occurs physiologically, as long as there is no cause for concern such as excessive blood loss. However, as a precaution, it is wise to have Syntometrine available.

Following the birth of the baby, if you ask the woman to bear down with the next contraction, the placenta is often expelled with ease. Using upright positions is often helpful. The third stage can average between 20 to 40 minutes. Provided there is no excessive bleeding and the mother's condition is satisfactory in other ways, you can afford to be patient. Putting the baby to the breast will help to increase oxytocin and stimulate contractions. If contractions seem to have lost power, leaving the pool is advisable to speed the delivery of the placenta.

Water embolism

Some obstetricians expressed anxiety about the potential for water embolism in the early days of waterbirth. This refers to the theoretical risk of water entering the uterus and being absorbed through the site of the placenta into the mother's bloodstream. No case of this occurring has been recorded among the tens of thousands of births in water that have taken place over the years, and this is acknowledged in a recent statement by the Royal College of Obstetricians and Gynaecologists.[8] Patricia Scott, a midwife at the Hospital of St John and St Elizabeth in London with over 16 years' experience of attending waterbirths, has written: 'immediately after birth, the vaginal walls touch one another, so the vagina is a potential cavity rather than an actual one. So it [water embolism] is extremely unlikely to happen.'[9]

8   RCOG Statement No. 1, January 2001
9   Patricia Scott, 'Water Birth Guidelines and FAQs', www.waterbirthfacts.com, February 2001

Because of the theoretical risk of water embolism, midwifery guidelines generally recommend the delivery of the placenta on land. As a result most women are asked to leave the pool after the initial mother/baby bonding and before the placenta emerges. In this case what is most important is that the mother holds the baby while getting out with cord intact and is kept very warm. With continuity of privacy and intimacy she can continue with a physiological third stage on land beside the pool. This is more of a priority than whether the placenta emerges in the pool or not.

> '*I got out for the third stage, which was the hospital's policy, and I was happy to comply with this. I got out holding the baby and sat down immediately to breastfeed.*'

How does one estimate blood loss in water?

In many waterbirths the water is often surprisingly clear following the birth, usually because of the minimal perineal trauma. You can use a sieve or fish net to collect any blood clots. It has become common to estimate blood loss as less than or greater than 500 ml, but it is difficult to judge precisely the amount of blood lost during and after delivery in water. With experience, midwives become more expert at gauging this by the colour and opacity of the water. If bleeding seems excessive then the woman should be helped to leave the pool. It may be more effective to observe the condition of the mother for any ill effects than to try and determine the blood loss in a pool of water. Women vary widely in their ability to cope with blood loss so you are looking for pallor and low blood pressure, rapid pulse rate and other physical signs indicative of a heavy bleed or post-partum haemorrhage.

If a mother feels faint she should be helped to leave the pool or the water should be drained. Midwives generally follow their intuition on this. In the case of a post-partum haemorrhage, take the following actions:

- Drain the pool and call for emergency medical help.
- Administer intramuscular Syntometrine.
- Help the mother out of the pool to lie down either on a floor mat or on the bed if it is close by. Ask the partner/colleagues to help you. Enable her to sit supported on the rim first (see Fainting, page 211) and then lift her legs over and assist her gently to the floor or bed.
- Wrap the woman in warm towels or a robe and rub up a contraction.
- Ensure that the uterus is firm and well contracted.
- Deliver the placenta, if not delivered, and check that it appears complete.
- Estimate the blood loss.
- Site an intravenous infusion, if required, and take a blood sample for cross-matching, a full blood count and clotting studies.
- Be prepared to administer a syntocinon infusion.
- Check that the woman has emptied her bladder. An indwelling catheter may be necessary.
- Check for any perineal trauma and suture as necessary.
- Record observations of maternal pulse and blood pressure and continue to observe maternal condition.

> '*I was asked to get out of the pool for the third stage, as blood loss could not be accurately ascertained in the water. I had a normal physiological third stage, the placenta being expelled approximately 15 minutes after the birth.*'

Water contamination

The general principle is that the mother's own body products do not usually present a risk of infection to the baby due to shared immunity, and the colonization with the mother's bacteria may offer some protection to the baby. The generally low incidence of infection at waterbirths supports this theory.

Debris can be removed with a plastic sieve. However, if the water is unpleasantly contaminated or becomes murky, visibility and estimation of blood loss may be impaired and it is considered best to ask the mother to leave the pool, drain it and replace with clean water. In the past there have been some concerns about faecal bacteria; therefore moderate to heavy contamination is generally considered a reason to leave the pool.

Care of the perineum

Water softens the tissues and makes it easier for the perineum to stretch, so deep tears tend to be less common in waterbirths. A slow, gentle delivery of the head regulated by the maternal breath is usually the best way to protect against tearing. Some women need more guidance than others, which is where having continuity of carer and building a relationship of trust between midwife and the woman in labour is helpful.

For occasions when the head is crowning for longer than usual, just changing position to being more upright or even to standing up will increase the help of gravity and aid the birth. Episiotomy is rarely needed and usually performed outside the pool.

If sutures are required following a waterbirth, it is best that they are done within an hour as this is less painful for the mother. The debate about the need to suture at all in some instances is topical in midwifery at present. The current view is that if the skin only has torn, sutures are not necessary, but if muscle has torn it is generally best to suture. This is an ongoing debate.

'The birth experience met all of my expectations, and the use of water was exactly how I imagined it would be. The pool was great – it gave me more mobility in labour and allowed me to stay in control. It helped me to feel 100 per cent more relaxed and definitely took the edge off the pain. Used as a form of pain relief, the pool enabled me to get through labour without pethidine. The water also gave me the ability to move easily in second stage, especially while the head was crowning, and this ensured an intact perineum. A wonderful waterbirth!'

A midwife's experience of the birth of her first baby

When should the woman leave the pool?

From the above it will be clear that there are times when it is advisable for a woman in labour either to stand up or to leave the pool. It's wise for parents to understand beforehand that the midwife's judgement about this is paramount and it is important to co-operate if the midwife requests that the mother leave the pool. Prior to the birth it's important to discuss this issue, and many birth units provide a workshop or antenatal session for women and their partners who are interested in using the pool. Reasons for the mother to leave the pool include:

- Foetal distress or potential compromise
- Insufficient pain relief
- Poor progress
- Potential complication

The key indications for this are summarized below:

- There are significant abnormal changes in the foetal heart rate.
- There is presence of moderate to thick meconium-stained liquor.
- The woman is exhibiting excessive fear, anxiety or loss of control.
- The contractions stop or slow down significantly.
- Augmentation of labour with Syntocinon or medical pain relief is required.
- There is lack of progress in the first, second or third stage.
- There is significant blood loss at any time.
- The woman has an abnormal rise in blood pressure.
- Assistance is needed to deliver the head or the shoulders.

Looking after yourself

In addition to taking care of the mother it's important for the midwife to consider her own comfort needs and any precautions needed for her own health and safety. The following questions are often asked by midwives.

Is there a need for the midwife to get into the pool?

With carefully designed pools that provide good access, birth attendants are easily able to touch, massage, monitor and assist the mother in the pool. It is not necessary or advisable for the midwife to get in the pool. However, midwives attending a waterbirth are advised to wear a light cotton top and trousers and top that can easily be changed as they are likely to get splashed. Water spillage can occur as the woman steps out of the pool, or leans over it. Be sure to clear up any water as soon as possible to prevent slipping. It is a good idea to place a non-slip bathmat at the side of the pool.

Is there an increased risk of HIV transmission during a waterbirth?

HIV does not easily survive outside its preferred environment. For this reason, it is possible that water provides a barrier to transmission of the virus rather than the reverse. However, it is becoming routine to offer antenatal HIV screening, and some hospitals have controversially denied women a waterbirth unless screening tests showed they were HIV negative. In any case, birth attendants are recommended to adhere to universal precautions against the transmission of infection, in particular the wearing of gloves. The following suggestions help to minimize the risk of transmission of infection:

- Wear gloves that are a half size too small to provide a watertight fit.
- Gauntlets are available, but because the latex is rather thick, they are not very comfortable to wear. Cut the fingertips off the gauntlets and wear them over regular gloves for better protection.
- Cover cuts and abrasions on the hands with suitable adhesive dressings.
- Keep the hands out of the water as much as possible. A 'minimal touch' delivery technique is advocated.

Hepatitis B and C

If a mother who is a Hep B or C carrier is insistent on using the pool, the main risk is to the carer ie. the midwife, not the mother or baby. The midwife should be taking proper universal precautions in every case as she will never know for sure which woman might have Hep C or not. In other words she should be caring for women as though they are all carriers of Hep C and take the appropriate precautions. Hep C is undoubtedly more infectious than HIV and Hep B but the midwife should be protected if she adopts standard precautions. If you know that a woman is a Hep C carrier it may be wise to be extra cautious. Use gauntlet gloves if you generally don't and more protective clothing such as a waterproof gown. The same recommendations as for HIV apply.

How can I prevent back strain?

In the UK's national survey on waterbirths (1995), out of 8,255 reports of women using water in labour, seven members of staff were reported to have suffered back problems. It is recommended that all midwives attend an annual moving and handling course and adhere to the recommendations. Active births and waterbirths require you to adapt to the mother's positions and movements. It is helpful for you to consider your own comfort in advance and to make sure you are provided with cushions and supports you will need to be comfortable when kneeling on the floor, sitting beside the pool and delivering the baby. While a low stool places you at the right height for communication with the mother in the pool, a chair, higher stool or birth ball, which seats you closer to the height of the rim, will enable you to lean forward from the hips, preventing back strain.

The following tips may be helpful for preventing back strain:

- Leaning over the pool from a standing position is hard on your back, so keep bending over the pool to a minimum. Sit on a stool or chair next to the pool or on a birth ball or kneel at the side of the pool.
- Make sure your knees are bent and try to be conscious of your posture when leaning over the pool. Always try to bend forward from your hips with knees slightly bent, rather than from your spine. With care and good postural habit, stress on the spine can be minimized.
- Wipe up any excess/spilt water from the floor and put away hoses to prevent falls/slipping.

- If you have a back problem or a concern, discuss this with your manager and occupational health department and consider regular physiotherapy or osteopathic treatment.
- Keeping fit and supple with simple yoga-based stretching exercises can help. There are a variety of exercise programmes available in gyms, health clubs and Pilates studios to promote and improve posture and structural integration. Regular attendance will promote your general wellbeing and help to prevent work-related injury.

Learning more

'I worked hard during the pregnancy to prepare both physically and emotionally. I think a lot of it was made possible by the midwife's absolute confidence and trust in me, the baby and the birth process. And her experience of active births and waterbirths. The education of midwives for this type of birth makes all the difference.'

I would highly recommend reading Dianne Garland's book, *Waterbirth – an attitude to care*, which offers an excellent guide to using water in midwifery practice. Dianne draws on her long experience of waterbirth at Maidstone Hospital and her visits to waterbirthing centres in America and Europe. She delves into the many issues that can affect midwives when setting up or using a waterbirth facility. She also explores issues of professional account-ability and legal responsibility, which relate particularly to midwifery prac-tice and waterbirth.

As knowledge and experience is gradually accumulated, waterbirth practitioners are gaining more understanding of how best to use water in labour and birth to avoid the occurrence of the potential problems described above. Childbirth can never be totally risk-free, and this is as true of land-based and medically managed births as those that take place with the assistance of water. Waterbirth midwifery guidelines aim for early detection and avoidance of problems by cautious exclusion of any potential risk that is identifiable in advance and may contraindicate the use of a birth pool. But however careful we are, on rare occasions unforeseen problems are bound to occur. Therefore it is essential to review anxieties and possible worst-case scenarios with colleagues and determine plans of action. The above guidelines will be useful when formulating such risk management procedures as will ongoing assessment and sharing of clinical experience.

Using water for labour and birth offers great benefits to mothers and also to midwives and midwifery students. It can be an increasingly rare opportunity these days to observe physiological births while training or practising as a midwife. Waterbirth enables you to both observe and to facilitate more of them. It is exciting and rewarding for all concerned to be able to witness the joy and fulfilment that the help of water can bring. Essentially, midwifery practice in this area is about the fundamental skills of being with women. This brings new life and enthusiasm to the ancient art of midwifery, which has been eclipsed for so long by the medical model. It is sensitive and proactive to the changes and innovations that women want. It also provides an exciting opportunity for midwives to increase and extend the knowledge base in this area by contributing to the growing body of midwifery research. The value and safety of waterbirth is increasingly validated by the evidence. It is an innovation that contributes significantly to women and to autonomous midwifery practice.

*'I went into labour and straight into regular contractions.
I had a bath and something to eat, put the TENS machine on
and plodded around to stay mobile. The midwife arrived as the
pool was filling. I got in and it was instant relief! As labour
progressed, I found the pool brilliant but, as it got really strong, I
found I needed to get out of the pool as I was too hot. So I got
in and out – I was quite restless. I think that the water made
strong labour very intense as, when I got out, it slowed the
contractions down and gave me a bit of relief! Then my waters
broke and I had a renewal of energy – things felt different and I
began to get a bit pushy. I had a long transition, which was
really hard, but I stayed in the pool. Then, suddenly, I began to
get expulsive urges to push and I could feel the head. He was
born, face up in the pool. I got out to deliver the placenta
(physiologically), which came 1 hour and 15 minutes later. Blood
loss was normal and there were no tears or stitches! The first
breastfeed was an hour after the birth. An amazing experience!'*

A midwife's experience of her own waterbirth

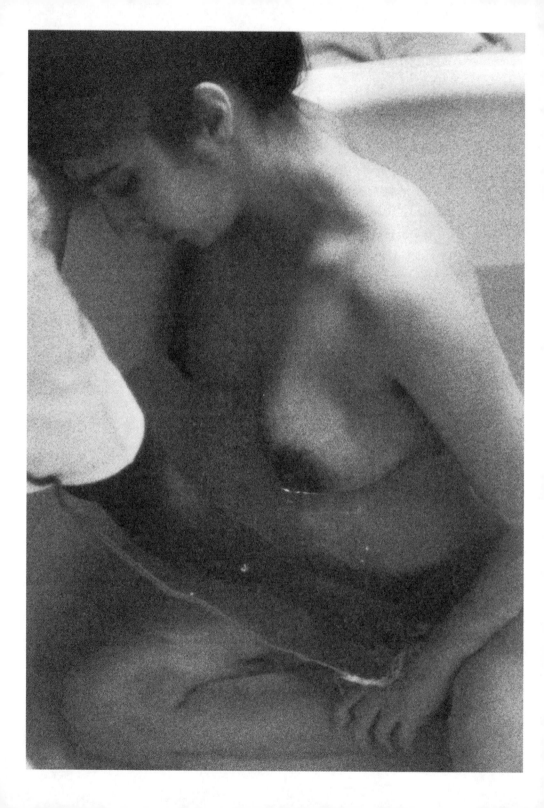

chapter nine

Medical backup for waterbirths

While you may be planning a waterbirth, what will happen during labour and birth remains unknown and unpredictable. It may be that you are faced with the unexpected and your agenda has to change. While most labours are potentially uncomplicated and the use of a birth pool helps to maximize this potential, it's important to keep an open mind and to be well informed about all your options. The use of a birth pool may no longer be an option if a problem or a complication arises or if you find that you need more pain relief than water can provide. In such circumstances you may need to take advantage of obstetric backup. This chapter will help to give you the information you need to understand the most common medical interventions. It will guide you in making the right decisions and gaining the most benefit, should you need or want obstetric care.

The following recommendations are based on the principle of the Hippocratic oath to 'first do nothing'. With this approach, the aim is to facilitate the natural birth process, using medical care as a last resort and if it becomes

Opposite: Midwife checks the baby's heartbeat with an electric foetal heart monitor.

necessary to intervene. It is important to understand how and when to use medical intervention most effectively to prevent side effects and ensure the best possible outcome for you and your baby. Being actively responsible and involved in making the decisions regarding all aspects of your care means that your birth is an 'active birth', whether you go through it naturally or opt for the help of medical intervention.

First try land

The first 'intervention' in a water labour that is not progressing is to get out of the pool and see how things go on dry land. Using upright positions may stimulate contractions in a birth that has slowed down. If the baby has been showing signs of distress, the change of position and environment may result in an improvement.

The benefits of upright positions include:

◦ **Optimal positioning.** It's easier for the baby to align itself in the best possible position for birth with the help of the downward force of gravity and your intuitive movements.
◦ **More effective contractions.** Gravity ensures that the baby's head is well applied to the cervix so contractions are more effective. This may result in faster dilation and a shorter labour.
◦ **Reduced pain.** Freedom of movement, free expression of sound and the natural forward tilting of the uterus help to modify the pain and may reduce the need for medical pain relief.
◦ **More space in the pelvis.** The movement of the sacrum, which forms the back wall of the pelvis, is not restricted as it would be if your weight was

resting on your lower back in a semi-reclining position. This allows the small degree of movement which is needed to increase the internal pelvic diameters so that the pelvis canal can accommodate the baby's head with maximum space as it descends during labour. In the final stages, the sacrum and coccyx are free to lift as you bend forward or squat, thus increasing the potential opening of the pelvic outlet by up to a third, to make more space for your baby to come out.

- **Improved blood supply.** Because of the tendency to lean forward in upright positions the blood flow to the placenta is optimal. There is no compression of the internal blood vessels from the weight of the heavy uterus, as there would be in the semi-reclining position. This helps to ensure that your baby has enough oxygen throughout labour and reduces the risk of foetal distress.

- **An easier birth.** During the actual birth, the help of the pull of gravity increases the power of the contractions, making them more effective, so that the baby's rotation and descent through the birth canal may be easier.

- **Enhanced first contact with your baby.** Gravity also helps the safe separation of the placenta once your baby is born. Sitting upright will make it easier for you to spontaneously hold your baby in a good position to breastfeed for the first time.

Medical pain relief

Although this book is primarily concerned with non-medical methods of pain relief, in some circumstances the use of conventional pain-relieving drugs may be necessary. If pain is severe and goes beyond what is normally expected or manageable, such medication may be the best solution. These days it is usually possible to combine the minimal use of medication with the principles of an active birth so that the overall experience is enhanced and you are left with a feeling that you made the right choices.

Drugs used to relieve pain in labour can be very helpful but may also have some side effects which can affect both mother and baby. While minimal use of such drugs helps to reduce the possibility of side effects, it is important to understand the potential risks of all drugs taken in labour and to weigh them up against the need for pain relief and the circumstances at the time. The following section will give you some further information.

If your labour is progressing normally and you are managing the pain well yourself, the risks of using medical pain relief probably outweigh the benefits. However, if you feel truly exhausted with a long way yet to go, or the pain is extreme, then the benefits of accepting some pain relief will probably outweigh the risks. Only you can tell when you truly reach your limit with the pain, so it's important that your birth partner and attendants know that. Although you may want them to encourage you to persevere without drugs in some circumstances, you also want them to hear and respond appropriately if you decide that you really do want some help.

Timing and dosage

To make the most of medical pain relief and minimize or prevent side effects, it is important to take the right dosage of the drug at the right time. Any drug you take will enter your bloodstream and cross over to your baby through the placenta. Minimal use at the right time, for the right reasons, will help to prevent any adverse side effects. It is important that cervical dilation is checked by an internal vaginal examination immediately before taking any drug in labour. While there are no rules, if you are getting close to giving birth (7–10 cm), it may be better to avoid narcotic analgesics or an epidural, as this may result in the need for an assisted or instrumental birth (see below). You could instead consider some of the suggestions in Chapter 7, or try gas and air (see below). However, if you need stronger pain relief, there is no point in being a martyr.

Narcotic analgesics

These analgesic (painkilling) drugs are derived from morphine. They act on the nerve cells in the brain and spinal cord (central nervous system) to alter the perception of pain. The pain impulses are present but the sensations may be modified. They are usually given as an intramuscular injection into the thigh or buttocks. Pethidine (meperidine/demerol in the US) and meptazinol (meptid) are the two narcotic drugs most commonly used in labour.

Potential benefits for the mother

- A minority of women who use narcotic drugs experience significant pain relief.
- A low dose can have a relaxant effect, which may help to improve cervical dilation in cases where anxiety and tension in reaction to the pain have led to very slow or ineffectual dilation.
- Narcotic analgesics can lower blood pressure, which may be beneficial when the mother has a problem with raised blood pressure in labour.
- They can be administered by a midwife at a home birth or in a birth centre.

Potential adverse effects for the mother

- As well as altering pain perception, narcotics alter consciousness. Some women feel that they lose control of the labour and do not experience effective pain relief.
- Nausea is a common side effect, so pethidine (meperidine/demerol) is often

given in combination with a powerful tranquillizer, to quell the nausea. This can cause drowsiness and prevent you from giving birth actively, increasing the likelihood of your needing other interventions. Metoclopramine (maxolon), which does not cause drowsiness, may be used instead, if needed.

- In high or repeated doses, narcotics may depress the mother's breathing. This means that there is a far lower concentration of oxygen in her blood compared to that of an undrugged mother who is moving and breathing deeply in reaction to the pain. This in turn can have an adverse effect on the baby.
- Narcotic drugs can make the mother less able to focus on her labour and, later, on her newborn baby.
- The use of narcotic analgesics may slow down the progress of labour.
- There is some evidence that the side effects of these drugs on the mother may contribute to postnatal depression.

Narcotic drugs taken by the mother in labour will be transmitted to the baby in the same concentration and can result in significant side effects, especially when large or repeated doses are given.

Potential effects on the baby

- The depressive effect of narcotics on the mother's breathing may lead to lowering of oxygen levels in her bloodstream, which reduces the oxygen supply to the baby. This puts the baby at greater risk of foetal distress.
- These drugs may depress the baby's breathing at birth. The effect on the baby is greater if large or repeated doses are given, or if the baby is small or premature. This may result in the baby needing to be given oxygen at birth and/or be given another drug to antidote the narcotics.
- If narcotic drugs are given to the mother late in labour, relatively high levels are likely to be present in the newborn. It can take several days before the

drug is eliminated from the baby's system. This can make the baby drowsy or sluggish, leading to slowness in starting to suck, which can impair the establishment of breastfeeding. In premature babies, this can increase the need for support systems to help them to breathe and feed.

◊ Narcotic drugs are known to affect consciousness, but we cannot know for certain how they make the baby feel in the uterus. However, there is evidence coming from research in Sweden suggesting a link between drug addiction in young adults and maternal use of pethidine during labour.[1]

Guidelines for use of narcotic pain relief

◊ Getting the dosage right is a crucial factor to maximize benefits and minimize possible adverse effects. The dose given needs to take account of your weight. The maximum dose usually recommended in hospitals is 150–200 mg. However, due to the possible adverse effects on both mother and baby, it is now thought best to use a much lower dose of 12–25 mg, with a maximum dose of 50 mg. This may have a relaxant effect and increase your ability to tolerate the pain rather than act as a painkiller.

◊ Wherever possible, the drug should be taken after 5 cm and before 7 cm cervical dilation.

◊ Ask for the drug to be supplied neat, without the addition of a tranquillizer.

◊ To avoid side effects on the baby, repeated doses are not recommended. If further help is needed, it is preferable to use a little gas and air or to have an epidural.

Epidural and spinal anaesthesia

An epidural is essentially a local anaesthetic introduced into the tiny epidural space around (epi) the membranes of the spinal cord (dura) which runs

1 Studies quoted in Michel Odent, *The Scientification of Love*, Free Association Books, 1999

through the centre of the spinal column. The anaesthetic is given by injection, through the opening between two vertebrae in the lower back. An epidural needs to be administered by a highly specialized anaesthetist, in a hospital. Great advances have been made in epidural technology in recent years.

An epidural blocks or numbs the transmission of pain signals along the nerve fibres from the uterus. Within a few minutes of insertion, all pain melts away, which can be a tremendous relief. The drugs used vary and may be derived from cocaine (sometimes called bupivacaine) or may be morphine-based or a combination of both may be used.

In many hospitals a 'low dose' epidural is offered that uses a minimal dose of anaesthetic, enabling the mother to be partially aware of contractions without feeling pain. The so-called 'mobile' epidural represents the latest advance in epidural technology. Whereas the more old-fashioned standard epidural used to numb the legs as well as the pelvic area, the low-dose and mobile epidurals tend to numb the pelvic area only. The anaesthetic effect lasts for about two hours when a 'top-up' can be given. Alternatively the anaesthetic may be administered continuously through an intravenous drip – however as the overall dosage tends to be higher this way, the 'top up' method is generally preferable.

Spinal anaesthesia

Similar to an epidural, but quicker and easier to administer, this form of anaesthesia is short-acting, lasting about two hours, and no top-ups are given. It anaesthetizes the uterus, vagina and perineum, and is often the first choice of pain relief for a forceps delivery or prior to a caesarean section. The quality of pain block is said to be better than with epidurals and the onset of anaesthesia is more rapid. The side effects are similar to those seen with epidurals but the incidence of headaches (see below) is lower. The lower dose of local anaesthetic used for spinals also has a lower risk of toxicity.

How is an epidural administered?

After you have met the anaesthetist and the procedure has been explained, an epidural is administered through a special needle that contains a very fine plastic tube or catheter. You are asked to sit on the bed and lean forward or to lie down in a foetal position to curl the spine and open the spaces between the vertebrae. A small local anaesthetic is injected into the area first so that the injection itself does not hurt. You will need to keep very still while the epidural is inserted. When the needle is withdrawn, the catheter is left in place and taped to your back so that it ends at your shoulder where there is a tiny cup and valve for the top-ups.

Potential benefits

- When successful, an epidural is the most effective form of pain relief during labour. Studies have shown that pain relief from epidural anaesthesia is satisfactory in over 80 per cent of cases. Many women who choose an epidural are highly satisfied with the experience – especially when pain levels have been intolerable, energy depleted and progress slow. It may work only partially with some women and fails for approximately five per cent of women.
- Pain relief can be easily sustained with repeated top-ups if necessary.
- An epidural can be very helpful in a prolonged labour if the pain becomes intolerable or if the mother is exhausted, thus enabling her to rest or sleep. Often this rest and relaxation results in progress and dilation may be

complete by the time the epidural wears off. It may or may not be necessary to induce contractions simultaneously (see induction below). This break from the pain may enable the mother to recover sufficiently so that she can regain her energy and push her baby out normally in the second stage.

- An epidural does not affect your mental state so you remain conscious.
- Epidurals or spinals are useful for a forceps delivery as they eliminate pain and reduce trauma.
- As a standard form of anaesthesia for caesarean section, epidurals enable the mother to remain conscious for the birth and enjoy early contact with her baby. Anaesthesia can continue in the next 24 hours for post-operative pain relief. As there is no general anaesthetic recovery tends to be rapid.
- Epidurals lower blood pressure and may be beneficial for mothers who have severe pre-eclampsia or a substantial rise in blood pressure.
- For some mothers who have suffered sexual abuse, a light low-dose epidural can be helpful if the sensations of labour are really intolerable. However, sometimes with the help of therapy and good preparation in pregnancy, going through a labour without anaesthesia can be a healing experience.

Potential risks

Many experts believe that the research into epidurals is insufficient to justify such widespread routine use, and often women are not fully informed about the potential risks before choosing to have an epidural. However, careful attention to the dosage and timing and selective use in the appropriate circumstances can help minimize the risks of this form of pain relief. Read through the rather long list of potential problems that follows bearing this in mind, and then look at the guidelines for some sensible ways to prevent them.

Possible adverse effects on the mother:

- Epidurals inhibit and interfere with the body's natural hormonal secretions and may slow down the progress of labour. This may mean that syntocinon (pitocin in the US), an artificial form of oxytocin, is needed to induce and stimulate contractions (see Inducing labour, below).
- Because she would not be moving and breathing deeply as in a natural birth, there may be less oxygen in the mother's bloodstream and reaching her baby. Over time this may increase the risk of foetal distress.
- Blood pressure may fall as the blood vessels in the lower body dilate causing the blood to pool within them. This can produce feelings of queasiness or faintness and may necessitate the use of additional drugs called vasopressors. A side effect of these drugs may be a reduction in blood flow to the placenta that may result in less oxygen getting to the baby. This in turn increases the potential for foetal distress. Because of this, every woman having an epidural needs to be on an intravenous drip to maintain her blood volume.
- Malpresentation (baby's head in an awkward position) is more likely with an epidural as the mother cannot help to position the baby with her instinctive movements as she would do normally, and the pelvic muscles are numb and less effective. This may necessitate an assisted delivery or a caesarean section. In some hospitals, because of foetal distress and malpresentation, up to 20 per cent of epidurals lead to forceps births. One study showed that 54 per cent of first-time mothers had a caesarean section or ventouse/forceps delivery following an epidural.
- Numbness of the area means that a catheter needs to be inserted into the urethra to empty the bladder. Painless at the time, this can cause minor discomfort the next day.
- Rarely, the anaesthetist may not be able to insert the epidural or may be able to achieve only partial blockage of sensation, so that pain or pressure may be

felt in one segment of the body, or on one side only.

♦ Occasionally, the needle may accidentally scratch the dura (the membrane that encloses the spinal cord), causing leakage of the spinal fluid. This can cause severe migraine-like headaches after birth and may disturb early contact with the baby. This is treatable but takes time to heal.

♦ Some women complain of backache after an epidural, which can become a long-term problem. This is usually caused by accidental injury to the lower spine and pelvic joints caused by over extension during birth that the mother cannot feel because of the anaesthetic effect.

♦ Shivering is a common side effect of epidurals.

♦ Approximately 20 per cent of women who have an epidural develop a fever known as 'epidural fever' and may need to take antibiotics. An epidural fever can mask a fever caused by something else.

♦ While the pain relief gained from an epidural can make birth a positive event, some women later feel that they were deprived of fully experiencing the labour and birth.

Potential effects on the baby:

Little is known about the long-term or subtle effects of epidurals on the baby, and there has been remarkably little research in this area. There is evidence that the anaesthetic is present in the baby's blood and brain cells after the birth. Some studies now show that epidurals do have an effect on the baby, altering breathing rate and blood sugar levels. However, there are no dramatic depressive effects as with narcotic drugs, and hence epidurals are favoured by paediatricians. Possible adverse effects include:

♦ An increased risk of foetal distress and an instrumental birth. Sometimes babies who have been exposed to large amounts of bupivacaine in the womb are born slightly blue in colour. This is due to reduced oxygenation of the mother's blood. These babies may be less responsive to their surroundings for a little while after birth.

- If the mother has epidural fever this may result in a rise in the baby's temperature too, and may lead to treatment with antibiotics or special care in a separate baby unit after birth.
- It is thought that the use of epidurals may contribute to irritability and inconsolable crying in some newborn babies who may be slow to 'settle' after birth. They may be very sensitive to noise and have some difficulty latching on to the breast at first.
- There is some evidence that epidurals may dull the babies reflexes to find the breast immediately after birth.

Guidelines for the use of epidurals

When epidurals are used minimally and as a last resort in pain management, the side effects can often be reduced or prevented.

- It's easy to progress from the pool to an epidural but impossible to change your mind once the anaesthetic is in place. Therefore it may be a good idea to try the pool for at least half an hour first if you can.
- Wherever possible, the epidural is best given after 5 cm and before 7 cm cervical dilation.
- You can ask the hospital what drugs they use for epidural anaesthesia and find out if the dosage can be kept as low as possible with top-ups instead of a continuous drip. The effect usually lasts about two hours. Make sure that top-ups are well timed to avoid 'breakthrough pain'. You could ask for your partner's help with this.
- You can help to prevent foetal distress and malpresentation by using

supported upright resting positions instead of reclining or semi-reclining. Remembering to do some relaxed deep breathing now and then will send more oxygen to your baby. Theoretically, a mobile epidural enables the woman in labour to stand, walk and change positions. However, in practice, most mothers do not feel like moving around very much, and although they can use their legs, they may not feel very sure where they are! Nevertheless, the use of simple, supported upright resting positions, such as kneeling over a birth ball or a bean bag or sitting on a chair leaning forward onto a few pillows on the bed, are possible with mobile or low-dose epidurals. This helps to encourage the baby's descent, improve circulation to the placenta and can significantly reduce some of the risks. If this is not possible, try lying well propped up on one side and changing sides from time to time with the midwife's assistance.

- An induction to boost contractions using a syntocinon (pitocin) drip is commonly used along with an epidural but is not always necessary. Sometimes keeping disturbances to a minimum and maintaining a very quiet, peaceful atmosphere in the labour room so you can rest or sleep is enough to encourage the secretion of natural oxytocin and thereby maintain the contractions.

- Always ask for an internal examination to check cervical dilation just before topping up – you may be close to giving birth. An epidural can be timed to wear off at the end of the first stage. Then you can be very slowly helped into sitting up on the edge of the bed and eventually standing and gently rolling your hips until full sensation is back and you are confident on your legs. This can be a slow process so it's important to allow plenty of time. Then you can try an upright position such as supported squatting or a standing squat, holding onto your partner's wrists or a firm support to bear down, once the desire to push returns (see page 190). Working with your contractions and gravity in this way will greatly increase the chances of a spontaneous vaginal birth.

Gas and air (Entonox)

This is a combination of 50 per cent nitrous oxide and 50 per cent oxygen similar to that used by dentists and sometimes called 'laughing gas'. It comes in a tank beside the bed in hospital and smaller portable tanks are available for home births. While widely available in the UK, there are some countries where this form of pain relief is not used during labour.

Compared to other forms of medication, minimal use of gas and air appears to be the most innocuous form of medical pain relief. However, it is medication and does enter your bloodstream and cross the placenta and should be used with care.

While some midwives require you to get out of the pool to use gas and air, others may support its use in the pool. I have heard of this working well in some cases, but would like to caution against overuse throughout labour. This, especially in combination with the relaxant effect of the water, can result in your becoming too 'spaced out' to make active decisions about your labour or muster yourself together for giving birth.

How to use gas and air

Gas and air is inhaled through a rubber mask or mouthpiece that you hold yourself. This has a valve that opens when you inhale and closes when you exhale. With the mouthpiece in place, you begin to inhale and exhale deeply just as you anticipate the start of a contraction and complete one or two cycles of the breath. The anaesthetic effect builds up and lasts for about a minute, taking the edge off the pain over the peak of the contraction without completely eradicating it. Each breath of gas and air may leave you feeling a little 'high' and may have the effect of wafting you over the peak of the contraction. Once the contraction reaches its peak, or if you have had enough, you can put the mask or mouthpiece down and the effects soon wear off.

Potential benefits

- Gas and air is self-administered so you can have total control of when and how much you take.
- You can stop using it if you do not like it, and the effects will soon wear off.
- Minimal use with good timing can be very effective for temporary pain relief.
- Gas and air can be used at home, in hospital and in an ambulance.
- While the available research is scanty, clinically there appear to be fewer immediate side effects on the mother and baby than with narcotics, especially with minimal use. However, we do not know how gas and air makes the baby feel or if there are long-term effects.

Potential adverse effects

- Extensive use of gas and air throughout labour may result in the loss of power and control, or active participation in your labour or birth. The 'high' may leave you feeling confused, dizzy or out of control.
- It's easy to feel 'hooked' on using it, and it can be difficult to stop.
- It can cause nausea and vomiting.
- Prolonged use is very dehydrating.
- The use of gas and air may delay the onset of the birth reflex and diminish your power to push.

Guidelines for the use of gas and air

- Gas and air is most beneficial when used late in labour for the final very strong contractions that occur when you are approaching full dilation, if you really feel overwhelmed by the pain. Bear in mind that this is a natural way to feel at this time.
- While giving birth there is a risk that you may focus on inhaling the gas and air rather than on pushing, and this may slow down the birth or diminish the power of contractions. It is generally best to avoid the use of gas and air at this time, or to use it very minimally.

Inducing and augmenting labour

Because inductions can lead to a cascade of other interventions, many women are reluctant to be induced. However most hospitals have a policy of routinely inducing labour after a certain date, commonly between 41 and 42 weeks. There are many doctors and midwives who are critical of routine induction policies and who prefer to follow an alternative approach which you can ask for if the issue arises. This involves assessing each woman who is 'overdue' individually and then deciding what would be best for her and her baby. The aim with this approach is to first determine whether the pregnancy is normal (albeit longer than the estimated average length), or whether there are any signs of post-maturity, or if there is any other medical reason or indication for inducing labour.

Very few babies are actually 'late' even though the due date may have passed. However, genuine post-maturity does occasionally happen and can endanger the baby. A thorough assessment will provide the information needed when deciding whether to induce or not. An induction is only worth considering if the risk of the baby remaining in the uterus is considered greater than the risks associated with induction. Sometimes, because of the risks of induction, a caesarean section may be the preferable option (see below).

The decision-making process should involve you and take your views into account. You are not obliged to agree to an induction, whether or not it is hospital policy. However, if there are convincing signs of post-maturity or if there is a medical or health problem, it is best to follow the advice of your midwife or obstetrician.

Reasons to induce may include the following:

- Progressive high blood pressure or pre-eclampsia
- Convincing indications of placental insufficiency and slow growth of the baby
- Significantly reduced amniotic fluid outside of the normal range
- Premature rupture of membranes with an extended period of no contractions (beyond 48 hours)
- Failure to progress in labour (induction at this point is called augmentation or acceleration of labour)

Estimated due date

The length of a normal pregnancy may be anywhere between 37 and 43 weeks and, very rarely, can even extend beyond this. If conception occurred later than the average estimate of day 14 of the menstrual cycle, the baby may not yet be ready for birth. Ultrasound scan estimates of the due date, though considered the most reliable, are approximate and may not be accurate. The usual method of estimating the average length of a normal pregnancy (nine months and one week since the first day of the last menstrual period) is known as Naegele's rule and was first established in the mid-19th century. There has been no satisfactory evaluation of this method, and it has been shown that only around five per cent of women go into labour on their due day according to this method. It has also been shown that the results from obstetric 'wheels' made by different manufacturers used to calculate the length of pregnancy by this method are not consistent.

The average length of a first pregnancy may be 41 weeks and one day for many women with a 28-day cycle. Ethnicity may also be a factor: studies have shown that Japanese and black women tend to have shorter pregnancies than white Americans. We can conclude that there is a wide range in the length of a normal pregnancy.

Additionally, the time babies take to be fully mature in the womb is variable. As we have seen, babies initiate labour themselves when their lungs are ready for breathing by releasing hormones that pass into the mother's bloodstream. This initiates the release of the hormone oxytocin, which stimulates contractions and starts labour. Being born too early may mean that maturation of the baby's lungs is not yet complete. That is why premature babies often need help to start and maintain breathing. If labour is induced when the dates are wrong, especially if you have a long cycle, the baby may be born prematurely increasing the risk of breathing difficulties and the need for special care.

Mother and baby's wellbeing

If careful checks reveal no sign of anything abnormal in either yourself or your baby, there is no pressing reason to intervene by inducing labour. Another approach is to reassess the situation on a daily basis and to continue waiting for nature to take its course, provided there are no problems. After 42 weeks, daily monitoring of the baby's heartbeat is recommended, which may necessitate a daily visit to the hospital. A consistently satisfactory heartbeat indicates that the baby is getting enough oxygen and the placenta is functioning normally.

An ultrasound scan can help to assess the size of the baby, the volume of amniotic fluid, the placental function and to provide more information about the baby's wellbeing. If clinical monitoring and an ultrasound scan confirm normal development of the baby, then the pregnancy can continue. If you re being pressurized to agree to an induction, you may be justified in seeking a second opinion. Try to find an obstetrician who supports a natural approach to birth and who will also recommend intervention if necessary.

Medical methods of induction

If the wisest decision after careful assessment seems to be to agree to induction, there is no need to feel you have failed in any way. Producing a live and healthy baby is an enormous achievement. So once you have given acknowledgement to your disappointment, let go of it and look forward to the birth of your baby, making it as good as possible under the new circumstances. There is a lot you can do to reduce the risks of an induction and make the experience more positive. The following information and guidelines may be helpful.

Prostaglandin

As this is the least invasive method of induction, it is generally recommended to try prostaglandin first. It is still possible to use a birth pool for labour or birth or to proceed with an active birth on land after successful induction with prostaglandin.

Prostaglandin in the form of a gel or pessary is inserted into the vagina by a midwife or doctor. This may help to soften and ripen the cervix and trigger the onset of labour. It needs to be done in hospital, as mother and baby's reactions are unpredictable. Contractions may begin very soon, or several applications at six-hourly intervals may be necessary. Some women are highly sensitive to prostaglandin; very rarely, extremely intense and painful contractions can occur which may deprive the baby of oxygen and potentially lead to foetal distress. Low doses of prostaglandin will help to prevent this. If prostaglandin induction is successful, labour can proceed as normal. If it does not result in contractions, then the next step is to induce with a syntocinon (pitocin) drip (see below). In this case, the prior administration of prostaglandin will help to prepare the cervix to dilate more easily – so it is always best to try prostaglandin first. Some doctors will agree to wait a day or so and try again, but this is not usually the case.

Amniotomy

This procedure, also known as artificial rupture of membranes (ARM), is no longer recommended as a method of starting labour on its own. It is, however, still often routinely done in conjunction with the use of prostaglandin or syntocinon (pitocin). You may request not to have the membranes ruptured as a matter of course when being induced, as intact membranes provide a protective cushion of amniotic fluid around the baby's head. Rupturing the membranes often stimulates the immediate onset of very intense contractions, and may increase the need for medical pain relief. It also increases the risk of infection through the vagina, by removing the protective barrier of the membranes.

Syntocinon (pitocin) drip

These days induction of labour can be carefully designed to mimic what would happen in a normal labour. However, it often makes labour progress more quickly and intensely. This is because the artificial hormone syntocinon is fed intravenously into the mother's bloodstream in much higher concentrations than the gradually increasing level of natural hormones produced in a normal labour. This means that contractions may be longer and stronger. The recovery time between contractions, when fresh oxygenated blood reaches the placenta, may be shorter. Therefore the risk is that, over time, the baby receives less oxygen than would otherwise be the case. This may be demanding on the baby and increase the potential for foetal distress and the likelihood of a caesarean section. Frequent or continuous monitoring of the baby's heartbeat to check how well the baby is coping is therefore essential when labour is induced. While syntocinon usually stimulates dilation of the cervix, it blocks the secretion of the natural 'love hormone' oxytocin and does not have the same altruistic effect which promotes bonding (see page 36).

More intense contractions also result in more pain, so you may need an epidural for pain relief. Up to 30 per cent of inductions fail to initiate labour, and in this case the baby needs to be born by caesarean section.

What you can do to minimize problems

The speed and concentration of a syntocinon drip is adjustable. You can request that the drip is introduced as slowly as possible to prevent overstimulation of the uterus, and you can ask for the drip to be slowed down to a comfortable level if you find it overwhelming.

By using comfortable upright positions such as kneeling on the bed over a beanbag, sitting on a chair leaning forward onto the bed, or lying well propped up on one side, you can ensure a better blood supply to the uterus than if you were lying on your back or semi-reclining. This will help to reduce the risk of foetal distress. It will also help you to cope better with the contractions. In second stage, supported upright positions that engage the help of gravity (see Chapter 7) will help you to push more effectively.

As contractions may be intense almost immediately, bear in mind that it will take about half an hour before your own endorphins can 'catch up'. It is helpful and reassuring to have someone with you at all times and to focus on breathing over the peak of the contractions (you can try long, slow out breaths through the mouth which 'take away the pain', with relaxed in breaths through the nose). Some women do manage without medical pain relief this way, but you can have an epidural if the pain is unmanageable.

Guidelines for medical induction:

- Before agreeing to an induction you can request a thorough assessment of the situation. This may include seeking a second opinion on the necessity of induction in your case, and an ultrasound scan. In the absence of a medical problem, you may decide to wait. Acupuncture, homeopathy, herbs and most complementary therapies can be helpful in getting labour started. Your midwife could perform an internal cervical massage – called 'sweeping the membranes'. After 42 weeks, daily monitoring of the baby's heart and reassessment of the situation is recommended.
- If you agree to a medical induction, try prostaglandin first. Request repeated low doses at six-hourly intervals for 24 hours before progressing to syntocinon (pitocin).

- Request the minimum effective dose of either prostaglandin or syntocinon.
- If a syntocinon drip is used, avoid lying on your back or semi-reclining (see above).
- Try to wait 30 minutes or so before deciding to have an epidural, to give your natural endorphins time to kick in. Ask for the drip to be phased in slowly and gently, and focus on 'breathing away' the pain with long exhalations through the mouth and relaxed inhalations.
- Have a support person with you at all times.
- If the idea of induction is not acceptable and the need to induce is urgent, elective caesarean is another option.

Inducing the delivery of the placenta

The third stage of labour ends with the delivery of the placenta. Strong contractions ('afterpains') separate the placenta from the wall of the uterus and expel it along with the membranes through the birth canal. These contractions usually occur within about half an hour of the birth, and are stimulated by first contact with your baby and the first sucking at the breast. The concern here is that the placenta should be delivered completely and without excessive bleeding.

In a 'managed' or induced birth, the standard routine for the third stage involves the administration of a drug known as syntometrine (pitocin) which contains oxytocin (to stimulate contractions of the uterus) and ergometrine (to reduce blood loss). This is injected into the mother's thigh or buttocks after the delivery of the baby's shoulders. Further interventions include early clamping and cutting of the cord to prevent the drug reaching the baby, followed by the manual removal of the placenta. Managed care in the third stage means that there is an abrupt cessation of the flow of oxygenated blood from the placenta, and the baby therefore has to make a sudden transition to air-breathing. In a natural or physiological third stage, on the other hand, breathing is established more gradually because of the continuing supply of oxygen through the cord blood, along with other important nutrients that the baby needs after the birth.

Louise Long, a midwifery lecturer at Kings College, London, makes the point that because so few midwives and obstetricians have extensive experience of observing physiological third stages, their understanding of this natural process is impaired.[2]

As with many forms of intervention in labour, there are situations in which active management is appropriate and safest for both mother and baby in the third stage, especially if labour was induced and the natural hormone secretion may have been suppressed. But for women whose labour and birth have been problem-free and without intervention, there is no reason to assume that the delivery of the placenta cannot also be allowed to take its course physiologically, provided privacy is maintained in a very warm room, first contact between mother and baby is undisturbed and blood loss is normal. At an early stage you should discuss with your midwife which approach to third stage you would prefer, depending on the circumstances.

Ways of assisting the birth

The simplest way of assisting the baby to be born quickly if there are difficulties, or in an emergency is by performing an episiotomy. This is generally done when the baby's head is crowning on the perineum, by making a small surgical incision in the vaginal tissues to enlarge the opening and hasten the birth.

2   Louise Long, *MIDIRS Midwifery Digest*, vol. 13, no. 3, Sept 2003

A local anaesthetic is injected into the tissues prior to the incision to prevent pain. Episiotomies used to be done routinely in some hospitals for all first births, allegedly to 'protect' the perineum and prevent tears. They are now much less common, since there is more evidence that a natural tear, should it occur, generally heals better. When birth is active, an episiotomy is very rarely needed.

There are two types of episiotomy – midline and medio-lateral. The midline extends directly backwards from the vagina, stopping short of the anus. The medio-lateral starts off like the midline, but then goes out to one side to avoid the anus. The midline cut is usually preferable because it runs between muscles, not through them, and is done as far as possible away from large blood vessels and nerves. It is also less painful while healing. During birth the midline cut may occasionally extend into the anus but a skilled midwife or doctor can prevent this kind of 'third degree' tear.

A tear is a natural hazard of birth. Most tears are minor, involving only the superficial layers of the vagina and the labia. They heal easily and are known as 'first degree' tears. Sometimes these do not require suturing. Occasionally more severe 'second degree' tears occur involving the underlying muscles, and in this case sutures are generally needed and should be done under local anaesthetic soon after the birth. Tears generally heal better and are less painful than episiotomies. The uneven line of the tear may be more awkward to stitch but the subsequent ease of healing makes up for this.

How to avoid tearing and episiotomy

- Pregnancy yoga and breathing, including pelvic floor exercises, will help to improve circulation to the perineum and enable you to learn how to relax and release these tissues when you are giving birth.

- Perineal massage in the last month of pregnancy may help to increase the stretchability of the tissues.

- The birth should not be hurried. The midwife will guide you to release the baby slowly, allowing the tissues time to release and relax. When the birth happens spontaneously in its own time without strenuous pushing at the end, tears are less common.

- The most effective way of avoiding a tear is to give birth in an upright position and to wait for the natural expulsive reflex to occur, thus avoiding strenuous pushing, especially at the very end. If you are lying on your back, the pressure of the baby's head is directed down on to the perineum and the muscles between the vagina and the anus are subjected to maximum tension. In vertical positions the pressure is brought forward and spread evenly throughout the vagina so that the perineum can expand spontaneously as the baby's head emerges.

- In the supported squatting positions, tears tend to be superficial, around the skin of the vaginal outlet instead of at the muscular back wall of the vagina. They are easily stitched if necessary, and do not cause much postnatal discomfort or pain. Second-degree tears are less common; third-degree tears are rare.

- If the baby is slow to emerge, supporting the perineum with warm compresses will bring blood to the tissues, helping them to release and stretch. After the birth of the baby's head, gentle delivery of the shoulders prevents tearing.

- In many cultures the liberal use of warm oil is common, and the tissues do produce their own natural lubricants.

- Labouring in water may soften the perineal tissues, allowing them to stretch more easily and thus prevent tearing or the need for episiotomy.

How an episiotomy is done

Episiotomies are traditionally performed with the woman reclining. A local anaesthetic is injected to numb the area and the incision is done during a contraction. At a waterbirth an episiotomy can be performed with the mother seated on the rim of the pool or even under water, but this is very rarely necessary.

When is an episiotomy necessary?

If the vaginal outlet is unusually tight, an episiotomy may be needed. It may also be required if forceps are used to deliver the baby. The size of the episiotomy can be kept to a minimum by removing the forceps when the head crowns so that the mother can give birth by her own efforts. Vacuum extractors or ventouse fit directly onto the top of the baby's head and do not stretch the vagina as much, so there is some debate about the necessity for an episiotomy. It may still be necessary to hasten the birth.

There is some disagreement as to whether an episiotomy should be routine in a premature birth to protect the baby's head. Although almost always unnecessary, if there is any delay and the head is under pressure, an episiotomy is done.

One argument often used in favour of episiotomy is that it prevents excessive stretching and reduces the risk of vaginal prolapse in later life. Vaginal prolapse has become much less common in the last 40 years or so but there is no evidence to suggest that episiotomy is the reason for this. The best prevention of prolapse is to practise pelvic floor exercises regularly during and after pregnancy.

Repairing tears and episiotomies

An episiotomy or tear is stitched by the doctor or midwife, often with the mother lying on her back with her legs in stirrups. Her head and neck should be comfortably supported by pillows and she may like to hold the baby. The best time to be stitched is after you have had a chance to hold your baby, but before the area feels tender. First a local anaesthetic is injected into the area to be stitched. This may be a little painful but quickly numbs the area. Breathe as you did during contractions and have gas and air to hand should you want it. Once the perineum is numb, the vaginal lining, the torn muscle and finally the external skin are stitched. Usually dissolving thread is used, and the stitches do not need to be removed.

Discomfort after the birth from stitches while sitting is often underestimated and can make early breastfeeding more difficult. Be sure to ask for help with positioning your baby for feeding if you need to do this lying down at first as this may not be as easy as sitting up.

Assisted (instrumental) deliveries

Babies can be assisted to be born with the help of forceps or ventouse. Forceps consist of two metal instruments shaped like large salad spoons with a hole in the middle. They are inserted through the vagina after an episiotomy and applied to each side of the baby's head. Alternatively, vacuum extraction, or ventouse, may be used. This is a rubber cup connected to a vacuum pump, which is applied through the mother's vagina to the baby's scalp. A vacuum is created so that the cup remains attached to the scalp by suction. Traction is applied to adjust the position of the baby's head and then help the baby out.

While forceps used to be more commonly used in the UK, the ventouse method is now becoming more widely available. In most European countries, forceps have been replaced by ventouse. Safety is thought to be comparable. Some discomfort or trauma may occasionally be caused to the baby with both methods, but the ventouse method is more comfortable and less invasive for the mother, and may not require the use of episiotomy or anaesthesia. If you would prefer to use ventouse should the need arise, discuss this beforehand with your attendants and find out if this option is available.

In some circumstances an assisted delivery can save the baby's life and prevent unnecessary damage or trauma. When this is the case, it is usually acceptable to the mother, and a good outcome and recovery follows. However, forceps or vacuum extraction are used in about 20 per cent of births, and a large number of these cases of intervention are avoidable.

When an assisted delivery is necessary

When the baby's head is large in relation to the mother's pelvis, or if the baby is in the occipito posterior (OP) position, contractions often slow down and an assisted delivery may be necessary. Forceps or ventouse are used to correct the abnormal position and to provide the additional force needed to deliver the baby. If the baby is breech, forceps are sometimes used to ease the birth of the head, especially if an epidural has also been given. An active breech birth in which the mother kneels or stands, engaging the help of gravity, does not usually require forceps. Caesarean section is often considered safer for the baby than a traumatic forceps delivery.

Assisted delivery is more common when epidural anaesthesia has been used because this can slow down contractions, remove the natural urge to bear down and push, and relax the pelvic floor muscles so that the baby's head is not encouraged to rotate in the second stage.

If the baby suffers severe foetal distress in the second stage of labour, forceps or ventouse can be life-saving by achieving rapid delivery. These interventions are also occasionally used to protect the mother. Women who have severe high blood pressure, lung or heart disease may be advised not to bear down, and an assisted delivery may be more appropriate.

Conditions for an assisted delivery:

- The cervix must be fully dilated and the bladder empty.
- The baby's head must be engaged in the mother's pelvis (if the head is still high a caesarean may be necessary).
- Sometimes delivery must be assisted when the baby's head is low down in the birth canal, but the mother is too anaesthetized or tired to push him or her out. This is known as a 'lift out' delivery, needing only a local anaesthetic to numb the birth outlet.
- Occasionally, if the baby is lodged a little further up the pelvic cavity (particularly in cases of OP presentation), forceps or ventouse are used in what is known as a 'mid-cavity' delivery. This usually requires an epidural or spinal anaesthetic. The other common reason for a mid-cavity delivery is when an epidural has affected the mother's urge to bear down.

A skilled obstetrician, aware of the possible effects on the baby, will sensitively apply the minimum possible force to assist the birth. Most babies make a rapid recovery after an assisted delivery but, because they may have a sore head and feel irritable, they may need to be handled very gently during the first few days. This usually subsides quickly, especially with the help of plenty of close body contact.

You can help to reduce trauma and bruising to yourself and your baby by taking the homeopathic remedy Arnica 200 just before the birth if possible, and then three times daily until bruising is gone. The baby can be given a dose of Arnica 6 as well, but discuss this first with a homeopath. In the first days or weeks following an instrumental delivery, a visit to a cranial osteopath experienced with postnatal work will help to heal the baby of any after effects, and will be equally good for you. In my view, this is essential after an instrumental birth as it helps to clear the nervous system of any trauma and to calm and heal the baby.

How you may feel

Women often feel sore and bruised, especially after a forceps delivery. If you know that your baby might not have been safely delivered without help you will probably feel relief and gratitude. If, however, you feel some disappointment at not having achieved a natural birth, it's wise to allow these feelings to surface, accepting that you are entitled to be disappointed if you wanted something that did not happen – at least for a little while. The amazing work of producing a healthy baby over nine months is really more important and a far greater achievement. However, your emotions will need to be understood and resolved after the birth. You could begin by talking to the midwife who takes care of you postnatally, as well as the doctor who performed the procedure. Usually these feelings can be resolved in a few weeks, but if they continue or are a source of postnatal depression or stress, you may wish to consider expert counselling.

Caesarean section

When a caesarean section operation is performed, the baby is delivered through surgical incisions made in the mother's abdomen and uterus. Then the placenta and the membranes are delivered and the incisions are closed with stitches. A caesarean section is performed either to protect the wellbeing of the mother or, more often, the safety of the baby. Possible reasons include:

- A baby thought to be too large to come through the mother's pelvis
- A baby in an untenable position for a normal delivery
- A baby suffering from foetal distress
- A prolonged labour
- A failed induction of labour

Reasons relating to the mother or baby's wellbeing include severe pre-eclampsia, severe bleeding, perhaps caused by placenta praevia (placenta in front of the cervical opening) or placental abruption (premature separation of the placenta from the wall of the uterus). Modern skill and expertise generally ensure a positive outcome for mother and baby if a caesarean proves to be essential.

Types of caesarean

When this type of delivery is planned for reasons known before the start of labour, this is known as an elective caesarean. When circumstances arise suddenly before or during labour that necessitate a caesarean, this is known as an emergency caesarean. Modern obstetric units are equipped to deal with such an emergency at any time.

Caesareans also differ in terms of the form of anaesthesia used. Until 20 years ago, all caesareans were performed under a general anaesthetic, which meant that the mother was unconscious throughout the birth and could not see her baby until she recovered. Today, epidural anaesthesia provides an alternative that allows you to remain conscious throughout the operation. Postnatal recovery is usually quicker, and an epidural is usually safer for the baby. An epidural caesarean cannot be commenced as quickly, so a general anaesthetic is always used in a true emergency. Moreover, some women find the prospect of being conscious during the operation unappealing and prefer a general anaesthetic. Hospitals generally do not allowing partners to be present if a general anaesthetic is used. However partners are encouraged to be there (beside you at the head end and behind a screen) during an epidural caesarean.

The operation

Before a caesarean section your abdomen is shaved and prepared for surgery. After anaesthesia is administered, a catheter (a narrow tube) is inserted into the urethra to the bladder to drain urine, and an intravenous drip is inserted into your arm. The skin of the abdomen is checked to make sure you don't feel anything before the surgeon cuts through the tissues to reach the membranes of the amniotic sac and the baby.

The surface incision is usually a horizontal 'bikini line' cut just below the pubic hair line across the bottom of the abdomen. This has the advantage of running along natural lines in the tissues, meaning less bleeding, less pain and faster healing. Very rarely in an emergency, a vertical cut is used, which runs from below the navel to the hair line. A little less awkward for the obstetrician, it results in a more disfiguring scar and is rarely done these days. The incision in the uterus itself is usually horizontal and made in its lower segment (called a lower segment caesarean). This reduces bleeding and minimizes the risk of scar rupture in a subsequent labour.

The baby is then lifted out, occasionally with the help of forceps. The time that elapses from the incision to the birth is about five minutes. The umbilical cord is clamped and cut, and the baby is handed to the assistant. If you are having an epidural caesarean, you will then be given the baby to hold or, if he is present, the father could take him or her.

The placenta is delivered and checked and then, while you are still anaesthetized, the layers of the uterus and abdominal wall are stitched with dissolving stitches. The skin will either be stitched or closed with small metal clips. It is common practice to leave a thin tube in the wound for a day or two so that excess blood and fluids can drain away. This is painlessly removed.

After the operation

Immediately after giving birth by caesarean you will be recovering in bed, usually in the postnatal ward. After a general anaesthetic, many women feel groggy and will find it difficult to focus on the baby for some time. You may be in pain, needing an injection of opiates until you are able to take ordinary painkilling tablets. If you have had an epidural, however, pain relief can be achieved by topping up the epidural before it is removed after the birth. You can expect to feel more comfortable within a few days. Movement may be restricted for at least 24 hours by the intravenous drip providing fluids and nourishment, but you may be surprised by how soon you will be encouraged to move about.

Mother and baby usually stay in hospital for about five days. The stitches or clips are removed after a week or less, and there is a postnatal checkup at six weeks. While most women recover surprisingly quickly, it can take others between six weeks and six months before full energy returns. Plenty of rest is essential.

Breastfeeding your baby after a caesarean

A caesarean should be no impediment to successful breastfeeding although it may be a bit difficult to get started. Much will depend on your own optimism and determination to succeed, and on the support of those around you. It is a good idea to begin as soon as possible after the birth. You will need help lifting and handling the baby, and your scar will need to be protected during feeds with a pillow. To do this, you can have the backrest on the bed raised and feed the baby semi-lying on one side, well propped up, with the baby tucked up beside you. Alternatively, you can try sitting a bit more upright with plenty of pillows to support your back and lay the baby's body under your arm on a pillow with head at the breast in the 'football hold'. Make sure that the baby's body is turned in well to face towards your body and that the mouth is directly opposite the nipple. You may need help from the midwife at first to get the baby latched on properly, so don't hesitate to ask. More breastfeeding and baby care guidance can be found in my book *Natural Baby* (see Resources).

When expectations are not met

Because the idea of a waterbirth seems so idyllic, it can be very disappointing when dreams of giving birth this way cannot be realized. It is especially sad when this disappointment lingers and results in feelings of failure or loss of self-esteem. This can be the very opposite of the empowering experience you may have been expecting. You are going to need time to recover and heal from this. The only way to do so is to acknowledge how you feel, to give yourself the time and space to share these feelings and get clear in your mind about what happened and why. This will undoubtedly involve talking through the experience with your birth attendants, partner, antenatal teacher or people you are close to, and possibly a session with a counsellor can be invaluable – sooner rather than later.

Modern interventions were not available to women as little as a hundred years ago. We need to keep things in perspective and remember how much safer birth is today with obstetric help readily available when it is needed. Sometimes, in retrospect, it seems that things or choices made at the time could have been different – could have been better – but since we are powerless to change the past we may as well accept that everything happens for a reason and we cannot change or control destiny – as hard as we may try.

Ultimately your baby is far more important than the birth. It's essential, once you have come to terms with the experience, to put it all behind you and get on with enjoying your lovely baby. It's also essential that you appreciate and congratulate yourself for what you have achieved. Every birth has its challenges and it takes even more courage and spirit to get to the other side when the going is tough. This experience will stand you in good stead for the many challenges that lie ahead and strengthen you as a parent in the long term.

Essentially this is your baby's birth, not yours, and if your baby is healthy and safe you have done a great job – no matter how you achieved it!

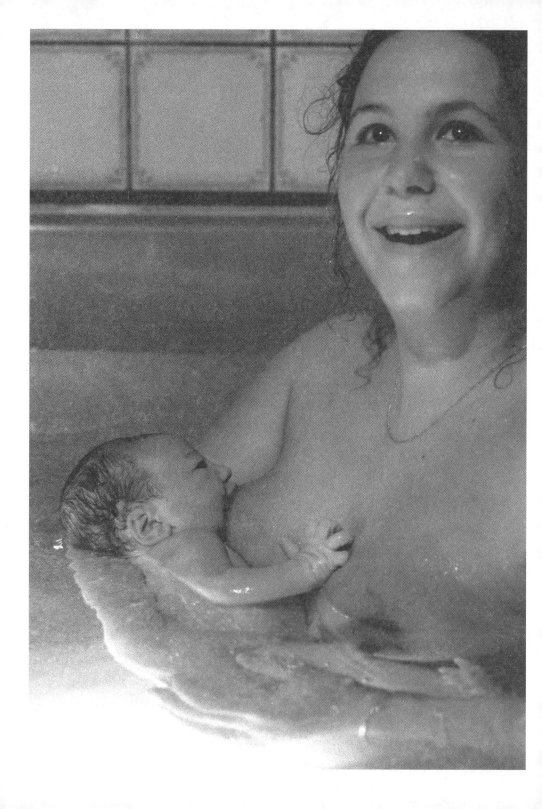

chapter ten

What women say

'The birth pool made my birth, though painful, much more relaxing and even "romantic" as steam rose off the surface in the candlelight at dawn.'

When women first stepped off the delivery table to labour and give birth in upright positions in the early 1980s, it was the start of a revolution in childbirth. They became active participants in their own birthing rather than passive recipients of a medicalized delivery. This reclaiming of the power of birth by women was historic; it will become legendary when we have enough distance to look back to the times when most women gave birth on their backs and no one knew any better.

When I founded the Active Birth Movement in 1981, I was one of the ordinary mothers who initiated, inspired and led this radical change in North London. The driving force behind this revolution was the power of true, personal experience and the recounting of these 'birth stories' to others. Such anecdotal evidence of women's common experience is arguably the most powerful and persuasive testament to the benefits of an active birth. Through this wave of enthusiasm and experience – passed on from woman to woman, witnessed by midwives and backed by scientific research – a better understanding of the nature of birth is gradually dawning among all concerned. Once free to move and adopt any position in labour, it is not surprising that women were attracted to the bath or shower; from this the idea of adding a pool of warm water to the active birth environment was a logical step.

The extraordinary fact that thousands of women all over the world are now using birth pools would have seemed like a dream to women in the late 1970s and 1980s who were fighting against the seemingly impenetrable obstacles of routine obstetric intervention and the medicalization of birth. While the idea of retreating into a deep bath of warm water for comfort and pain relief in labour readily appeals to our common sense, there have also been some new discoveries and benefits we could not have anticipated. The first of these is the power of water to stimulate, enhance and shorten labours; and the second is the potential for the baby to be born more gently into the world through water. While we must remember that no single way of birth can be appropriate for everyone, the widespread experience over two decades is telling us that more women could have easier labours and better births by using a birth pool.

In addition to the evidence and conclusions of scientific studies, we need to hear what women all over the world have been saying for more than two decades about their experience of water labours and births and their water babies. Time and again we hear that being in water made a huge difference to the quality of this peak experience in their lives. When the birth takes place in water, mothers often say that the baby seems unusually contented and relaxed.

Giving birth naturally can be joyous, mystical and deeply sexual. It is the source, in all its richness, of the profoundest motherly love. When thousands of women are experiencing this, in contrast to what most women say about medically managed births, it is time for the world to sit up and listen.

Our thanks go to the women who have contributed the stories that follow. They are at the same time unique and typical of the shared similar experiences of women all over the world. Because some of them preferred to remain anonymous for the sake of privacy in sharing such intimate experiences, I have made the decision to omit or change names and leave out places. Where the midwife is mentioned by name I have used only an initial.

First baby, born at home

'My feelings about the use of the birth pool at home are nothing short of evangelical. On getting into the pool, I felt instant relief and a change of pace that allowed me to relax, sleep and recover strength over the next hour or so before contractions lengthened to about two and a half minutes each, with virtually no break between. Even during this time, I felt that the pool allowed me to centre my thoughts, relax my body and focus on my breathing. I was able to maintain my calm throughout the labour and birth and had a wonderful experience. My daughter was born underwater and I gently lifted her to the surface between my legs. Having skin-to-skin contact with my baby and partner (who had jumped in the pool after the birth) helped us to feel a family and enjoy our first few moments together in an atmosphere of peace and calm.'

First and second babies, born in hospital

'I wouldn't have chosen waterbirth. The midwife suggested it when I arrived at the hospital. I found the warmth of the water and the buoyancy it offered helped me to relax, especially as you don't know what to expect with a first baby. I could change position easily when the contractions became intense and during transition. I used gas and air but realized that I wasn't really using it properly – hardly breathing it in, just as a way to control my breathing (I'd done a yoga course a few years back). If anything, I found the gas and air made me sleepy and the warmth of the water slowed the process down. The midwife got me out of the water about 40 minutes before my son was born. She said I was too relaxed, which probably meant I wasn't progressing as she'd like. The four-metre walk to the bed was excruciating but seemed to push things along. I was helped onto the bed and gave birth on all fours about 15 minutes later.

'Spending my labour in the pool made the whole process seem timeless. I wasn't obsessed with the clock and the "centimetre per hour" issue. I was very proud of myself – I had my first child in a natural way with hardly any pain relief. No other achievement in my life matched this. (May 2002)

'In September 2003 I had my second baby – only 16 months after the first! I was absolutely sure I wanted to labour in water again. This time I stayed at home for most of my labour. I was 6 cm dilated when I reached the hospital. After initial monitoring I got into the pool at 2.15 a.m., had two very painful contractions, had my show and then my waters broke. I started bearing down very quickly and 10 minutes later my second son was born. It all happened so fast that I don't think being in the water made much difference. I was in transition before I got into the water. However, it was marvellous actually to give birth in the water this time. My little baby shot out very quickly and was brought to the surface looking all clean and pink. He cried as soon as he hit the air, which the midwife said was quite unusual with water babies. This time I didn't need or want any pain relief – I wanted the experience to be crystal clear this time. Even so, looking down at my body and seeing the umbilical cord hanging out was very surreal. I would certainly want a waterbirth again and I'm very grateful to all the midwifery team at the hospital for making my experiences so positive.'

Third baby, born at home

'My waters broke around 1 a.m. and the midwife arrived around 2.30 a.m. She examined me and then left as I was not yet dilated and was having only mild contractions. I put on the TENS machine and started filling the pool. I called the midwife again about an hour later. Contractions were building up, but were still very bearable. A vaginal examination at about 4 a.m. showed I was about 3 cm dilated. After this contractions built up very quickly, and 20 minutes later they were so strong I felt very close to not being able to cope. At around 4.30 a.m. I entered the pool (I had not done so earlier because I didn't want to slow down the labour), and this brought intense relief and made the remainder of the first stage bearable. The second stage went very smoothly. My baby's head came out after a few strong pushes and he floated under water until the next contraction when I pushed him out. My partner was able to watch him at this stage. We both held him and then the midwife passed him through to me (he was born behind me) so that my partner could cut the cord. Using the pool definitely made all the difference and it was a fantastic experience.'

Second baby, born at home

'I first considered a home birth when I realized my local hospital didn't have waterbirth facilities. I was so determined that this time I was going to give it a go as, with my first baby, most choices had been taken out of my hands. I'd been induced at 12 days overdue so wasn't able to have a waterbirth, and I had endured a painful labour lasting three days. This time I figured I had an idea of how bad the pain could get, and if I could move around I would be able to cope. I had always felt comfortable in water. Any period pain, stress or just a bad day at work and I was straight in the bath, so I knew about the healing power of water.

'I felt so sure this baby would also be overdue. My due date came and the house was in chaos. My husband had decided to build decking in the garden, and since the adjoining kitchen/living area was my "birth room", the birth pool was surrounded by power tools and sawdust. I tried not to stress about it and thought perhaps tempting fate was a good thing! I left the builders to it and drove to the airport with my three-year-old son to pick my mum up, as she was arriving to help out with childcare. By the time we got home again I realized that labour was starting, as my niggling back pain seemed to be getting stronger. My husband and mum were a bit sceptical. After all, this was my due date and babies hardly ever come on time, do they?

'That evening, there were two significant and exciting develop-ments: a show, and the decking was finally finished! My partner and mum tidied up and fitted the pool liner as I tried to get my first child to sleep. I walked downstairs again into a beautifully tidy and clean room, with the pool all set up in the centre. I felt ready to get in the water right there and then! We called the maternity unit at about midnight, still not knowing if I would be able to have the waterbirth as planned. I was delighted when both midwives arrived an hour later and saw that J, who had earlier made a home visit to explain the waterbirth procedure to us, was on our case. I was 1^1/2 cm dilated, and they left me with a canis-ter of Entonox and instructions to call back when I felt the labour had progressed. My husband filled the pool and fitted the ther-mal cover. I told both him and mum to go off and get some sleep, as there was no point in everyone feeling exhausted when things really started happening. I used this time to relax and think posi-tively, and enjoyed the sense of being alone and peaceful. I rolled on my birth ball through contractions while singing along to a video of *Funny Girl* and walked around the garden as the sun was coming up – it was going to be a beautiful day.

'I woke my husband as it was starting to get to that stage in labour where nothing felt comfortable. The pain was all in my backside and nothing seemed to help, so I decided to go for a bit of Entonox and keep rolling and rocking on the birth ball with my partner's support and encouragement. It was such a good feeling to have him to hold on to. When the midwives J and B returned, I was only 3 cm dilated, and the next few hours were spent dealing with contractions as the rest of the household was chatting, making tea and toast etc. It was so relaxed and lovely to be home that the time seemed to go very quickly. However, I was thinking I was there for the long haul – after my first experience of birth I really did expect to be there all day and probably the following night. Looking back, I should have realized that all births are very different.

'J knew I was finding it hard to get into a position where I felt comfortable as I was changing how I knelt or lay with every contraction. She kept telling me to just hold on for 10 a.m. when she was going to examine me again, so I had something to aim for and didn't take my eye off the clock! At the "magic hour" I was 5 cm dilated and was told I could get in the pool. The sun was shining on the surface of the water – a most enticing sight and one I'll never forget. I can't explain how I felt as I got in the water. I'd had such high hopes for the pool and was actually scared that I might be disappointed or feel "lost" in there. Would I feel uncomfortable or out of control? No – I can only describe it like a religious experience! My husband had gone back and forth checking on the water temperature, and when I sank back into the warm water I knew immediately that everything was going to be all right. I actually cried with gratitude as I said "thank you, thank you" over again, I don't know to whom. I remember saying it felt like a thousand hands supporting me, holding me up, helping me. I floated on my back and used the time between contractions to find a comfortable "space". It felt good to lean on the rim of the pool with my legs bent to either side a bit like a frog, opening my pelvis as wide as possible. The beauty of it was that it was so easy to change position. If something didn't work for me I could move my legs or get from my back onto my knees in a matter of seconds – try doing that on dry land!

'At this point my friend arrived as planned to offer her support. She'd had her second baby in water so had experience of the whole thing and was able to help me concentrate on my breathing. B went off to the hospital to get more Entonox, but just as she left I told J I had to push. She told me to hang on and pant my way through as she wasn't sure I was ready yet – this was only around 20 minutes after getting in the pool. As I reached under the water I could actually touch the baby's head inside me, so J told me to listen to my body and go with it. I pushed through the burning pain and felt my waters break. With the next contraction I gave a huge push and felt the amazing sensation of the baby being born and shooting through the water behind me. I think it took everyone by surprise and we all cheered – it must have sounded like a party (actually, that's what it felt like!).

'My husband had rushed round and saw our baby calmly float to the surface, so he was first to see that we had a daughter. I can still hear him saying "It's a girl!" with so much emotion and joy in his voice. It was such a great moment. He held her as J suctioned her mouth. She took to the breast immediately as we sat on the step inside the pool and my husband cut the cord. I got out of the pool more easily than I'd expected. J delivered the placenta on dry land as my mum and son arrived back from a trip to the shops and met the new addition to the family for the first time. We were all so happy that we laughed and laughed for ages afterwards, perhaps in a mix of shock, relief and incredulity that it had all been so easy. What an amazing, wonderful, incredible morning!

'We kept the pool for the rest of that week, moved it to the new decking and the family used it to cool off in as the temperature hit 100 degrees. I really did not want to give it back! My daughter is the most "chilled out" baby you could imagine. I'm sure this was because she spent hardly any time squashed in the birth canal and was born into such a homely, calm and stress-free environment. If she cries she only has to be put in the bath and she's immediately relaxed and happy.'

First baby, born in hospital

'After visiting Maidstone Hospital I was keen to have a waterbirth, so I was pleased that the pool was available when I went into labour. My labour was very straightforward. I used a TENS machine when contractions started and gas and air when I reached the hospital. I got into the birthing pool when I was 5 cm dilated. The labour was seven hours in total, three and half hours of which were spent in the pool, including the delivery. The third stage lasted just over 30 minutes. Being in the water helped to ease the pain of contractions and assisted mobility. I'm positive that the mobility that waterbirths allow helped the quick delivery. My son was alert but calm when he was born and the whole experience was less frightening than I had expected it to be. I would definitely recommend a waterbirth to others.'

First baby, born at home, written by dad

'My partner had a complicated 40-hour labour. It was made more painful by compound presentation, in which one of the baby's hands was on the face and the elbow extending out. My partner entered the pool once strong labour was established. Although she reached 9 cm dilation fairly quickly, she laboured for many hours trying to ease the head and hand past the anterior lip [front rim of the almost fully dilated cervix]. She said "the pool was a godsend to help with the pain". Encouraged by the independent midwives in attendance, she tried a variety of positions, both in and out of the pool. Eventually she was able to give birth in the pool, an experience she describes as "amazing for all concerned".'

Second baby, born at home

'The labour of my second child started shortly after midnight, just after I'd gone to bed. The contractions were about five minutes apart and fairly easy to deal with by breathing through them. After a while I woke my partner – I wanted him to fill the pool while I got on with the labour. (I now wish I'd got him up quicker, as then maybe the pool would have been filled in time for me to get in when I needed to). I got up, made a drink and got a plastic sheet, birth mat, sheets and towels ready. Moving about made the contractions more intense and much closer together. I noticed a heightened sense of colour, which made me think I might be further on than I had first thought. I rang the hospital to tell them I was in labour, but didn't feel I needed anyone yet — they sent a midwife anyway, which was a good thing.

'I was 5 cm dilated when she arrived and the labour was cranking up a few gears very quickly. The vaginal examination was long and during a contraction, which made me very nauseous. By 4 a.m. I would have loved to have got in the water, but the pool wasn't full enough and was also too hot. My partner had to stop holding my hands and encouraging me through the contractions to rush up and down stairs with buckets of cold water to top up the pool. Although I wanted to be in the water, I stayed relaxed by rocking in the all-fours position over the birth ball, with the midwife rubbing my back. I could feel the pressure of the water bag, which was hard to cope with. The contractions were only seconds apart now. At last the pool was deep enough and I got in. My next contraction was much more comfortable — I could breathe through it and moan softly, instead of shouting as I had been doing out of the water. The difference was amazing.

'The pressure of the head and water bag was immense now and hard to deal with. I think I had one or two more contractions and then an almighty one that didn't subside. The midwives said "go with what you feel", so I pushed. The baby and water bag moved into the birth canal and the waters broke. I felt I'd exploded! With two or three more pushes, my son was born — 7lb 15oz and very beautiful. We gazed into each other's eyes for a few minutes while he started to breathe. He was very calm and peaceful. The cord was cut when it stopped pulsating and I was asked to leave the pool to deliver the placenta. I gave the baby to his daddy. I leaned over the ball again to deliver the placenta. Our new baby cried a little and his big sister awoke and came downstairs to meet him. Four months on, and our son still really enjoys bath time and swimming.'

Fourth baby, born at home

'I first heard about waterbirth over 20 years ago while in France. There is no other way I would want to give birth to my babies. I have had four children this way – in water and at home. [Giving birth in water] I feel in control of my peace of mind and health. I believe the water helps with relaxation and breathing. It may also be responsible for my not tearing and for the calmness of my babies on entering the world. Dim lighting and the warmth of the water are just what common sense tells me a baby needs in its first moments of life.'

First baby, born in hospital; second baby, born at home

'My first birth experience was a very positive one. It started with my waters breaking. I phoned the hospital and they told me to stay at home unless I started to bleed. Half an hour later, I started bleeding (a show) so we went up to the hospital. We thought we would be sent home again as I had only had half an hour of contractions. After being examined I was 7 cm dilated, and I asked to go into the pool. I stayed there apart from being examined on land at 9 cm and finally 10 cm dilated. It took a further two hours until I gave birth to my daughter in the pool. To deliver the placenta I was on a mat on the floor. I left the ward after six hours as I couldn't get any rest and decided home was a better option!

'My second birth was much more relaxed. I felt completely in control of my pain. I suppose I knew what to expect and how to deal with it. I used a TENS machine which I thought worked well.

'My waters broke while I was resting in bed. The contractions didn't start until half an hour later but we phoned the midwife to let her know. I walked up and down the stairs to try to get things going, and very quickly the contractions became more regular and S, the midwife, arrived. It was so relaxing to see a friendly familiar face. She examined me and I was 7 cm. I then entered the pool. Very quickly (45 minutes) I dilated and felt like pushing. I thought I would have to be taken out to be examined again (which was the practice in the hospital) so I kept asking if I was 9 cm yet! The midwives were smiling and saying "I think so!" When I asked if I could push, S said to "do what your body is telling you", and I just felt such a sense of relief and excitement. The first push my little girl's head came out, and with the second she was here!

'My hospital birth was a very positive one, and when I compare it to my home birth I suppose the hospital birth lacked the caring supportive environment you can create in your own home. I knew the midwife from my first pregnancy so a friendly face put me at ease. I had two midwives in the hospital, and the only one with any waterbirth experience was the student midwife who, while delivering my baby, informed me with a very scared face "I can't do it!" "Yes you can!" I said back, and she did, and my little girl was born. I had a similar experience at home. I found out later that the midwife who delivered the baby had never delivered in water and the other midwife had never attended a home birth. I'm glad I didn't know it beforehand! The midwives at home were more relaxed than the hospital ones and I felt much more at ease. The noticeable difference is the facilities – at home I knew everything was clean and I could use my own shower after the birth, which was definitely lovely!

'Both my births were very positive experiences and I can say that I enjoyed giving birth to both my children. My first birth will always be special as it was such an exciting new experience. You are struck with the awesome miracle of life. The second birth was an amazing experience as well but it was much more personal sharing it with people who really mattered. (My husband and best friend supported me throughout the labour.) The most magical time was when everyone had gone and we sat in bed with our new baby, looking down on the bundle of joy, knowing hours earlier we had been just a family of three. Truly magical and I'm so lucky to have experienced a birth at home and also two births in water. I can't imagine what a dry land birth feels like as I have found the water very comforting and enclosing. It's as if the pool is an extension of your body. I don't know if I have been incredibly lucky but I have not experienced 'pain' as described by some women. In labour I found it very intense but never unbearable. I think the water softens the sharp edges of pain. A lot of the time I felt like I was in a trance looking down on the event. I think the water gave me the amazing feeling of relaxation. I have never taken drugs so I can't compare this feeling to them!

'I also think the water helped to soften the skin for the appearance of the head. My first baby weighed 8lb 6oz and I didn't need any stitches, which I put down to waterbirth and also to perineal massage. Referring to my first birth, my community midwife told me that had I delivered my baby on land, it would have been an assisted delivery for sure. I don't know if there has been a lot of luck involved but I feel the use of water and home make an excellent combination and I would definitely do it again.'

Second baby, born at home

'I waited to get into the pool until I was 6–7 cm dilated. Once in the pool, labour progressed rapidly and just 35 minutes later I felt the urge to push. Our baby was born three and half minutes later. The pain was so well controlled that I couldn't believe the birth of our daughter was imminent; neither could our fantastic independent midwife. The water was so relaxing; this was my only form of pain relief. This birth was so different from my previous experience when I had our son without access to a pool. It was fantastic that our baby daughter entered the world calm and relaxed with no complications – a wonderful experience for all of us.'

First baby, born at home

'I woke up at 3 a.m. on Thursday with contractions. I had a warm bath as contractions picked up and spent time leaning on a birth ball or on my husband. All day the contractions gradually intensified until by 3 p.m. the frequency had increased to three to four minutes apart. The midwife came over as contractions were more regular and intense. She identified the baby as being posterior and told me that labour was likely to be much longer than usual. At 10.15 p.m. I was given an internal and was 4–5 cm dilated. The midwife went home and came back at 2.30 a.m. when I started using the TENS machine. Contractions were one minute long and coming every three minutes by now.

'At 4.30 a.m. I put on music and lit candles and got into the pool. The second midwife arrived at 8 a.m. The contractions became very intense and quite painful due to the baby still being posterior. The pool was really helping. I couldn't take the weight on my joints outside the pool. I was coping but I was extremely exhausted. I needed supporting in the pool due to fatigue. We discussed the options of breaking the waters or going into hospital. I didn't want these. The baby was finally born at 10.43 a.m. Her heart rate didn't rise at all during this long labour. I was so pleased that this was the way I chose to have my baby and that I could spend time bonding with her in the pool afterwards. I eventually delivered the placenta while my husband spent time alone with the baby. I would definitely choose to have a home waterbirth next time. I don't think I could have had a natural birth without the pool to help me because the labour was so long.'

Second baby, born at home

'My first birth two years previously was fairly rapid, so it was no surprise that this one was too. For about a day I was in pre-labour, which stopped at around 10 p.m. I then slept until 1 a.m. when I was woken by a fairly strong contraction. Fortunately, we had set up the birthing room the night before. I used only TENS while on the birthing mat. We called the midwife at about 2 a.m. and she arrived shortly after. I got into the pool at 2.50 a.m. and contractions became very strong quite rapidly. Labour was very intense and at times I found it difficult to cope, but with support from my husband and midwife, I managed to stay on top of it. Alexander was born into my hands in the water at 3.42 a.m. and I brought him to the surface. He breathed fairly quickly and then fell asleep! He woke 20–30 minutes later for a feed. I feel very proud to have birthed a 10lb 6oz baby in such a natural way. It was very empowering.'

First and second babies, born in hospital

'I had wanted a waterbirth even before wanting to have children. It seemed to me a romantic, atavistic experience. One thing I have always been aware of is that one must treat the act of giving birth with an open mind because it can be very unpredictable. Ideally, I wanted a waterbirth but I decided to wait and see how things evolved during labour. As it turned out, I arrived at the hospital fully dilated, and my daughter was born 10 minutes after I reached the delivery room. All in all, the birth of my first child felt far too quick and I had not had time to understand what was happening to me.

'I was determined that the birth of my second child would be a much more positive experience. The midwives at the hospital had been warned that this time round I would ring to announce I was coming in so that they might prepare the birthing pool for me.

'Although my second labour was also quick, I did manage to get to the hospital two hours before giving birth. The pool was ready for me, but I was not sure whether I would use it. I started by sitting on a large ball, which helped as it relieved some of the pressure on the pelvic floor. All the time I was eyeing the pool, and half an hour later I ventured inside.

'The results were immediate. The water worked against gravity, relieving the pelvic floor even more than the ball had. It also acted as a buffer zone against the pain. It felt wonderful to be able to move slowly inside the water. I felt very contained and safe, but also very fluid and agile. I could move freely and without interruption. I imagine that the baby in my womb could feel this too. The midwife reinforced my sense of security and containment with her quiet authority, her empathy and warmth. She knew exactly when to guide me, and when to simply let me be. She helped make my second labour the wonderful experience it was, and I am utterly grateful to her for this.

'When I finally pushed my baby out, he came straight up through the water and into my arms. It was as though he and I were both floating inside a larger womb. His entrance into the world, it seems to me, was gentle and warm, and as reassuring as it can be for a newborn. He did not have the shock of suddenly finding himself naked, in the light, on dry land after nine months of darkness, movement and water. The change was gradual: first the light, then a wider embrace, a different kind of water, and then, finally, the air. Now when I put him in the water, he becomes very quiet and pensive. I like to think that perhaps he remembers something of his coming into the world.'

Second baby, born in hospital

'My son showed no sign of arriving on his due date, despite weeks of niggles and pre-labour. I got very tired and fed up. I didn't want a 'sweep' as I'd been having too much discomfort in my pubis and around the cervix. So I took homeopathic remedies and put clary sage essential oil in my bath and in a massage oil. On the day before the birth, I woke up at 4 a.m. I felt tightenings with slight pain every 10 minutes for a couple of hours, then very irregularly – sometimes every four minutes, then nothing for 30 minutes. I went to the birth unit at 9 a.m. I had the foetal heart monitor on for 15 minutes with infrequent mild contractions. At about 9.45 a.m. I walked to the lounge. As I walked I had a couple of huge contractions close together. I felt a bit faint. The midwife put on the TENS machine but it was a bit too late – it seemed I was ready to deliver.

'I lay on my side for about 10 minutes and then got into the water because the pains were quite bad. Amazingly, the contractions stopped for about 10–15 minutes. I was able to calm down and talk normally about how to deliver. The midwife advised me to go at my own speed, pushing as and when I wanted. Contractions resumed very gradually. One or two were very severe; the rest were mild to moderate. The atmosphere was very relaxed. The midwife said we could "afford the time", and this was great advice. I had pain in my back but I was able to stretch in the water to stop it. I could feel the head, and when I was ready I gave a push so the head appeared with the sac intact. I held on to my partner with arms straight and sat back. As I finally delivered my baby, the waters broke. He seemed to slither and swim and was very relaxed. He started to feed at once and stayed attached for quite a time as he went from greyish to pinkish. Then my partner cut the cord and I delivered the placenta. A remarkable labour – I didn't know they existed like that!'

First baby – hospital birth unit

'I had been absolutely terrified of childbirth since I was four years old when I saw a picture of a woman giving birth which I was both traumatized and mesmerized by. I was in a state of fear for most of my pregnancy and this included panic attacks and intense feelings of claustrophobia, particularly in the last trimester. I worked through how I could manage by talking about my fears in therapy and I also did a course in self-hypnosis and visualization that was incredibly helpful. I did lots of yoga and meditation and was very careful about my diet.

'There was no way I could have a home birth because I was so scared and my partner is very squeamish. I went to visit my local hospital and all they talked about were all the things that could go wrong. One male midwife even demonstrated the use of a ventouse on his own bald head. I was horrified and left in tears, thinking I would have to have an elective caesarean. Then I found a hospital birth unit that specialized in active and water births. I liked their ethos and was attracted to the idea of a water birth. I love baths – I often have two in a day. It's the first thing I do if I am in any pain or discomfort. I spent most of my childhood summers by a beautiful river in Wales. I used this imagery as a safe place in my visualization and so it made a lot of sense for me to want to give birth in water.

'I went into labour two weeks early and had what I would call twinges at first. I wasn't sure what was happening. It felt like my maternity trousers were too tight and were pinching me so I changed into some tracksuit bottoms. I kept thinking, it can't be this, this thing I have been fearing all my life! I couldn't work out what all the fuss was about. I had some friends come over in the evening for a Chinese take away, and I was actually in labour, although I didn't really quite realize it. We laughed a lot and I kept leaving the table to roll over the birth ball while my friends rubbed my back. At around 10.00 p.m. my partner came home from a work dinner and my friends left. He kept saying, "Let's not go into hospital yet – it's probably a false alarm", and I was convinced we would be turned away and told to come back next week and that I was only imagining it. So then I had a bath and the contractions gradually became a lot more intense.

'My partner was very tired and needed to rest and was struggling to stay awake to time the contractions. Deciding I needed more support, I phoned the birth unit and they thought I had a long way to go and suggested I start using the TENS machine, which I did. They said I should come in whenever I wanted and that they would give me a room even though I sounded like I still had a long way to go.

'We arrived at 1.00 a.m. in the morning. The midwife examined my notes and they said "fear of childbirth, panic attacks, claustrophobia, partner liable to faint". She seemed calm but I guess she was bracing herself for a long night! Then she examined me, found I was 8 cm dilated, and said "Your baby is nearly here." I burst into tears and cried out, "Turn on the taps and get the pool filled!"

'The sound of the pool filling up was just great. The midwife gave my legs a lovely massage with essential oils while I sat on the loo. I was still using the TENS, I had a relaxation tape playing meditation music that I had worked with in my pregnancy and the room was lit by candles. I breathed through the contractions and visualised being in the river to the sound of the pool filling up. I also used lots of positive affirmations like "I can do this, I'm doing really well." Then I got into the pool at about 2.00 a.m. and my baby was born by 3.30 a.m. in the water. So I went through the last centimetre of dilation, the transition and the pushing in the water. It was just wonderful. I hung onto the sides and was in a squatting position. The midwives examined me with a mirror and a torch – their skill was amazing.

'The pushing lasted abut half an hour and was the worst bit for me, with the head coming in and out with the contractions. The pool gave me my happiest environment for my worst pain. The midwife was incredibly strict at the end about when I should push, to great effect as I had no tear or even a graze. At that point I asked for pain relief and she said that there wasn't any time to go looking for the gas and air and that anyway I had done so well so far and the end was so close. And then out he came. Once the head was out it took just one more contraction to deliver his body and she put him into my arms. I looked down and saw these huge balls and I was completely shocked because I was convinced I was having a girl. I gave birth to the placenta on land out of the water and drank some sweet tea because I was shaking a bit. I was euphoric – I felt like a goddess. I totally marvelled at what my body had done – a birth beyond my wildest, wildest dreams!'

Resources

Useful Addresses

UK and Europe

Active Birth Centre
25 Bickerton Road
London N19 5JT
Tel: +44 (0)20 72816760
Fax: +44 (0)20 72638098
www.activebirthcentre.com
For birth pool hire, water birth
information, workshops and
resources

Active Birth Pools
25 Bickerton Road
London N19 5JT
Tel/fax: +44 (0)20 72721311
www.activebirthpools.com
Europe's leading installed and
portable birth pool supplier

AIMS (Association for Improvements
in the Maternity Services)
5 Ann's Court
Grove Road
Surrey KT6 4BE
Tel: +44 (0)870 765 1453

Fax: +44 (0)870 765 1454
info@aims.org.uk
www.aims.org.uk

Albany Midwives Practice
Peckham Pulse
10 Melon Road
London SE15 5QN
Tel: 020 75254995
E-mail:
albanymidwives@ukonline.co.uk
A self-employed and self-managed
group contracted into the NHS who
practise individual caseload
midwifery in a socially deprived
inner-city area.

ARM (Association of
Radical Midwives)
6 Springfield Road
Kings Heath
Birmingham B14 7DS
Tel: +44 (0)121 444 2257
www.radmid.demon.co.uk

Doula UK
PO Box 26678
London N14 4WB
E-mail: info@doula.org.uk
www.doula.org.uk

Edgware Birth Centre
Edgware Community Hospital
Burnt Oak Broadway
Edgware
Middlesex HA8 0AD
Tel: 020 87326777
Fax: 020 87326773
www.birthcentre.co.uk

Hospital of St John and
   St Elizabeth Birth Unit
60 Grove End Road
London NW8 9NH
Tel: 020 72865126
www.hje.org.uk

HNE Diagnostics
35 Portanoor Road,
Cardiff CF2 2 HB
For waterproof heart monitors

Independent Midwives Association
1 The Great Quarry
Guildford
Surrey GUI 3XN
Tel: +44 (0)1483 821104
E-mail: c.f.winter@city.ac.uk
www.independentmidwives.org.uk

Maidstone Hospital
Hermitage Lane
Maidstone
Kent ME16 9QQ
Tel: +44 (0)1622 729000

Dr Gowri Motha
Jeyarani Centre
34 Cleveland Road
South Woodford
London E18 2AL
Tel: +44 020 8530 1146
Email: gowrimotha@jeyarani.com
www.jeyarani.com

MIDIRS
9 Elmdale Road
Bristol BS8 1SL
Tel: +44 (0)117 925 1791, 0800 581
009 (UK only)
Fax: +44 (0)117 925 1792
www.midirs.org

National Childbirth Trust
Alexandra House
Oldham Terrace
London W3 6NH
Tel: +44 (0)870 444 8707
www.nct-online.org

Oxford Instruments UK
1 Kimber Road
Abingdon
Oxon OX14 1BZ
Tel: +44 (0)1235 533433
Fax: +44 (0)1235 559745
www.oxinst.com (international)
For sonicaid waterproof fetal
heart monitors

Primal Health Research Centre
59 Roderick Road
London NW3 2NP
Fax: +44 (0)20 7267 5123
E-mail: modent@aol.com
www.birthworks.org/primal health/

Royal College of Midwives
15 Mansfield Street
London W1G 9NH
Tel: +44 (0)20 7312 3535
Fax: +44 (0)20 7312 3536
E-mail:info@rcm.org.uk
www.rcm.org.uk

Shaw Method (of swimming)
27 Greenway Close
London N20 8ES
Tel: +44 (0)20 8446 9442
Fax: +44 (0)20 8632 9570
www.artofswimming.com

Silverlea Textiles
Units 3 and 4 Silverhills Buildings
Silverhills Road
Decoy Industrial Estate
Newton Abbot TQ12 5LZ
Tel: +44 (0)1626 331 655
Fax: +44 (0)1626 335 171
For lifting slings

Watsu for Pregnancy Training
Watsu Instituut Nederland
Saskia van Rees
Scheyvenhofweg 12
6093 PR Heythuysen
The Netherlands
Tel: +31 (0)495 65 1735
Fax: +31 (0)495 65 2375
Email: info@watsu.nl
www.watsu.nl

Viveka
Women's Health Centre
27A Queen's Terrace
London NW8 6EA
Tel: +44 020 7483 0099
Fax: +44 020 7483 3988
Email: vision@viveka.co.uk
www.viveka.co.uk

US

Global Maternal/Child Health
   Association, Inc.
PO Box 1400
Wilsonville
Oregon 97070
Tel: +1 503 673-0026
E-mail: info@waterbirth.org
www.waterbirth.org
This comprehensive site contains
references to major organizations
and suppliers in the field of
waterbirth in the US, Canada and
international

American College of Nurse Midwives
(ACNM)
818 Connecticut Ave
NW Ste 900
Washington DC 20006
Tel: +1 202 728-9868
Fax: +1 202 728-9860
E-mail: info@acnm.org

Birth Works
PO Box 2045
Medford
NJ 08055
Tel: +1 888 862-4784
E-mail: cathyd@birthworks.org
www.birthworks.org

Coalition for Improving Maternity
   Services (CIMS)
PO Box 2346
Ponte Vedra Beach
FL 32004
Tel: +1 904 285-0028
E-mail: cimshome@bellsouth.net

Doulas of North America (DONA)
PO Box 626
Jasper
IN 47547
Toll-Free: 888 788-DONA
Fax: +1 812 634-1491
e-mail: Doula@DONA.org
www.DONA.org

Worldwide Aquatic Bodywork Assn
PO Box 889
Middletown
CA 95461
Tel: +1 707 987-3801
E-mail: info@waba.edu
www.waba.edu
Watsu for pregnancy information

Karil Daniels
Point of View Productions
2477 Folsom Street
San Francisco
CA 94110

Tel: +1 415 821-0435
Fax: +1 415 821-0434
Email:Karel@waterbirthinfo.com
www.waterbirthinfo.com
Award winning video on waterbirth.
National and international
contact list

Lamaze International
2025 M Street
Suite 800
Washington DC 20036-3309
Tel: +1 202 367-1128
Toll-Free: (800) 368-4404
Fax: +1 202 367-2128
www.lamaze-childbirth.com

Midwives Alliance of North America
   (MANA)
PO Box 1121
Bristol
VA 24203
Tel: +1 615 764-5561
www.midwife.org

National Association of Childbearing
   Centers
3123 Gottschall Road
Perkiomenville
Pennsylvania 18074
Tel: +1 215 234-8068
Fax: +1 215 234-8829
E-mail:
ReachNACC@BirthCenters.org
www.birthcenters.org

Australia and New Zealand

Birth International
ACE Graphics
PO Box 366
Camperdown
N.S.Wales 1450
Australia

Tel 0061 (0) 295642322
Fax 0061 (0) 295642388
email info@birthinternational.com
website www.acegraphics.com.au

Portable pool hire companies

UK

Active Birth Centre
25 Bickerton Road
London N19 5JT
Tel: +44 (0)20 7281 6760
Fax: +44 (0)20 7263 8098
www.activebirthcentre.com
Leading nationwide birth pool hire
service and booking service for
trainings and workshops with Janet
Balaskas

BirthWorks
58 Shalmsford Street
Chartham
Canterbury
Kent CT4 7RH
Tel/fax: +44 (0)1227 730081
www.birthworks.co.uk

BubbaTubs
30 Albemarle Ave
Cheshunt
Hertfordshire EN8 0EY.
Tel/fax: +44 (0)1992 302449
www.bubbatubs.com

Gentle Water
50 North Way
Lewes
East Sussex BN7 1DJ
Tel: +44 (0)1273 474927
www.gentlewater.co.uk

Splashdown Water Birth Services Ltd
17 Wellington Terrace
Harrow on the Hill
Middlesex HA1 3EP
Tel: +44 (0)870 444 4403
www.splashdown.org.uk

US

Global Maternal/Child Health
Association, Inc. PO Box 1400
Wilsonville Oregon 97070
Tel: +1 503 673-0026
E-mail: info@waterbirth.org
www.waterbirth.org
Provides US and international
waterbirth resource and pool hire
contacts.

Further reading

Balaskas, Janet, *New Active Birth*, HarperCollins, 1989

Balaskas, Janet, *Natural Baby*, Gaia Books, 2001

Balaskas, Janet, *New Natural Pregnancy*, Gaia Books, 1998

Balaskas, Janet, *Preparing for Birth with Yoga*, Thorsons, 2003

Bertram, Lakshmi, *Choosing Waterbirth*, Hampton Roads Publishing Company, 2000

Beech, Beverley A. Lawrence (ed.), *Water Birth Unplugged*, Books for Midwives, 1996

Dull, Harold, *Watsu – Freeing the Body in Water*, Worldwide Aquatic Bodywork Assn., 1997

England, Pam, *Birthing From Within*, Partera Press, 1998

Freedman, Françoise, *Aqua Yoga*, Lorenz Books 2000

Garland, Dianne, *Waterbirth: An Attitude to Care*, Books for Midwives, 2000

Gordon, Yehudi, *Birth and Beyond*, Vermilion, 2002

Gurmukh, *Bountiful, Beautiful, Blissful*, St Martin's Press, 2003

Harper, Barbara, *Gentle Birth Choices*, Healing Arts Press, 1994

Heston, Lauren, *Water Baby*, Element Children's Books, 1999

Johnson, Jessica and Odent, Michel, *We are all Water Babies*, Dragon's World Ltd, 1994

Kitzinger, Sheila, *The New Pregnancy and Childbirth*, Dorling Kindersley, 2003

Leboyer, Frederick, *Birth Without Violence*, Inner Traditions, 1995

Lichy, Dr Roger and Herzberg, Eileen, *The Waterbirth Handbook*, Gateway Books, 1993

Morgan, Elaine, *The Descent of Woman*, Souvenir Press, 1985

Morgan, Elaine, *The Aquatic Ape Hypothesis*, Souvenir Press, 1997

Napierala, Susanna, *Waterbirth: A Midwife's Perspective*, Greenwood Press 1994

Odent, Dr Michel, *Water and Sexuality*, Arkana, 1990

Odent, Dr Michel, *The Scientification of Love*, Free Association Books, 1999

Odent, Dr Michel, *The Nature of Birth and Breast-feeding*, Bergin and Garvey, 1992

Odent, Dr Michel, *The Farmer and the Obstetrician* Free Association Books, 2002

Odent, Dr Michel, *The Caesarean*, Free Association Books, 2004

Rachana, Shivam, *Lotus Birth*, Greenwood Press, 2000

Ray, Sondra, *Ideal Birth, Celestial Arts*, 1985

Van Rees, Saskia, et al, *Women Giving Birth*, Celestial Arts, 1992

Ryrie, Charlie, *The Healing Energies of Water*, Gaia Books, 1998

Shaw, Steven, and D'Angour, Armand, *The Art of Swimming*, Cygnus Books, 1996

Sidenbladh, Erik, *Water Babies*, A & C Black, 1983

Vincent Priya, Jacqueline, *Birth Traditions and Modern Pregnancy Care*, Element, 1992

Index

accessories 101, 157
accountability 229
Active Birth Centre 207
Active Birth Movement
    271
active phase 63–4, 164
activists 16
acupressure 151
acupuncture 83, 112, 140,
    255
adrenaline 40, 41, 42, 43,
    44, 181
afterpains 192, 256
AIMS 96
Albany Midwifery Practice
    14
Alexander Technique 129
alpha brainwaves 48
amniotic fluid 67, 137, 170,
    187, 252–3
amniotic sac 26, 266
amniotomy 253
anaesthetics 266, 267
anecdotal evidence
    271–94
antenatal classes 78, 88,
    118
anterior lip 180
anxiety 57–8
apnoea 208
Apsu 25
aquatic mammals 31–2
aromatherapy 94, 112,
    125–7, 151–3, 164, 176
artificial rupture of
    membranes (ARM) 253
assisted deliveries 236,
    243, 261–4
attachment parenting 38
attitude 17–18

audits 20
augmenting labour
    249–61
Australia 9, 21, 91, 98
Austria 21
Ayurveda 29

back strain 228–9
backache 60–1, 244
baptism 27
bathing 125
Belgium 9
benefits of waterbirth
    34–73
birth 78–9, 180–91
    balls 115–16, 190
    centres 97–8, 145
    environment 45–7
    positions 189–91
    reclaiming 4
    reflex 43–4, 248
    stools 145
    stories 271–94
birthing pools
    benefits 73
    booking 100
    entering 160–2, 206–7
    filling 155–7
    getting out 173–4, 225–6
    guidelines 203, 204–26
    hiring 92–101, 207
    hospitals 95
    labour 164–9
    leaving 192–4
    midwives 203, 226
    positions 82
    trials 128–9, 134
blood loss 222–2, 226
blood pressure 64–5, 81,
    86

labour 161
    medical backup 237,
        242–3
    midwives 210–11, 222–3,
        226
Boulvain, M. 56
breastfeeding 35–6, 38, 44
    birth 191, 194, 198
    caesareans 268
    medical backup 239, 261
    preparation 106
breathing
    awareness exercise 110
    mechanisms 20–1, 32
    reflex 39, 216
breech position 82, 114,
    262
British Medical Journal
    (BMJ) 11
buoyancy 56, 58–9,
    129–30, 172, 211
bupivacaine 244

caesarean section 46, 82,
    84–7
    labour 138, 170
    medical backup 242–3,
        250, 254, 256, 262–3,
        265–8
    midwives 202
catecholamines 40, 56, 63
catheters 243, 266
Central America 5
central nervous system
    51
cephalic presentation 60,
    77, 81, 83
cervix 135–6, 141–3, 146
    labour 172–3, 178, 192
    massage 255

medical backup 234, 237, 246, 253
midwives 206
cetaceans 32
Chamberlen, Peter 4
Charles I 4
childcare 134
China 27, 29
Christians 25, 26, 27
Chumash dancers 5
complementary therapies 80, 112, 142, 147–55, 255
conception 1–2, 35
conserving energy 166–7
contractions 37–44, 48, 54–5
  assisted delivery 262
  birth 159–69, 182–3, 187–91
  delivery 215–16
  induction 255
  labour 134, 137, 141–8, 152
  placenta 198
  prostaglandin 253
  transition 178–80
  in water 58–9, 62
contraindications 80–1, 83, 88
counselling 120, 264, 269
cranial osteopathy 112, 140, 264
crowning 187–8, 189, 257, 260
Cumberledge, Baroness 17

Daniels, Karil 15
death 10–11, 22, 42
dehydration 206
demerol 237
Denmark 21

Department of Health 10, 13
depth of water 174, 205–6
Dhanjal, – 70
dilation 41, 50, 63, 135
  labour 142–3, 160, 162, 172–3, 178, 180
  medical backup 234, 237, 241, 246
  midwives 206–7
disabilities 65–6
dive reflex 21, 66–9, 187, 208, 214–15
doctors 9, 12–17, 21, 42, 48
  medical backup 261, 264
  role 67, 82, 87
dolphins 9, 31, 32
double-blind trials 19
doulas 16, 46, 98–9, 175
drug addiction 239
due date 138–40, 249, 250–1
Dull, Harold 122
duration of labour 62–4
dystocia 52–3, 216–18

early labour 141–7, 154
Edgware Birth Centre, London 13–14, 98
Egyptians 5, 25, 26
ejaculation 36, 42
Eldering, Gerd 21
emotions 116–22, 191, 264
endorphins 36, 55, 63, 147, 153, 255, 256
entonox 247
environment 62, 90, 94, 189, 197
epidurals 14, 46, 52, 65, 80
  fever 244–5

labour 148, 160, 164
  medical backup 236, 239–46, 254, 256, 262–3, 266–7
  midwives 202
episiotomies 13, 202, 224, 257–61
equipment 101
ergometrine 256
essential oils 125–7, 148, 151–3, 164
estimated due date (EDD) 138–40, 249–51
ethnicity 251
Europe 4, 6, 9, 16, 29, 262
examinations 210, 212
exercises 83
  breathing awareness 110
  partner 123–4
  water 130–1
expectations 121–2, 201, 268–9
expulsive reflex 181–2, 259

faintness 210–11, 223
Family Birthing Centre, Upland 15
fear 118–19, 147, 226
fitness 112–13
flotation tanks 30
foetal distress 68, 81, 86
  labour 170
  medical backup 238, 243–5, 255, 263, 265
  midwives 207, 209, 225
foetal monitoring 40, 50, 65
  labour 170–3
  medical backup 252, 255
  midwives 207–9, 211
  role 68, 94

foetus ejection reflex 42–4, 181, 212
football hold 268
forceps 242, 260–4, 267
France 4, 7–8
frank breech 83

Ganges, River 26
Garden Hospital 12
Garland, Dianne 12, 207, 217, 229
gas and air 164, 236–7, 247–9, 261
Gate Control theory 54
General Hospital, Pithiviers 8, 10, 15
Genesis 25
gentle birthing 71–2
Gilbert, Ruth E. 22, 219
Global Maternal/Child-health Association 16
gloves 227, 228
Gordon, Yehudi 12, 204, 208–9
gravity 59, 83, 108, 113
labour 173–4, 189, 197
medical backup 234, 246, 255, 262
Greeks 5, 29
guidelines 12, 81–2, 137
induction 255–6
labour 142, 163–4
medical pain relief 239, 245–6, 249
midwives 201, 203–26, 230

Harbin Hot Springs, California 122
Hardy, Alister 30
Harmsworth, – 70
Harper, Barbara 4, 5–6, 15

Hawaii 5
healing 119–20, 264, 269
hepatitis 227–8
Hindus 26, 27
Hippocrates 29, 233
hire companies 16, 58, 63, 92, 96, 99–101
history of waterbirths 1–23
HIV/AIDS 81, 227
home births 4, 11, 16–17, 41
choosing 85, 88–93
labour 134, 137, 155, 174
role 41
homeopathy 12, 83, 94, 101
labour 134, 148–51, 164
medical backup 255, 264
midwives 211
preparations 112
hormones 7–8, 35–41, 46–7, 63
labour 136, 178, 181, 195, 198
medical backup 254
midwives 212
preparations 109, 113, 116
role 63, 75
Hospital of St John and St Elizabeth, London 12, 204, 219–21
hospitals 3–4, 8–9, 12, 14
birth 41, 46, 51
history 16, 18
labour 151, 155
medical backup 267
midwives 203
role 81–2, 85–6, 88–9, 93–7, 101
hydrotherapy 29, 48, 78
hypertension 65, 210

hyperthermia 206
hypnotherapy 56, 120
hypothalamus 36–7
hypoxia 68, 208, 209

independent midwives 8, 11, 57, 85, 91
India 26, 29, 107
induction 14, 38, 52, 137
natural 139–41
role 241–3, 249–61, 265
Institute of Child Health, London 22
instrumental deliveries 236, 261–4
inter-uterine life 2
International Water Birth Conference 17, 208
interventions 10, 13, 18–20, 38
facilities 86, 98
role 79, 202, 234, 269, 272
unnecessary 46, 52–3
ions 28
Italy 21

James I 4
Japan 9, 21, 251
Jews 25, 27
John Radcliffe Hospital, Oxford 20, 67
Johnson, Paul 20–1, 67

key studies 20–3
Kings College, London 257
kneeling 184–5

labour duration 62–4
labour pains 146–7
Laing, R.D. 2
land births 188–91

latching on 198, 245, 268
laughing gas 247
Leboyer, Frederick 2–3, 78
Lichy, Roger 11–12
lift out deliveries 263
limbic system 125
local health authorities 90–1
Long, Louise 257
lotus birth 195
Lourdes, France 26

McRoberts position 217
Maidstone Hospital 12, 229
Malta 9, 21
Maoris 5
massage 151–3, 164
maxolon 238
Mecca, Saudi Arabia 26
meconium 81, 170, 208–9, 226
medical backup 232–70
meditation 109–11, 117, 124, 127–8, 133–4
Melzack, Ronald 54
menstruation 5, 36, 54
meperidine 51, 81, 237
meptazinol 237
meptid 237
meridians 151
Mesopotamia 25, 27
metoclopramine 238
mid-cavity deliveries 263
Mikvah 27
mobility 59–60
Moon 27
morbidity rates 22
Morgan, Elaine 30–1
mortality rates 22
motherhood 35, 102–31
Muscat, Josie 9

Muslims 26, 27
Myers, Estelle 9

Naegele's rule 251
narcotic analgesics 236, 237–9
National Health Service (NHS) 12–13, 16–17, 91
National Perinatal Epidemiology Unit, Oxford 12
Native Americans 27
neo-cortex 36–7, 40
New Zealand 9
newborn babies 1–3, 21, 25
  medical intervention 238–9, 244–5
  polycythaemia 220
  treatment 193, 197–9
  water benefits 67–8, 71–2
Newton, Niles 42
Nile, River 26
non-intervention 50
North Pole 9
Norway 9
Nu 25, 26

observations 209–10
obstetricians 21, 80–1, 84, 86, 87
  labour 192
  medical backup 250, 257, 263, 266
  midwives 202–4, 221
  role 86–7
occiput anterior 60, 82
occiput posterior (OP) 61, 82, 262, 263
Odent, Michel 7–11, 15, 31, 37

birth 180, 180–1, 181
breech babies 83
caesarean sections 85
environment 46
hormones 36, 39–43
labour duration 62
relaxation 48
oestrogen 38
omega-3 fatty acids 31
one-to-one midwife schemes 17, 57, 202
O'Neill, Anita 12, 205
orgasm 36, 36–7, 37
Ostend, Belgium 9
Otigbah, – 70
ovulation 36
oxygen shortage 68
oxytocin 36–9, 41, 44, 55, 94
  labour 140, 142, 161, 173–4, 192, 194–5
  medical backup 246, 251, 256
  midwives 207, 214
  wave 63–4

paediatricians 11–12, 22, 81, 244
pagans 26
pain relief 8, 21, 49, 51–9
  coping strategies 78, 80, 88
  labour 142, 148, 153–4, 160, 162–4
  medical 234–49, 254, 267
  midwives 225
pain threshold 53
Parliamentary Health Select Committee 17
partners 46, 88, 94, 96, 99

labour 143, 164, 174–80,
190
medical backup 245,
266, 269
preparations 120–1,
123–4, 126
squatting 185–6
Patanjali 107
pelvic floor exercises 260
perineum 187, 215, 222,
224–5
medical backup 240,
257–9, 261
midwives 224–5
personal experiences
271–94
pethidine 51, 55, 81, 164,
237, 239
physiotherapists 29
Pithiviers, France 8, 10, 15
pitocin 38, 62, 160, 243,
246, 253–6
pituitary gland 37, 63,
63–4, 64, 109
placebo effect 19
placenta 37, 39, 44–5, 55,
67
abruption 265
delivery 188–9, 191–6,
198, 216, 219–23,
256–8
labour 143, 174, 177, 188
praevia 86, 265
polycythaemia 193, 220
Ponette, Herman 9
positions 4, 8, 59–60, 78,
82–4
birth 179–80, 183–7,
189–91
delivery 213–14
McRoberts 217
pool 165–6

preparations 108, 128
upright 144–6, 183, 207,
221, 234, 246, 255, 259,
271
post-partum haemorrhage
222–3
postnatal checkups 267–8
postnatal depression 264
power of water 24–33
pre-eclampsia 65, 242,
265
pre-labour 135–41
precautions 227–8
pregnancy 122–31
premature babies 7, 239,
251
Priessnitz, Vincent 29
primal period 1
primates 30–1
privacy 45–7, 50, 57, 90, 92
labour 143, 165–6
medical backup 222
Priya, Jacqueline Vincent
138–9
prolactin 36
prolapse 260
prostaglandin 38, 67,
140–1, 252–3, 255–6
prostaglandin E2 39
psychology 2

randomized control tr[...]
(RCT) 19, 52
rebirthing 30, 1[...]
reclaiming o[...] [...]
reduced [...]ty 65–6
reflexo[...] [...]40
relati[...] [...]nips 120–1
rel[...] [...]on 53, 56, 58, 78
[...]ur 147, 160
[...]edical backup 258
midwives 210

preparations 127–8
research 18–23, 48, 63, 90
midwives 201, 230
role 242, 244, 248, 272
resuscitation 209
reviews 20
ring of fire 187
risks 22
rooting reflex 198
Rosenthal, Michael 16
Royal College of Midwives
10, 13–14, 77, 95, 201
Royal College of
Obstetricians and
Gynaecologists 221
rupture of membranes 52,
77, 137, 140, 253
Russia 3, 7, 21

safety precautions 131
science 18–19, 21, 25,
Scott, Patricia 12, 2[...]
221
second opinio[...]
second sta[...] [...], 263
sedation[...]
Selke[...] [...]1
Sh[...] [...]d 129
[...]0, 112, 122, 140,
[...]
[...]oulder dystocia 52–3,
216–18
show 136
Sidenbladh, Erik 7
skeletal pain 65–6
sleep patterns 134
South Pacific 5
Southampton General
Hospital 52
special care rates 22
spinal anaesthesia
239–46, 263

spinal problems 65–6
squatting 86, 114–15, 129, 145
  labour 166, 176, 183, 185–6, 190
  medical backup 259
  midwives 213
standing up 186–7
Staritsky, Jennifer 12
starting labour 132–57
stirrups 261
structural engineers 93
Sumerians 27
supplements 134–5, 137–8, 141, 167, 211
sutures 224–5
Sweden 10, 21, 160, 239
swimming 129–31, 134, 140
Switzerland 50, 122
Syntocinon 38, 62, 160, 226, 243, 246, 253–6
syntometrine 221, 223, 256

tears 21, 69–70, 187, 224, 258–9
TENS machines 54, 94, 148, 153–5, 163–4
Thai massage 112, 151
Tiamat 25
Tjarkovsky, Igor 3, 7, 67
Tjarkovsky, Veta 7
Tookey, Pat A. 22, 219
traditional Chinese medicine 29
training 14–15, 46, 91, 95
transition 41–3, 178–80, 212

ultrasound scans 250, 252
umbilical cord 22, 177, 192–6

circulation 67
guidelines 217–20
medical backup 267
midwives 214, 216
United Kingdom (UK) 10–17, 21
  choices 84, 87–8, 90–1, 95, 98
  medical backup 247, 262
United States (US) 4, 9, 15–16
  choices 84, 91, 98
  conference 21
  medical backup 237, 243
  midwives 203
  pain relief 51
upright positions 59–60, 144–6
  labour 183
  medical backup 234, 246, 255, 259, 271
  midwives 207, 221

vacuum extraction 260, 261
vasopressin 64
vasopressors 243
Vedas 26
ventouse 260–3

Wall, Patrick 54
water
  contamination 224
  cultural associations 26–7
  depth 156–7, 174, 205–6
  embolism 193, 221–2
  exercise 130–1
  healing energy 29–30
  human affinity 30–1
  inhalation 22, 32, 67–9, 208–9

physical qualities 28–9
power 24–33
role 47–9
temperature 67–9, 83, 156, 174, 205–6, 212
waterbirth
  benefits 34–73
  choosing 74–101
  criteria 77
  delivery 214–16
  history 1–23
  labour 158–99
  medical backup 232–70
  midwives 158–99
  origins 5–6
  personal experiences 271–94
  pioneers 7–8
  power 24–33
  preparation 102–31
  spread 9–11
  starting labour 132–57
  United Kingdom 11–15
  United States 15–16
Waterbirth International 16
waters breaking 137–41
Watsu 30, 122–3
websites 106
Weisel, Serge 56, 64
whales 31, 32
Winterton Report 17
workshops 204, 225

yin-yang 27
yoga 56–7, 88, 104–9, 112–13
  labour 133, 140
  medical backup 258
  midwives 229
  preparations 117–19, 123, 130

S P E C I A L   O F F E R

Order these selected Thorsons and Element titles direct from the publisher and receive £1 off each title! Visit www.thorsonselement.com for additional special offers.

Free post and packaging for UK delivery (overseas and Ireland, £2.00 per book).

NCT Breastfeeding for Beginners Caroline Deacon (ISBN 0-00-713608-0)	£6.99 - £1 = £5.99
NCT Help Your Baby to Sleep Penney Hames (ISBN 0-00-713605-6)	£6.99 - £1 = £5.99
NCT First Foods and Weaning Ravinder Lilly (ISBN 0-00-713607-2)	£6.99 - £1 = £5.99
NCT Potty Training Heather Welford (ISBN 0-00-713606-4)	£6.99 - £1 = £5.99
NCT Toddler Tantrums Penney Hames (ISBN 0-00-713609-9)	£6.99 - £1 = £5.99

Place your order by post, phone, fax, or email, listed below. Be certain to quote reference code **713P** to take advantage of this special offer.

Mail Order Dept. (REF: **713P**)   Email: customerservices@harpercollins.co.uk
HarperCollins*Publishers*   Phone: 0870 787 1724
Westerhill Road   Fax: 0870 787 1725
Bishopbriggs G64 2QT

Credit cards and cheques are accepted. Do not send cash. Prices shown above were correct at time of press. Prices and availability are subject to change without notice.

BLOCK CAPITALS PLEASE

Name of cardholder   _____

Address of cardholder   _____

                                       _____

                                       _____

Postcode   _____

Delivery address (if different)

                                       _____

                                       _____

                                       _____

Postcode   _____

I've enclosed a cheque for £_____, made payable to HarperCollins*Publishers*, or please charge my Visa/MasterCard/Switch (circle as appropriate)

Card Number: _____

Expires: __/__   Issue No: __/__   Start

Date: __/__

Switch cards need an issue number or start date validation.

Make
www.thorsonselement.com
your online sanctuary

Get online information, inspiration and guidance to help you on the path to physical and spiritual well-being. Drawing on the integrity and vision of our authors and titles, and with health advice, articles, astrology, tarot, a meditation zone, author interviews and events listings, www.thorsonselement.com is a great alternative to help create space and peace in our lives.

So if you've always wondered about practising yoga, following an allergy-free diet, using the tarot or getting a life coach, we can point you in the right direction.

www.thorsonselement.com